Penfolds

THE REWARDS
OF PATIENCE

— FIFTH EDITION —

A DEFINITIVE GUIDE TO CELLARING AND ENJOYING PENFOLDS WINES

By Andrew Caillard MW

EST 1844

Peter Gago wishes to thank the Penfolds *Rewards of Patience Fifth Edition*
stewards: Pat Connors, Neil Hadley, Rhonda Finlay, Amanda Pulford,
Dani Richie, Michael Murphy and Nicola McConnell.

Special thanks to Valmai Hankel for her help with the John Davoren
story research.

Caillard, Andrew
The Rewards of Patience:
A Definitive Guide to Cellaring and Enjoying Penfolds Wines.
Fifth Edition

ISBN: 1-877082-37-6

Photography: Richard Humphrys, Adelaide
and Fosters Wine Estates' Image Library (unless credited otherwise)
Designed: Evocatif Pty Ltd, Sydney, Australia
Distributed by Gary Allen

Copyright © Penfolds 2004

EST 1844

INTRODUCTION

"...we must not be afraid to
put into effect the strength of
our own convictions, continue
to use our imagination in
winemaking generally, and
be prepared to experiment in
order to gain something extra,
different and unique in the
world of wine."

– MAX SCHUBERT

EST 1844

Although with Penfolds for barely 15 years, I have always been captivated by its rich heritage and commitment to fine wines. As I progress through the 2004 vintage with our winemaking and viticultural teams, it is appropriate to pause to reflect upon the recent fifth *Rewards of Patience* tastings. In doing so, it is fitting to recount the milestones of the last 160 years that have brought us to this point.

The story of Penfolds is inextricably linked to South Australia's colonial settlement and Australia's subsequent journey to nationhood and the modern era. In 1844 when Penfolds was founded, the colony had been established for a mere eight years. Migrating from near Brighton, England, the young Dr Christopher Rawson Penfold and his wife Mary purchased "the delightfully situated and truly valuable estate of Mackgill for the sum of £1,200... comprising 500 acres of the choicest land". Named after Sir Maitland Mackgill, the suburb, as well as the Penfolds property itself, is now known as Magill.

Like many medical practitioners of the time, Dr Penfold firmly believed in the medicinal value of wine. The couple used vine cuttings brought with them from the South of France to establish their vineyard. Mary Penfold farmed Magill Estate while her husband operated a busy medical practice from their stone cottage, 'The Grange'. By all contemporary accounts Mary Penfold was responsible for the management and early winemaking on the fledgling wine estate. Initially the wines were prescribed as tonics for anaemic patients. The famous slogan: '1844 to evermore' harks back to these origins.

By 1870, the year in which Christopher Rawson Penfold died, the Grange Vineyard comprised over 60 acres with several different grape varieties including Grenache, Verdelho, Mataro (Mourvèdre), Frontignac and Pedro Ximenez. The Estate produced fortified, sweet, dry red and white table wines for a growing market in the eastern Australian colonies of Victoria and New South Wales. Mary Penfold established a partnership with her highly ambitious and devoted son-in-law Thomas Hyland and her cellar manager Joseph Gillard. In the latter part of the nineteenth century Penfolds and Co. claimed to be responsible for over one-third of South Australia's wine production.

> The story of Penfolds is inextricably linked to South Australia's colonial settlement and Australia's subsequent journey to nationhood and the modern era.

THE REWARDS OF PATIENCE

Mary Penfold died in 1896 having set Penfolds on the path to becoming Australia's most significant winery. Her remarkable contribution to Australia's wine industry, however, remains largely overshadowed by her husband's position and profile. Through their daughter Georgina's marriage to Thomas Hyland, the family lineage was secured. The Hyland grandchildren affectionately adopted the surname Penfold-Hyland, with both Herbert Leslie (Leslie) and Frank joining Penfolds in the 1890s. The story of Penfolds can be divided into three eras, each of approximately 50 to 60 years duration, and this generational change marked the beginning of the company's second era.

By the late 1940s Penfolds had acquired or planted vineyards in the Barossa Valley, Eden Valley, McLaren Vale, Auldana, Griffith, the Hunter Valley and Minchinbury.

Between them, the two brothers oversaw a substantial expansion of Penfolds and enjoyed all the trade benefits of the newly formed federation of Australia. Leslie ran the South Australian office, whilst Frank established the New South Wales arm of the business. Frank, based in Sydney, considerably expanded the business in New South Wales during this period. Fortified wine production dominated the industry throughout the first part of the 1900s, but sparkling wine also became fashionable and was reflected in Penfolds' 1912 acquisition of a sparkling wine facility at Minchinbury, now a western suburb of Sydney. During this same period, Leslie established cellars in McLaren Vale and, in 1911, built the Nuriootpa winery in the Barossa Valley that would ultimately become the company's winemaking hub. In 1943 Penfolds acquired the highly regarded and valuable Auldana Vineyard and winery adjacent to their Magill Vineyard. In 1945 Penfolds purchased the Kalimna Vineyard in the Barossa Valley, at the time the largest vineyard in South Australia. By the late 1940s Penfolds had acquired or planted vineyards in the Barossa Valley, Eden Valley, McLaren Vale, Auldana, Griffith, the Hunter Valley and Minchinbury.

In the late 1940s the Australian wine market began to change rapidly as soldiers returned from World War II and new immigrants from Italy, Greece and Eastern Europe settled in Australia. With this emerging multi-culturalism came a new orientation towards dry table wine.

Max Schubert had joined Penfolds' Nuriootpa winery in 1931 and had risen from errand boy to assistant winemaker at Magill prior to enlisting for service in World War II. His return to

Penfolds after the war saw him quickly promoted to full control of winemaking at Magill by 1948. Finding favour with the Penfolds family and Board of Directors, he was the first non-family member ever sent on an overseas trip and visited Europe in 1950 to expand his winemaking knowledge. His mission was to learn about Sherry production but it was to be a side trip to Bordeaux that would ultimately lead to the extraordinary development of Penfolds Grange. Schubert returned inspired and immediately set about creating the first experimental vintage of Grange Hermitage in 1951. This wine's creation marks the beginning of the third, or modern era in the Penfolds story.

During the 1950s an exciting time of experimentation and research underpinned the winemaking regime at Penfolds. Ray Beckwith, the brilliant Penfolds research chemist, introduced the use of pH meters to control bacterial spoilage. Indeed, under Schubert's growing authority as the company's lead winemaker, Penfolds embraced major advances in winemaking techniques. Also in the 1950s, the highly skilled and innovative senior Penfolds winemaker, John Davoren, created the elegantly styled St. Henri Claret at the Auldana winery.

The 1960s was a period of enormous activity and innovation at Penfolds. Max Schubert's creativity was extraordinary as he oversaw what he called a "dynasty of wines (which) may differ in character from year to year, but all bear an unmistakable resemblance and relationship to each other". These wines included the creation of Penfolds emerging red wine portfolio – Bin 389, Bin 707, Bin 28, Bin 128 and Bin 2, as well as the legendary Penfolds Bin 60A. Also during this time a phenomenal number of experimental or one-off 'Special Bin' wines were made and entered into Australian Wine Shows. Even today old bottles with previously forgotten Bin numbers or vintages turn up at auctions and Penfolds Red Wine Re-corking Clinics.

Over the ensuing years Penfolds began to concentrate on red wine production and its vineyard and cellar assets in South Australia. In 1973 Max Schubert stepped down as Penfolds Chief Winemaker. The baton was passed to veteran off-sider and senior Penfolds winemaker Don Ditter. Max officially retired in 1975 but remained actively involved with Penfolds until his death in 1994.

During the 1950s an exciting time of experimentation and research underpinned the winemaking regime at Penfolds.

THE REWARDS OF PATIENCE

Don Ditter's contribution to and refinement of house style is palpable. The remarkable reintroduction of Penfolds Bin 707 in 1976 illustrated Penfolds commitment to a premium Cabernet Sauvignon. Within just a few years, Bin 707 was recognised as one of Australia's leading wines. The Penfolds wine style was, and still is, immensely popular at every price level because it delivers quality and reliability. In 1976 Koonunga Hill Claret, later called Koonunga Hill Shiraz-Cabernet, was introduced and met with the enthusiastic approval of consumers.

> The Penfolds wine style was, and still is, immensely popular at every price level because it delivers quality and reliability.

The introduction of a single vineyard wine, Magill Estate Shiraz, in 1983 was an important addition to the Penfolds stable. The fruit from the Magill Estate Vineyard, mostly replanted to Shiraz in the early 1950s, had been periodically used for Grange. However, it was felt that this remaining small patch of vines on barely 13 acres should be put to a more singular use. The idea was to provide a link to the past by creating a Shiraz from the vineyard planted by Dr Christopher and Mary Penfold in 1844. Doing so meant that this important vineyard site would be protected from further suburban encroachment. The evolution of the Magill Estate wine is fascinating because it has embraced both house style and the character of a single vineyard site without compromise.

In 1986 John Duval, understudy of both Max Schubert and Don Ditter, took over as Penfolds Chief Winemaker, ensuring a smooth transition of winemaking philosophy. Refinement of the house style continued throughout the 1980s. John Duval's outstanding technical ability and instinctive nature were decisively illustrated in his handling of the profoundly opulent and beautifully balanced wines of the 1986 vintage. These are important milestones in the evolution of Penfolds wines. The 1990 and 1991 vintages, both remarkable Penfolds years, underscore his considerable talents as a team leader and Chief Winemaker.

The fortunes of Penfolds went arm-in-arm with Australian wine's exponential success in export markets. Max Schubert had retired, but was still on the scene as a mentor. In recognition of his contribution to wine and the emerging importance of Penfolds in world markets, he was named (UK) *Decanter Magazine's* 1989 'Man of the Year'. This was followed by John Duval winning International Winemaker of the Year at the 1989 International Wine and Spirit Competition in London.

The next decade saw the introduction of a number of new wines to the Penfolds portfolio amid a time of renewed winemaking trials. The search for new wine expressions and experiences during this period was reminiscent of the 1960s.

Penfolds embarked on a flagship white wine project which signalled Penfolds ambition to produce a white counterpart to Grange. This resulted in the release of 1995 Penfolds Yattarna Chardonnay in April 1998. The barrage of media attention was extraordinary, demonstrating the level of public interest in Penfolds wines. There were also red wine trials in the 1990s, resulting in the May 2000 release of the Penfolds first Barossa Shiraz, 1997 Penfolds RWT (Red Winemaking Trial). It presented an innovative expression of this classic Australian regional/varietal combination, with the wine matured in French oak in direct contrast to the more regular use of American oak.

During this time, Penfolds recognised the need for improved access to the very highest quality grapes, through which it aimed to meet the forecast growth in demand for its top-end red wines. Project Max (named in honour of Max Schubert) was initiated to expand and improve premium vineyard holdings and has enabled Penfolds winemakers to gradually increase production without compromising quality.

The 1990s also saw an exceptional level of critical acclaim for both Penfolds wines and its winemakers. John Duval won Red Winemaker of the Year at the 1991 International Wine Challenge in the UK. In August 1995 Robert Parker Jr., the world's most influential wine critic, wrote in his self published *Wine Advocate*, that Grange was "a leading candidate for the richest, most concentrated dry table wine on planet earth". At the end of that year *Wine Spectator* named the 1990 Penfolds Grange its Wine of the Year.

In Australia too, Penfolds has won considerable acclaim. Since 1991, Penfolds Grange has held pride of place at the head of Langton's Classification of Australian Wine. The elite Penfolds Bin 707, St Henri, Magill Estate and Bin 389 are also included in this internationally recognised benchmark listing of Australian wines.

> The barrage of media attention was extraordinary, demonstrating the level of public interest in Penfolds wines.

THE REWARDS OF PATIENCE

The strength of
Penfolds is that the
wine comes first.
We are custodians of a
wonderful Australian
tradition steeped in
wine lore and the
spirit of generosity.

Penfolds Red Wine Re-corking Clinics, held in Australia's major centres and subsequently abroad in London, New York, Chicago and Auckland are an ongoing project, emphasising the aging qualities and secondary market importance of Penfolds wines. In the past 12 years, over 45,000 bottles have been certified through the Re-corking clinics.

In 2001 we celebrated the 50th anniversary of Penfolds Grange at Magill Estate, where plans were announced to return the winemaking of Grange to its original home. The following week a rare bottle of 1951 Grange Hermitage, in perfect condition, sold at auction for a record AUD$52,211. The National Trust of South Australia made the remarkable gesture of listing Penfolds Grange as a Heritage Icon in 2001. This is a badge of considerable pride.

In 2002 grapes destined for Grange were specifically crushed and vinified at Magill Estate for the first time since 1973. It was also the year that I received the baton of Penfolds Chief Winemaker. I am mindful of the extraordinary heritage of Penfolds and its importance to Australian winemaking culture. So many of the ideas and innovations at Penfolds have permeated through our wine industry.

Max Schubert's legacy is profound. Yet, like the great Australian cricketer Sir Donald Bradman, he was the star batsman in a team of outstanding players. The Penfolds winemaking effort is team-based and generational. Former winemakers Don Ditter, John Duval and John Bird retain a mentor role, sharing their wisdom and instincts for the wines with myself and the present winemaking team: Steve Lienert, Oliver Crawford, Glenn James, Andrew Baldwin, Kym Schroeter and Emma Dal Broi. This group's collective loyalty and passion for our wines and winemaking is a tribute to the contribution of all those who have been before them.

The strength of Penfolds is that the wine comes first. We are custodians of a wonderful Australian tradition steeped in wine lore and the spirit of generosity. Penfolds' *The Rewards of Patience* is a review of our wines and winemaking philosophy. This is, perhaps, the last time we will be able to construct such a comprehensive museum tasting back to their inaugural vintages.

Although Penfolds bottles and Grange collections will come up for auction from time to time, many early vintages from the 1950s, 1960s and experimental Bin wines have become impossibly rare. Wine, of course, is very much a living thing. As such, I sincerely hope that you find *The Rewards of Patience* not only a fascinating testimony to the rich heritage of our past, but also a working guide to enjoying your own collection of Penfolds wines at their drinking peak.

Peter Gago

Penfolds Chief Winemaker
Magill Estate
February 2004

The Rewards of Patience, now in its revised fifth edition, is a unique publication which tracks the fortunes of almost all Penfolds wines through the senses of an independent international tasting panel.

This historic tasting, comprising a comprehensive catalogue of wines, took place over four days early in the Australian spring of 2003 at several locations – Mount Lofty House in the Adelaide Hills, Penfolds' Nuriootpa cellars, Penfolds' Kalimna Vineyard in the Barossa Valley, and at the South Australian Parliament House in Adelaide.

I have been involved in three editions of The Rewards of Patience – first as an observer and compiler of text, the second time as co-writer, and the third, as the author. As an Australian specialist wine auctioneer, I enjoy a unique perspective on Penfolds. In preparing this book I have played the roles of researcher, historian, market analyst, wine taster and independent Penfolds expert.

As I look back on the two previous editions, I notice in photographs that over the last ten years I have become older and greyer. I wonder how some person (or panel) in the sky would rate my evolution. Have I cellared well or am I past it? Tasting wine is a deeply personal experience. Perspective and truthfulness play an important part in assessing wine. I don't believe, for instance, that the same wine tasted in New York or London will taste exactly the same in Sydney or Singapore. The character of wine changes with humidity, temperature and with the myriad fragrances and emissions which pervade and bombard our senses. Nor do I believe that wine tasters, even those sitting in the one room, can possibly perceive exactly the same nuances. For all its wonder, wine is complex and unstable – and we human beings are little different. That is why the language of wine is spoken in many tongues.

Despite these differences, there was a symmetry and common understanding among the panel. After four days the language and observations became intertwined. The Rewards of Patience is a very revealing experience. I enjoyed Ch'ng Poh Tiong's gentle, generous and concise approach. Joseph Ward's tasting notes are precise and matter-of-fact, sometimes a hilarious commentary about the battle between fruit and tannins. Joanna Simon's contribution is intuitive, well considered and insightful. Her evocative notes and commentary were always close at hand. James Halliday's beautifully written, perspicacious observations are poetic and sometimes whimsical. He is able to capture the essence of a

REWARDS OF PATIENCE FIFTH EDITION

Tasting Panel:
(above, left to right)

• *Ch'ng Poh Tiong*
  (Singapore)

• *Joanna Simon*
  (United Kingdom)

• *James Halliday*
  (Australia)

• *Joseph Ward*
  (United States of America)

• *Huon Hooke*
  (Australia)

AUTHOR'S NOTES

wine with remarkable ease. Huon Hooke's notes are extraordinarily comprehensive, academic and authoritative – even occasionally mischievous. When woven together these perspectives provide Penfolds collectors and wine enthusiasts with an 'all-round' view of Penfolds wines – a multi-regional blend of opinion, the perfect companion to Penfolds' winemaking philosophy.

The fifth edition of *The Rewards of Patience* comprises a wealth of information about Penfolds – its history, its vineyards, its winemaking and its wines. The tasting notes and commentary provide readers with a detailed overview of most Penfolds vintages. There are some gaps, but these relate mostly to old curios and experimental wines of minor interest.

> The 5th edition of Penfolds' *The Rewards of Patience* comprises a wealth of information about Penfolds, its history, and its wines.

The bar accompanying each tasting note signifies the wine's 'drinking window'. This is the period over which the panel believes the wine will be drinking at its best. The bar typically bleeds away at the end because wine fades. It also shows that predictions are not necessarily definitive. Indeed, there is a tendency for conservatism in *The Rewards of Patience* tastings. As was the case with previous tastings, panel members and winemakers were sometimes surprised by the evolution of vintages. Some wines have defied expectations, either cheating the prediction of an early death or evolving in rather unexpected ways. It is important, therefore, not to take the 'Now' indication too literally. It means that the panel sees no likelihood of further improvement. The 'Past' indication suggests that the wine is either at or very near its end. In the case of older vintages of Grange, these wines still remain valuable as collectables, but in all likelihood they are past their best.

A star indicates exceptional vintages within each tasting bracket. Once again a comparison of starred wines across five editions will reveal some have risen while others have fallen. Largely though, there is a consistency of view – 1962, 1963, 1971, 1976, 1986, 1990, 1991, 1996 and 1998 are generally recognised as great Penfolds vintages. A few wines detailed were not, in fact, tasted during *The Rewards of Patience* tasting week. However, they are included for the sake of completing the record of all wines made under any given label, with notes constructed from either my own or Chief Winemaker, Peter Gago's, tasting experience. For clarity, these wines appear in italics wherever they appear within the text.

> The language of wine is spoken in many tongues. Despite these atmospherics, there was a symmetry and common understanding within the panel.

Throughout the text, at the end of each commentary, a key to the tasters' intials appears to remind the reader of the identities of the panel members. Periodically, however, other comments are included from the following:

PG – Peter Gago – *Penfolds Chief Winemaker*
JD – John Duval – *former Penfolds Chief Winemaker*
SL – Steve Lienert – *Penfolds Red Winemaker*
OC – Oliver Crawford – *Penfolds White Winemaker*
JB – John Bird – *former Penfolds Senior Winemaker*
AC – Andrew Caillard – *Author*

All the wines tasted for this book came from Penfolds museum cellars and were stored under optimum conditions. Cellaring conditions (see Perspectives) are important because temperature and humidity can accelerate or retard the aging process. Readers should therefore understand that whilst *The Rewards of Patience* is a consumer's guide, the best way to enjoy your own wines is to open the bottles and drink them!

Andrew Caillard

Andrew Caillard MW
March 2004

THE VINEYARDS

QUALITY BEGINS IN THE VINEYARD

Whilst the Penfolds name is shrouded in winemaking lore, the selection of vineyard sites and the quality of its fruit have always underpinned its reputation. In 1844 Dr Penfold was congratulated for purchasing a well-sited vineyard. The South Australian Register of 8 August, 1844 reports the arrival of Dr Penfold in the colony, noting, "He is the fortunate purchaser of the delightfully situated and truly valuable estate of Mackgill for the sum of £1,200".

One hundred years later, Penfolds had become a major landholder with vineyard and winery holdings throughout New South Wales and South Australia producing an array of light table and sparkling wines, ports and sherries. Today, however, Penfolds is predominantly a South Australian winemaker, sourcing its fruit from its own vineyards and from independent growers, many of whose families have supplied grapes to the company for generations.

The move towards table wine production really began during the 1940s. While the importance of vineyard site and quality fruit was well recognised by growers and winemakers, the overall consumer market was yet to appreciate the highly evocative and compelling idea of vineyard provenance. Indeed, the emerging Penfolds red winemaking ethos of multi-district blending was a natural progression from the days of fortified winemaking where house style played a critical role in capturing the loyalty of the consumer. The concept of multi-district blends built on a keen sense of multi-vineyard provenance is still central to the Penfolds winemaking philosophy. However, in more recent times Penfolds has evolved to embrace the contemporary enthusiasms for single vineyard and regionally defined wines.

The acquisition of vineyards by Penfolds during the 1940s was effectively placing an each way bet on the future of post-war Australian wine culture. Frank and Jeffrey Penfold-Hyland knew the market would change irrevocably with the arrival of returned soldiers, refugees and immigrants. Initially providing fruit for its fortified wines, these vineyards were to become an important source for Penfolds' emerging table wine portfolio. Some of the early vineyards have now disappeared, mostly sold off because of intense urban pressure. These include the Auldana Vineyard

> Penfolds has evolved to embrace the contemporary enthusiasms for single vineyard and regionally defined wines.

THE VINEYARDS

(the original source of St. Henri) and the Modbury Vineyard (further north in the Adelaide foothills). A small portion of the historic Grange Vineyard, now known as Penfolds Magill Estate, was saved and is now heritage listed and thus protected.

Today Penfolds not only has significant vineyard holdings of its own in the Barossa, but also draws fruit from a number of independent growers.

Other Penfolds vineyards have gone from strength to strength. Kalimna Vineyard, purchased in 1945, was once the largest vineyard in Australia, and remains an important source of high quality Shiraz and Cabernet Sauvignon. Penfolds Bin 28 was originally a single vineyard Shiraz, but evolved as a multi-vineyard blend. Located in the Barossa heartland, Kalimna is regarded as Penfolds' mother vineyard because it contributes core fruit to many of its best wines, including Grange. The Koonunga Hill Vineyard, also in the Barossa, was established in 1973. It not only inspired the Penfolds Koonunga Hill label, but also produces such high quality fruit that it is considered a sister vineyard to Kalimna.

Today Penfolds has significant vineyard holdings of its own in the Barossa and also draws fruit from a number of independent growers, many of whom are members of the elite Penfolds Grange Growers Club because of the exceptional quality of their grapes.

Penfolds' investment in vineyards extends throughout South Australia's premium wine districts. Penfolds was an early investor in the Coonawarra, purchasing vineyards in the early 1960s. Penfolds Bin 128 Coonawarra Shiraz was initially a single vineyard wine, but now draws fruit from several vineyard sites in Coonawarra. Penfolds also owns vineyards in McLaren Vale, Clare Valley, Padthaway and the emerging viticultural areas of Bordertown and Robe along South Australia's Limestone Coast.

The sheer diversity and quality of regional provenance, vineyard sites and independently grown fruit provide winemakers with a rich palette of colour, aroma and texture – a superb resource which allows a remarkable consistency of style and quality across the Penfolds portfolio.

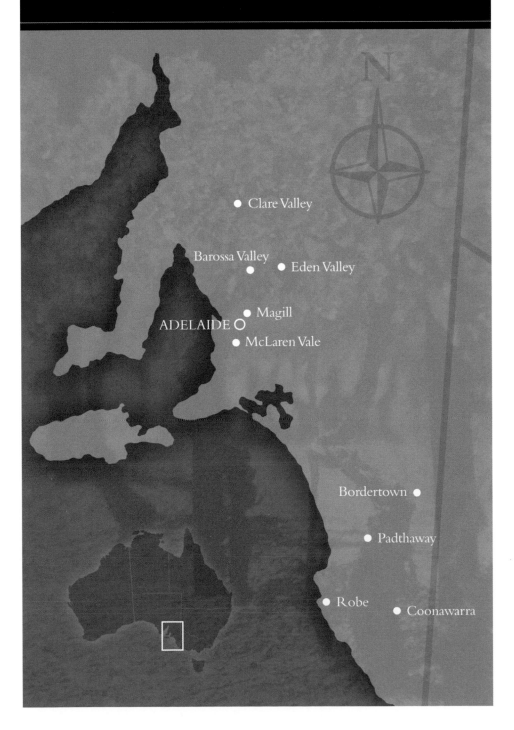

PENFOLDS VINEYARDS
IN SOUTH AUSTRALIA

N

● Clare Valley

Barossa Valley
● ● Eden Valley

● Magill
ADELAIDE ○
● McLaren Vale

Bordertown ●

● Padthaway

● Robe   ● Coonawarra

THE VINEYARDS

MAGILL ESTATE

The historic and heritage protected Magill Estate Vineyard was established in 1844 by Dr Christopher Rawson and his wife, Mary Penfold just eight years after the foundation of Adelaide. It was originally known as the Grange Vineyard, named after their new homestead, 'The Grange'. This cottage still stands intact amongst the vines. In later years this vineyard would inspire and supply fruit for Penfolds Grange, the most prized of all Australian wines.

The vineyard was first planted with vine cuttings taken from the south of France. At its peak in 1949, the vineyard, planted to several different grape varieties on rich chocolaty red-brown soils, covered 120 hectares (296 acres) of gentle north-west and west facing slopes. During the 1950s and 1960s it was replanted with Riesling, Cabernet Sauvignon, Shiraz and Mataro (Mourvèdre), reflecting the waning demand in fortifieds and the increasing interest in table wines. Urban pressure (largely through commercially unsustainable land rates) and compulsory acquisition gradually forced the diminution of this vineyard to its present size of 5.24 hectares (12.94 acres).

The Magill Estate Vineyard, one of the few city vineyards in the world, is now planted entirely to Shiraz. Viticulture follows organic principles, largely because of superb drainage and predictable afternoon sea breezes during the growing season. The contour-planted, dry-grown, gnarled old vines established over half a century ago are extremely low yielding and bear fruit of exceptional concentration, flavour and balance. At vintage the fruit is hand-picked block by block. The very best parcels are used for the limited release, single vineyard Penfolds Magill Estate Shiraz. Most recently, in 1996 and 1998, both exceptional years, the vineyard produced parcels of very opulent powerful fruit, some of which was selected for inclusion in Penfolds Grange.

VINEYARD DETAILS

Climate: Warm

Location: Magill – Adelaide 8km east of CBD.

Vineyard: Situated at the base of the Adelaide Hills. Gentle, west-facing slopes range from 130m-180m (430ft-600ft) above sea level.

Soils: Fertile red-brown soils.

Rainfall: Average rainfall is 502mm (20 in). About 221mm falls during the growing season.

Irrigation: All dry grown.

Viticulture: Original Shiraz vines on the existing site were planted in 1951, with most recent plantings in 1985. Hand pruned and hand harvested. Yields on average less than 35 tonnes of grapes.

Grape Varieties: Shiraz only.

THE VINEYARDS

KALIMNA

Penfolds draws fruit from a combined vineyard area of 618 hectares (1526.5 acres) in the Barossa region of South Australia. It owns several of its own vineyards, but also purchases fruit from independent growers. Settled by Silesian and English immigrants in the mid 1800s, the Barossa is about 70km north of Adelaide. In 1911 Penfolds established a winery at Nuriootpa. It relied entirely on independently grown fruit in the Barossa for the production of fortified wines. The move towards table wine production resulted in a vineyard acquisition and replanting programme during the 1940s and 1950s.

In 1945 Penfolds purchased the highly significant Kalimna Vineyard, originally planted to vines by George Swan Fowler about 1888. Previously the land was used as a source of firewood by D and J Fowler Ltd, the family fruit preserving company. George Fowler named the vineyard Kalimna, which means 'pleasant view' in the local Aboriginal language. The vineyard lies on gently undulating slopes with elevations as high as 340m. Located at the northern end of the Barossa Valley, about 4km north of Nuriootpa, the Kalimna Vineyard represents an important chapter of Australia's wine heritage.

In 1903 the Kalimna Vineyard covered 132 hectares (317 acres). Some of the unproductive land was sold off during the 1950s and 1960s. During the 1970s, at the height of Australia's red wine boom, all the white varieties were removed. Today the 290 hectare property (700 acres) comprises 153 hectares (378 acres) under vine, mostly planted to Shiraz and Cabernet Sauvignon. Many of the vines are over 50 years of age, illustrating the extraordinary provenance of this vineyard. A classic First Growth vineyard in Bordeaux, for instance, would be lucky to claim an average age of over 40 years.

The Kalimna Vineyard is planted on rich brown soils and alluvial sands. The soil profiles, however, vary widely across the vineyard from deep and sandy soils on the ridges to sandy loams on the slopes and heavy, red-brown clay soils on the flats. The vines are planted in blocks. Trellising systems vary according to when each block was established or redeveloped. Varieties are carefully matched to soil profiles to achieve optimum performance. Yields are generally between 1 and 4 tonnes per hectare (0.4–1.6 tons/acre). This is low to extremely low by wine growing standards.

VINEYARD DETAILS

Climate: Warm to hot.

Location: Northern Barossa, about 4km north of Nuriootpa.

Vineyard: Undulating slopes and flats with elevations to 340m (1100 ft).

Soils: Deep and sandy soils on the slopes to sandy loams and heavy, red-brown clay soils on the flats.

Rainfall: Average rainfall is 508mm (20 in). About 201mm falls during the growing season.

Irrigation: In some blocks supplementary irrigation is used.

Viticulture: Original Cabernet vines were planted circa 1888. A succession of plantings and re-trellising has followed. Many blocks are mechanically pruned and harvested. Older blocks are hand picked. Yields 1-4 tonnes/hectare (0.4 - 1.6 tons/acre).

Grape Varieties: Shiraz, Cabernet Sauvignon, Mataro (Mourvèdre) and 8 rows of Sangiovese (planted in 1984).

Block 42, planted around 1888, stands out as a very special piece of viticultural dirt. These vines, producing remarkably vibrant, beautifully balanced fruit, are thought to be the oldest Cabernet Sauvignon in the world. Over the last sixty years Block 42 (also known as the Golf Course block) has played an important role in the development of the Penfolds reds. It contributed to the red table wine trials of the late 1940s and early 1950s Grange experiments, in particular the rare 1948 Kalimna Cabernet and 1953 Penfolds Grange Cabernet.

Block 42, planted around 1888, stands out as a very special piece of viticultural dirt. These vines, producing remarkably vibrant, beautifully balanced fruit, are thought to be the oldest Cabernet Sauvignon in the world.

Although the vineyard provides unusually high quality fruit in most vintages, limited yields meant that Block 42 could not be relied upon as a core source of fruit for Max Schubert's Grange experiments. The development and continued success of Penfolds Bin 707 Cabernet Sauvignon, however, is in some part due to the contribution of Block 42. To highlight the exceptional provenance of this vineyard within a vineyard, Penfolds released a Special Bin 1996 Block 42, a wine with impressive concentration, balance and finesse.

The Kalimna Vineyard provides core fruit for Grange, RWT, St. Henri and Bin 28. It also provides an essential element to many of Penfolds Special Bin wines, illustrated by the renowned Penfolds Bin 60A, often cited by critics as one of the finest Australian wines ever made.

While it is romantic to think of old vines as the determinant of quality, the Kalimna Vineyard's age is only one of several contributing factors to its unique status. The focus of vineyard management is to achieve well-balanced fruit. This goes beyond the shape and age of the vine. Penfolds' viticulturalists are constantly seeking ways of improving vine performance through vine selection and replanting, refinement of trellising systems and shoot positioning, optimising soil moistures as well as reducing pest and disease pressure.

THE VINEYARDS

KOONUNGA HILL

Named after a nearby landmark, the Koonunga Hill Vineyard is located on the drier northern edge of the Barossa Valley. Originally 32 hectares (79 acres) of grazing land, it was planted with Shiraz and Cabernet Sauvignon in 1973. The vineyard inspired the name, Penfolds Koonunga Hill, which was originally released as an entry point to the Penfolds portfolio of wines. This low yielding vineyard on flat, well drained soils has become a consistent producer of Grange and Bin 707 quality fruit. Aged over 30 years, the vines are in their prime and also produce core premium fruit for Penfolds St. Henri, Bin 389 and Bin 28.

The vineyard is trellised to allow mechanical pruning and harvesting. In keeping with modern 'precision' viticulture techniques, 'capacitance probes' are situated throughout the vineyard to measure soil moistures. If a particular block of vines is stressed, controlled drip irrigation can be delivered to the exact location to relieve the stressed vines, while leaving the remainder of the vineyard dry. In 1996 an adjacent property of equal size was purchased and planted to Shiraz. These relatively young vines are now quickly reaching an ultra-premium level of maturity and potential quality, illustrating how optimised vineyard management plays a vital role in delivering high quality fruit at vintage time.

VINEYARD DETAILS

Climate: Warm to hot.

Location: Northern Barossa, about 5km north-east of Kalimna.

Vineyard: 64 hectares (158 acres) of original flat grazing land at an elevation of 280m (930 ft).

Soils: Red-brown earth over heavy clays.

Rainfall: Average rainfall is around 508mm (20 in). About 201mm falls during the growing season.

Irrigation: Supplementary drip irrigation is available for use.

Viticulture: Planted in 1973. Vines are trellised (single wire) for mechanical pruning and harvesting.

Grape Varieties: Shiraz and Cabernet Sauvignon.

THE VINEYARDS

WALTONS

The worldwide interest in Barossa Valley wine has intensified over the past decade, creating a scarcity of valuable premium grapes in the valley. Independent growers provide Penfolds with a vital element of supply, but Penfolds recognises that it must also improve and develop its own vineyards. The 317 hectare (783 acre) Waltons property, located on classic Barossa Valley heartland soils, is an important recent development. Over 130 hectares (321 acres) have already been planted, mostly to Shiraz, Cabernet and Mataro. This is a contemporary vineyard – planned, planted and managed with extreme precision.

The entire vineyard has been mapped and monitored to optimise vine performance and fruit quality. One of the main issues is the use of water, a scarce resource. Although many vineyards are dry grown in the Barossa, the use of supplementary irrigation is an important insurance against drought and vine stress. Technology has allowed better water management in recent years. The capacitance probes placed throughout the vineyard are able to monitor soil moistures, which vary according to the depth and structure of the soil. If needed, water can be directed to the areas of the vineyard which need replenishing without wasting this valuable resource.

Penfolds has great hopes for this vineyard. The oldest Shiraz vines, planted in 1999, are already producing impressively concentrated and flavoursome Shiraz with some of the best parcels strong contenders for inclusion in Bin 28. Such an achievement bodes well for future supply of super-premium quality fruit for the very best Penfolds wines.

VINEYARD DETAILS

Climate: Warm to hot.

Location: Central Barossa, about 3km south of Tanunda.

Vineyard: 317 hectares (783 acres) of undulating Barossa heartland. 130 hectares (321.1 acres) planted.

Soils: Sandy loams and red-brown soils.

Rainfall: Average rainfall is around 508mm (20 in). About 201mm falls during the growing season.

Irrigation: Supplementary drip irrigation is available for use.

Viticulture: Planted in 1999. Vines are trained on high trellises for mechanical pruning and harvesting. Yields are about 3-4 tonnes/hectare (1.2 to 1.6 tons/acre).

Vine Density: 1667 vines/ hectare (675 vines/acre).

Grape Varieties: Shiraz, Cabernet Sauvignon and Mataro (Mourvèdre).

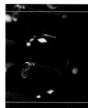

THE VINEYARDS

VINEYARD DETAILS

Location: Stonewell Road, central Barossa – 4km west of Nuriootpa.

Vineyard: 33 hectares (80 acres) on undulating slopes.

Irrigation: Supplementary drip irrigation is available for use.

Viticulture: First planted in the early 1970s, but a replanting programme was introduced when Penfolds purchased the vineyard in the early 1990s. Vines are trained on trellises for mechanical pruning and harvesting. Yields are about 5.5-6 tonnes/hectare (2.2 to 2.5 tons/acre).

Vine Density: 1667 vines/hectare (675 vines/acre). Average age 10 years.

Grape Varieties: Shiraz (23 hectares/67 acres), Cabernet Sauvignon (5 hectares/12 acres), Grenache (0.8 hectares/2 acres), Semillon (2 hectares/5 acres) and Chardonnay (1.9 hectares/ 4.7 acres).

STONEWELL

Established in the 1970s, the Stonewell Road Vineyard was purchased in the mid 1990s and is now producing quintessential Barossa Valley Shiraz with some of the crop also being used for Penfolds RWT and Penfolds St. Henri.

As well as being an enormously significant source of Penfolds fruit, the Barossa Valley is home to many of the company's key growers – independent vineyard owners whose longstanding relationship with Penfolds is pivotal to the consistency of quality grapes delivered to the winery each vintage. Penfolds' growers are discussed in detail later in this book (pp 42-44).

PARTALUNGA

Although technically situated in the Adelaide Hills region, the beautifully sited Partalunga Vineyard in fact hugs the slopes of the High Eden Ridge in the Barossa Ranges. It was first planted in 1981. With elevations from 460–520m, this is a much cooler location than the Barossa Valley floor. Water is limited. Planted on shallow slate and granitic soils, the vines take longer to ripen, but produce fruit of great finesse and elegance. It is a large vineyard covering approximately 82 hectares (201 acres).

Significant parcels of Chardonnay were used during the Penfolds flagship white wine project and the Partalunga Vineyard is a now a regular source of fruit for Yattarna Chardonnay. The elegantly structured qualities of its Shiraz are also an extremely useful element in the St. Henri blend. Also a small parcel of the Pinot Noir clone MV6 consistently reaches the Cellar Reserve Pinot Noir blend.

VINEYARD DETAILS

Location: Northern Adelaide Hills, bordering High Eden Ridge.

Vineyard: 82 hectares (201 acres) of contour hugging vineyard.

Soils: Shallow red clay soils and sandy-silty loams interspersed with schistic gravels. Many rocky outcrops.

Rainfall: Average rainfall is around 760mm (19 in). About 283mm during the growing season.

Irrigation: Supplementary drip irrigation is used.

Viticulture: Planted in 1981. Vines are trained on high trellises for mechanical pruning and harvesting. Yields are Shiraz 5 tonnes/hectare (2.2 tons/acre) and Chardonnay 7.5 tonnes/ hectare (3.03 tons/acre).

Vine Density: 2055 vines/hectare (833 vines/acre). Average age 13 years.

Grape Varieties: Shiraz, Chardonnay, Pinot Noir (Cellar Reserve).

THE VINEYARDS

McLAREN VALE

Sometimes referred to as the Southern Vales, McLaren Vale has been called Australia's mid-palate, reflecting the hallmark mid-palate richness and opulence of its Shiraz wines. In 1837 John Reynell wrote in his diary, "We started ascending first a very gradual hill, and traversing afterwards through a most rich and beautiful country and encamped on the banks of the Onkaparinga River, a most delightful little spot." A few years later he planted the first commercial vineyard at Reynella beginning a tradition of viticulture and winemaking in McLaren Vale.

By the early 1900s, McLaren Vale was producing over three million litres of wine; much of it "dark-coloured full bodied red table wine" destined for the United Kingdom. Penfolds has been sourcing fruit from this region since at least the early 1950s. Indeed an association with this region goes back to 1882 when Joseph Gillard – who managed Penfolds Magill Vineyard until 1905 – purchased a 16 hectare (39 acre) vineyard at Clarendon. Climatically McLaren Vale is warm and maritime with elevations of between 50m to 200m. The undulating landscape is framed by the Sellicks Hill Range to the south and Reynella to the north. Although the region benefits from the moderating effect of the Gulf of St Vincent, the best vineyard sites are protected from afternoon southerly breezes.

Rainfall is relatively low during the growing season. Supplementary irrigation is used although there are many dry grown vineyards. There are three distinctive soil types: the sandy loams of Blewitt Springs; the darker soils of McLaren Flat; and the terra rossa over limestone soils near Seaview. Penfolds sources both company-owned and independently-grown Shiraz and Cabernet Sauvignon from high quality vineyards such as Aldersley, Bethany, Blencowe, Booths, Park Hill, Roscor and Vine Vale. Depending on vintage some components are used for Grange, St. Henri Shiraz and Bin 389.

VINEYARD DETAILS

Climate: Warm with significant maritime cooling influence from the Gulf of St Vincent.

Location: 37 km south of Adelaide.

Soils: Sandy and reddish-brown loams.

Rainfall: Average annual rainfall 660mm (26 in). About 180mm falls during the growing season.

Viticulture: A full spectrum of modern, trellised vineyards with drip irrigation, through to free-standing 100+ year-old Shiraz blocks. Yields are approximately 3.2 tonnes hectare (1.3 tons/acre).

Grape Varieties: Shiraz and Cabernet Sauvignon.

THE VINEYARDS

CLARE ESTATE

The Clare Valley Estate Vineyard lies 5km south-east of Clare on the eastern slopes of the Clare Hills about 130km north of Adelaide. The vineyard was purchased on the recommendation of Max Schubert, who recognised the potential of this region as a premium grape supplier.

The Clare Valley is essentially a corrugation of hills and gullies. The climatic data suggests a hot region. However, the Clare Valley Estate, like many other vineyards in the Clare, is elevated at 430 to 470m. While the Clare Hills protect the vines from strong south-easterly winds, the vineyard benefits from moderating cool breezes that funnel up from the south. Planted in 1978, the vineyard now comprises a fruit salad of varieties, including: Cabernet Sauvignon, Shiraz, Merlot, Malbec, Petit Verdot, Sangiovese, Riesling, Chardonnay, Semillon, Sauvignon Blanc and Traminer. It is located in the famous Polish Hill River Valley, first settled by Polish migrants in the 1840s.

This huge vineyard of 350 hectares (218 hectares planted) is situated almost on the edge of a desert. Rainfall, which occurs mainly during autumn and winter, decreases by an 'inch per mile' east of the Clare Hills. During summer the climate is generally hot, dry and continental with a high level of evaporation. Penfolds has a philosophy of 'low-input' viticulture in all its vineyards. The Clare climate reduces the risk of disease, making it possible to grow vines without the assistance of man-made herbicides, pesticides and fertilisers. Thus, 52.6 hectares (127 acres) of the Clare Estate is organically grown and is certified by the National Association for Sustainable Agriculture Australia Limited (NASAA).

The vineyard is trellised to allow machine pruning and harvesting. Soils vary ranging from shallow brown earths over broken clay slate subsoils on higher ground to red–brown soils over clay and deep, black alluvial clay loams below. Drip irrigation is used throughout the vineyard to provide supplementary water when necessary during summer.

VINEYARD DETAILS

Climate: Warm to hot.

Location: Polish River Valley, about 5km south-east of Clare.

Vineyard: 350 hectares (861 acres) and 218 hectares (538 acres) planted on the eastern slopes of the Clare Hills.

Soils: Soils vary. Shallow brown earths over broken clay slate subsoils on higher ground. Red-brown soils over clay and deep, black alluvial clay loams with a high level of organic matter on lower elevations.

Rainfall: Average rainfall is around 657mm (26 in), mostly falling in autumn and winter.

Irrigation: Supplementary drip irrigation is used.

Viticulture: Planted in 1978. Vines are trained on high trellises for optimal pruning and harvesting.

Grape Varieties: Cabernet Sauvignon, Shiraz, Merlot, Malbec, Petit Verdot, Sangiovese, Riesling, Chardonnay, Semillon, Sauvignon Blanc and Traminer.

THE VINEYARDS

COONAWARRA

The Penfolds Coonawarra vineyards are located on over 100 hectares (250 acres) of prime terra rossa soil. The vines are all trained on high single wire trellises. Yields are approximately 4-5 tonnes/hectare.

The original vineyard, Sharam's Block, was purchased from Redmans in 1960. At the time Coonawarra was barely known as a premium wine district, although Penfolds had been sourcing fruit from various vineyards there. Indeed, Max Schubert was sceptical about Coonawarra fruit, believing that it was difficult to achieve the optimum ripeness required for the Penfolds style. Initially he preferred Coonawarra Shiraz to Coonawarra Cabernet Sauvignon because it was more reliable.

The success of Bin 60A was a turning point. However, Penfolds has only occasionally released 100% Coonawarra Cabernet Sauvignons. The Penfolds house style is largely based on warm climate fruit. Hence, in cooler but well regarded Coonawarra vintages such as 2000, the Cabernet Sauvignon is not always suitable for Bin 707. Vineyard management has progressed substantially over the last 40 years, with fruit now supplying many of Penfolds Bin wines including Bin 128, Bin 407, Bin 389 and Bin 707. The Penfolds Coonawarra vineyards are now entirely planted to premium red wine varieties, in particular Cabernet Sauvignon and Shiraz.

The region is flat and largely unprotected, but the unique confluence of cool maritime and warm continental climates is ideal for Cabernet Sauvignon and Shiraz. With the added benefit of natural aquifers and groundwater, vineyards can be tuned almost perfectly throughout the growing season. Drainage is excellent, but frosts can be a problem and have been known to decimate vineyards. Overhead sprinkling devices are sometimes deployed when temperatures drop in early spring – the danger period.

Three blocks within the Coonawarra vineyards are of particular note: Blocks 6, 19 and 20 are an important source of Penfolds Bin 707. They are located about 0.5 and 2kms south of the Coonawarra township, on the eastern side of the Riddoch Highway, which bisects the Coonawarra region. Penfolds is also able to access fruit from independent growers and other vineyards in Coonawarra to supplement its own Coonawarra intake.

VINEYARD DETAILS

Climate: Cool to temperate with significant cooling influence due to proximity of Southern Ocean.

Location: Far south of South Australia.

Soils: Terra rossa – friable, vivid red clay loams over well drained limestone subsoil.

Rainfall: Average annual rainfall 593mm (25.5 in). About 209mm falls during the growing season.

Viticulture: Vines trained on high single wire trellis with overhead sprinkler system for use in combating frost. Yields are approximately 4-5 tonnes/hectare (1.6-2.0 tons/acre).

Grape Varieties: Shiraz and Cabernet Sauvignon.

THE VINEYARDS

OTHER VINEYARDS

Penfolds has developed vineyards in **Bordertown** close to the South Australia/Victoria border. The region was first settled in the early 1850s following the establishment of Alexander Tolmer's Gold Escort base camp on the banks of the Tatiara Creek. Bordertown was located on the major supply route between the Victorian goldfields and Adelaide. The Bordertown district is warm and has the most continental climate of the sub-regions within the Limestone Coast. The land is gently undulating, punctuated by large stands of eucalyptus trees.

Penfolds has been sourcing fruit from Bordertown for over ten years. Impressed by the sheer quality of the fruit (the Cabernet has been selected for Bin 707), Penfolds recently planted its own 180 hectare vineyard and believes that the Bordertown Vineyard will make a significant contribution to Penfolds reds in coming years.

Penfolds also draws premium fruit from over 400 hectares of vineyards planted in the moderate-warm region of **Padthaway**. With a patchwork of soils from deep yellow duplex to red loams over limestone subsoils reminiscent of those found in Coonawarra, the region is regarded as prime viticultural ground. The Penfolds vineyards date back over 35 years, consistently contributing to wines across the portfolio. Cabernet Sauvignon is frequently used in Bins 707, 407 and 389, as well as Shiraz in Bin 389 and occasionally Grange.

Penfolds' **Robe** Vineyards are located close to the Southern Ocean and benefit from its moderating influence. These relatively young vineyards, planted during the mid 1990s on weathered limestone terra rossa soils, are producing fruit of excellent definition and palate structure. The Cabernet Sauvignon and Shiraz are more refined than Coonawarra fruit, but both have masses of sweet fruit and depth.

The Robe region is centred around the small townships of Robe and Beachport. Penfolds' Robe Vineyard is located on the eastern slopes of the relatively low lying Woakwine Ranges. Protected from the prevailing winds, the maritime climate is marginally warmer in spring than in Coonawarra, whilst summers are slightly cooler. The vineyard is well drained, but also benefits from an artesian basin – a plentiful source of ground water. The overall standard of fruit quality is extremely high, with the highly aromatic Shiraz, for instance, used as a top note in the Bin 389 blend.

The Bordertown district is warm and the most continental of the sub-regions within the Limestone Coast. The land is gently undulating, punctuated by large stands of eucalyptus trees.

Grange Growers Club members, Neville and Howard Kies. Their family has supplied Barossa Valley grapes to Penfolds for five generations. *Photograph courtesy of: Martin Mischkulnig.*

Penfolds contracts well over 200 independent growers, many of whom have supplied the company for generations. In the past, all growers were paid for their crop on a $/per tonne basis. Today, Penfolds rewards its growers for their patience and commitment to quality-focused viticulture, forming the elite Penfolds Grange Growers Club, for whom payments are now made on a per hectare basis, 'rain, hail or shine'. Bonuses are offered if the fruit exceeds expectations.

The majority of Penfolds growers in fact are located in the Barossa Valley. One such person is John Kalleske, whose great grandfather established the family vineyard at Greenock on the north western edge of the Barossa Valley. This 40 hectare (100 acre) vineyard, mainly dry grown, is planted on sandy loams over red clay. Peppered with ironstone, the soils are rich in nutrients ideal for the production of high quality Shiraz. Optimum fruit quality is associated with small, highly flavoured berries and high skin-to-juice ratios. This can be achieved only by creating a balanced, well-managed vineyard where yields are kept low.

During the year John Kalleske and his son Kym are provided with advice and technical support by Penfolds viticulturalists and grower liaison officers. Penfolds' input covers a range of issues from soil and vine management to employing the latest innovations in technology. Penfolds' aim is to encourage the development of the best available fruit by providing the best possible support and advice to its growers.

Vineyard assessment and monitoring are vitally important. Premium vineyards are visited regularly at pruning time, flowering and veraison. Penfolds' viticulturalists, winemakers and growers walk each block together, discussing its attributes and potential. During the growing season they look at growing tips, lateral growth and shoot length. They also observe periderm development, leaf condition and fruit exposure.

Close to harvest, each vineyard block is likely to be assessed several times by winemakers who scrutinise grape quality and flavour development, and monitor chemical residues, while grower liaison officers watch for potential disease and predict harvest dates. Understanding the quality and variability of each vineyard block enables winemakers to match and batch fruit for specific Penfolds wines.

Penfolds contracts to well over 200 independent growers, many of whom have supplied the company for generations.

PENFOLDS GROWERS

The relationship between growers and Penfolds is an important one. Growers are given every opportunity to improve their knowledge and refine their vineyard management skills.

Over a period of time both growers and Penfolds are able to predict vineyard performance within the context of seasonal conditions. Growers are given grade level targets, an internal alpha-numerical grading system. A-1 Grade fruit is likely to find its way into Penfolds Grange. The fruit at this level must be sublime, with superb colour, flavour and tannin ripeness.

Paul Georgiadis, who is in charge of looking after Penfolds' growers, maintains that you can recognise a top vineyard by its appearance and by the look and taste of its fruit. "We look beyond Baumé, pH and acidity. The fruit that scores the highest points invariably has grapes with concentration, richness, chewiness, and plenty of sweetness and flavour length. The spit test is usually a very good indicator. If it's got the colour of dark purple ink, it's a winner."

The relationship between growers and Penfolds is an important one. Growers are given every opportunity to improve their knowledge and refine their vineyard management skills. Field days, regional workshops, and a range of planned feedback sessions are offered throughout the year. The use of field digital technology has allowed Penfolds to further improve the capture of information and feed it back to growers.

Belonging to the Penfolds Grange Growers Club, or the Penfolds Yattarna Growers Club are the ultimate accolades for those growers who are able to achieve the highest fruit quality. Aside from the financial rewards, they belong to an elite group of growers who take pride in producing, on a regular basis, some of Australia's finest wine grapes. While refinement and hard work in the vineyard can reap dividends for growers, vineyard site is the tangible yet enigmatic wild card. The late Max Gersch, a veteran Grange grower, once said, "If we all knew the answer to making such high quality fruit, everyone would be growing grapes for Grange".

Digital records help to monitor canopy and crop developments. *Photograph courtesy of: Martin Mischkulnig.*

Is winemaking art or science? Or is it a craftsman's philosophy? At Penfolds the role of the winemaker is to make the best possible wine from the gifts of each vintage. A deft hand, initiative, precision, a touch of guile and a sympathetic understanding of nature's colour and order are the tools in trade.

The Penfolds house style emerged from a fortified wine producing culture. It has evolved as a winemaking philosophy – a way of making wine – which has had a profound influence on the entire Australian wine industry. This house style embraces the concepts of multi-regional blending, optimum fruit quality, the use of fine-grained American (and increasingly French) oak and, most often, barrel fermentation and maturation. The development of red table wines during the 1950s and 1960s was underpinned by an investment in new vineyards, winemaking equipment, skilled personnel and, perhaps most importantly, research and experimentation.

Penfolds already had a reputation within the wine industry for its ground-breaking work during the 1930s and 1940s, overcoming spoilage and wine stability problems, which were industry-wide concerns. It employed a full-time chemist, Ray Beckwith, to investigate and research every aspect of the winemaking process and to develop ways of improving all Penfolds wines.

Ray Beckwith's contribution underpinned the extraordinary creative development of Penfolds Grange and St. Henri by Max Schubert and John Davoren during the 1950s. A preventative winemaking regime, a team of highly intuitive and imaginative winemakers, and benevolent, production-orientated owners (particularly Jeffrey Penfold-Hyland) provided an atmosphere of creativity and innovation. Max Schubert's well-known article, The Story of Grange, (see pp260) is an insightful and remarkable account of the times. When he was ordered to stop production of Grange in 1957, Penfolds was already set on an irrevocable course towards table wine production.

The friendly rivalry between Max Schubert and John Davoren resulted in a broad rather than narrow winemaking perspective. Whilst the development of Grange had a major impact on Penfolds' overall winemaking culture, St. Henri, a traditional style, inevitably played a more singular role.

The Penfolds house style emerged from a fortified wine producing culture. It has evolved as a winemaking philosophy – a way of making wine – which has had a profound influence on the entire Australian wine industry.

Max Schubert, who was appointed production manager at Magill Estate in 1948, was an early proponent of regional definition. His fascination and specific demands for fruit quality resulted in a comprehensive understanding of vineyard performance, summarised as, "The development of a new commercial wine, particularly of the high grade range, depends on the quality and availability of the raw material, the maintenance of standard, and continuity of style".

He achieved this by identifying specific vineyard sites and developing relationships with growers. While developing Grange, he once observed that using Shiraz from two specific vineyards would "result in an improved, all-round wine". During the 1950s Schubert searched widely for suitable fruit, particularly in the foothills around Adelaide, in McLaren Vale and the Barossa Valley.

Without the constraints of a single vineyard, winemakers chose the best possible fruit, showcasing the outstanding characteristics of each vineyard.

Both Max Schubert and John Davoren were mindful of the vinification and maturation practices of Europe. The development of both Grange and St. Henri was modelled, to some extent, on Claret styles. The availability of Bordeaux grape varieties in South Australia, however, was limited. Schubert soon favoured Shiraz, largely because of the spectrum of ripe flavours, tannin structures and the relative ease of supply. He struggled initially with Cabernet Sauvignon because of its scarcity and capricious nature in the South Australian climate. John Davoren was similarly constrained, though both winemakers used Cabernet to add perfume and structure to their wines. The release of Bin 389 in 1960, a Cabernet-Shiraz blend now considered the quintessential Australian wine, reflects the winemaking attitude of the time. It was thought that Cabernet Sauvignon did not have the power or mid-palate intensity to be made as a single wine. Many years of improved vineyard management, site selection and winemaking resulted in the subsequent development and releases of Bin 707 and Bin 407 Cabernet Sauvignon.

The concept of multi-regional and vineyard blending, a feature of the Penfolds house style, exemplifies the 'all-round' wine style. Without the constraints of a single vineyard, winemakers chose the best possible fruit, showcasing the outstanding characteristics of each vineyard. This idea gathered pace during the 1960s, as a result of the success of Bin 389 and experimental cross-regional blends such as Penfolds Bin 60A. This method of fruit selection also contributed to

a consistency of style. As the volume of production increased over the years, a method of classification was introduced to earmark particular fruit for individual Bin numbers. This selection process has since been further refined, permitting extraordinary blending options. *The Rewards of Patience* tasting showed that optimising fruit quality in blends does not compromise vintage character.

The felicitous choice of American oak was based on availability. Max Schubert had noticed during his visit to Bordeaux in 1950, that some winemakers used new, 'raw' oak during vinification and maturation. In fact, he had stumbled across a rare practice. At that time, few Clarets completed fermentation in the barrel. While it was true that the leading chateaux employed new oak during maturation, the percentage used depended on the quality of the vintage. His experiments with Shiraz and American oak were profound. He discovered that if the wine completed fermentation in new American oak, the two components would generate a tremendous "volume of bouquet and flavour." Max Schubert remarked, "It was almost as if the new wood had acted as a catalyst to release previously unsuspected flavours from the Hermitage (sic) grape".

Penfolds' release of Bin 128 Coonawarra Shiraz and Bin 28 Kalimna Shiraz in 1962 preceded the contemporary enthusiasm for regional definition by about 25 years. Max Schubert applied many of the techniques used in the research and development of Grange, once more using American oak and barrel fermentation to great effect. All the same, the difference between the ripe, opulent Bin 28 and the elegant, structured Bin 128 (as shown in *The Rewards of Patience* tasting) demonstrated strong regional differences.

James Halliday, influential Australian wine critic and *Rewards of Patience* panel member, has written, "The so-called 'Penfolds style' is so distinctive that to miss it means either I or the wine was off-colour".

Maturation in oak following fermentation is also a key to the Penfolds house style. Penfolds Grange, which is matured in American oak for 18 months, benefits greatly from the aging process, whereupon aromas and flavours derived from both fruit and oak evolve, while tannins polymerise and soften. At the other end of the spectrum is Penfolds St. Henri, which benefits from the maturation effect rather than from the influence of new oak.

The Rewards of Patience tasting showed that optimising fruit quality in blends does not compromise vintage character.

WINEMAKING PHILOSOPHY

John Bird has commented, "Curiously there is some kind of similarity between St. Henri and Grange of between 10 and 15 years of age. There is no doubt about which stable they come from".

Research and development continue to play an important role in the evolution of Penfolds.

While American oak has played a central role in the development of Penfolds red wines, French oak has been used increasingly in the evolution of new wines, particularly RWT and Yattarna. Don Ditter, who became Chief Winemaker in 1973, introduced French oak to the elegantly structured Bin 128 as a way of refining the style and emphasising its regional characteristics. RWT Barossa Shiraz, which is barrel fermented, is also particularly suited to the savoury nuances of French oak. Nowadays, French oak barrels are used in the maturation of around two thirds of Magill Estate Shiraz and approximately half of Bin 407 Cabernet Sauvignon. All premium white wines are fermented and/or matured in French oak (usually barriques).

Research and development continue to play an important role in the evolution of Penfolds wines. The Penfolds flagship white wine project, quickly dubbed by media, 'The White Grange Project', resulted in the release of Penfolds Yattarna Chardonnay, thus rising to Max Schubert's challenge of "making something different and lasting". Penfolds continues to experiment with new varieties, new vineyards and new winemaking techniques while improving on the tried and tested.

The Penfolds approach to winemaking has percolated through the Australian wine industry over the last 50 years. The use of American oak and barrel fermentation, for instance, is these days considered a traditional Barossa winemaking practice. The techniques employed in the research and development of Penfolds wines are astonishing. Max Schubert and his team pioneered major advances in: yeast technology and paper chromatography, the understanding and use of pH in controlling bacterial spoilage, the use of headed down/submerged cap fermentation, the technique of rack and return, cold fermentation practices, the use of American oak as a maturation vessel, and perhaps most critically, partial barrel fermentation.

The Penfolds winemaking philosophy is the accumulation of more than half a century of knowledge and winemaking practice initiated by Max Schubert and subsequently refined by Don Ditter, John Duval and Peter Gago. In the end, of course, the wines must speak for themselves and this is the essence of this fifth edition of Penfolds' *The Rewards of Patience*.

RAY BECKWITH

Ray Beckwith receiving Life Membership of the Australian Wine Industry. *Photograph courtesy of: Craig Arnold.*

Ray Beckwith is one of the unsung pioneers of the modern Australian wine industry. His contribution to quality control and wine stability is of major significance. His influence has been far reaching, yet his name is barely known.

In 1932 he returned to Roseworthy Agricultural College with a cadetship in oenology, a paid position, after having graduated earlier in the year with an Honours Diploma in agriculture. His interest in the performance and efficiency of winemaking yeasts led to an important association with Alan Hickinbotham, a pivotal figure in Australian wine science, whose work on pH and malo-lactic fermentation had a profound generational effect on winemaking philosophy. The project involved the identification and analysis of a high performance yeast of Portuguese origin, a yeast later designated as A1 and used commercially by Penfolds in the production of millions of litres of fortified wines.

After a brief stint at Thomas Hardy, working with Colin Haselgrove and Roger Warren, Ray Beckwith was poached by Leslie Penfold-Hyland, who had read about his findings and the potential economic benefits of pure yeast culture in an Australian Brewing and Wine Journal. Beckwith joined Penfolds at Nuriootpa in January 1935. He was immediately impressed by "the row upon row stacks of American oak hogsheads (300 litres) filled almost exclusively with port", the drink of preference at the time. Submerged cap fermentation, still a classical method of vinification, was used extensively throughout Penfolds cellars even prior to the production of Grange.

In 1935 Penfolds did not own any vineyards in the Barossa. All the grapes were purchased from independent growers, many of whom still used "German wagons and horses" to deliver their crop. Indeed the only company vehicle at Nuriootpa was a "heavy masher dray pulled by a Clydesdale horse". Wine left the winery by rail in hogsheads. As soon as he arrived, Ray Beckwith set about building a new laboratory, turning an old gin still into a yeast propagation tank.

Observation and innovation resulted in new ways of making wine at Penfolds. Ray Beckwith introduced a highly analytical and practical winemaking regime, which included many practices that are now standard in the modern Australian wine industry. Bacterial spoilage of wine, however, was a major problem in the early 1930s.

His contribution to quality control and wine stability is of major significance. His influence has been far reaching, yet his name is barely known.

RAY BECKWITH

Ray Beckwith introduced a highly analytical and practical winemaking regime, which included many practices that are now standard in the modern Australian wine industry.

Initially his role was to find ways to treat the wine through fining agents, ozone injection, pasteurisation and refermentation. The quest for stability led him down new pathways and culs-de-sac. As one problem was solved, fresh problems arose. Out of frustration, he introduced a philosophy of preventative winemaking which was to become a key to Penfolds' reputation.

Ray Beckwith's interest in wine acidity led, in 1936, to his important and far reaching conclusion: "pH may be a useful tool in the control of bacterial growth". He knew of John Fornachon's work with the disastrous sweet wine disease, identified as being caused by lacto-bacillus, which was damaging Australia's reputation in its key United Kingdom market. On reading Fornachon's report, Ray Beckwith understood the influence of pH.

He persuaded Leslie Penfold-Hyland that Penfolds needed a gas electrode pH meter with the Morton glass electrode, a very expensive piece of equipment. He then experimented and applied new winemaking standards using the addition of tartaric acid, a natural constituent of wine, to lower the pH. He is noted as saying, "Maybe it's overstating the case that bacterial spoilage could go through a winery like a bushfire, but with proper control, a winemaker could sleep easy at night".

Certainly his discovery was critically important to the development of all Penfolds dry red wines, most notably Grange. He also noticed that on adjusting pH to his new standard, the "colour brightened and with it a sheen". Interestingly, many believe Ray Beckwith was the first in the world to discover the application of pH to the control of bacteria in wine.

In later years the drainings (the last free run but highly concentrated runnel of new wine from the press) would be sent down to Max Schubert at Magill to strengthen some of the premium and special Bin reds. Beckwith observed, however, that "the heat of fermentation was a major problem because too much heat resulted in a loss of quality and the prospect of bacterial spoilage".

Crude copper heat exchangers that used bore water were brought in around this time. Later these would be replaced by stainless steel. Presses, must pumps and crushers were driven by a shaft with

pulley and belt drive, all powered by 60HP electric motors. These had only recently replaced a powerful steam engine that was mounted on the front deck opposite the boiler house.

Vigilance, care and attention to detail were important to Ray Beckwith. He developed systems which are now standard throughout the industry. This went beyond the laboratory to practical winemaking solutions at every quality level. The list of his innovations and inventions is extraordinary. He designed and improvised new plant and equipment, introduced new technology, and implemented quality control procedures. He was the first person to introduce paper-chromatography as a test for the completion of malo-lactic fermentation. He designed quality standards at a time before consistency and standardisation became an industry norm. His early work with the mass production of Flor Sherry and in finding solutions to the issues of contamination was critical to the success of Penfolds during the 1940s and 1950s.

Ray Beckwith was the quintessential winemaker's 'boffin', a brilliant chemist and scientist. Clearly Max Schubert relied greatly on his intuition and quiet determination. History will remember Max Schubert as the creator of Grange. Ray Beckwith's contribution, however, should also be recognised.

He designed quality standards at a time before consistency and standardisation became an industry norm.

PENFOLDS WHITE WINES

"All winemakers should
possess a good fertile
imagination if they are to
be successful in their craft."

– MAX SCHUBERT

EST 1844

> "The oak is very well handled and the fruit is fresh and clear." – JAMES HALLIDAY

OVERVIEW: Rawson's Retreat is named after Christopher Rawson Penfold's original stone cottage which still stands among the vines at Magill Estate in Adelaide, South Australia. The whites are 'entry level' wines produced in relatively large quantities and sold at everyday prices. They are fresh, easy drinking, fruity wine styles made for immediate consumption. The wines embrace the Penfolds winemaking philosophy of multi-district blending. This allows for consistency of quality each year, even though vintage conditions may vary throughout South Australia. If the style or quality of the fruit from one area is unsuitable in a particular year, Penfolds has the resources to replace it with fruit from other areas.

Winemakers are looking for fruit with good definition and flavour. The Semillon Chardonnay is a more aromatic style with lemony aromas and plenty of ripe fruit on the palate, underpinned by some smoky oak. The Chardonnay is a classic Australian 'sunshine-in-a-glass' style with clear tropical fruit aromas, creamy flavours and a touch of oak. James Halliday regards the Rawson's Retreat whites as well made commercial wines. "These are cleverly made wines that should be drunk right away. The oak is very well handled and the fruit is fresh and clear. These wines are not made for cellaring. We tasted three vintages from 2002 to 2000. The youngest wines are the most satisfying to drink."

PENFOLDS RAWSON'S RETREAT SEMILLON CHARDONNAY

First Vintage: 1995

Variety: Semillon and Chardonnay

Origin: Multi-district blend from South Australia. Predominantly McLaren Vale and Riverland. May vary considerably depending on vintage conditions.

Fermentation: Stainless steel tanks. Some components undergo malo-lactic fermentation.

Maturation: Some components are matured in oak for three months.

PENFOLDS RAWSON'S RETREAT CHARDONNAY

First Vintage: 1998

Variety: Chardonnay

Origin: Multi-district blend from South Australia. Barossa Valley, McLaren Vale, Clare Valley, Riverland and Adelaide Hills. May vary considerably depending on vintage conditions.

Fermentation: Stainless steel tanks. Some components undergo malo-lactic fermentation.

Maturation: Some components are matured in oak for three months.

PENFOLDS KOONUNGA HILL
SEMILLON CHARDONNAY & CHARDONNAY

Penfolds
KOONUNGA HILL
CHARDONNAY

OVERVIEW: The release of the Koonunga Hill Chardonnay recognised that market sentiment was evolving. Emerging export markets demanded a Penfolds white wine. With access to several company vineyards throughout South Australia, Penfolds was able to match its resources to this market need. The Koonunga Hill Chardonnay was first released in the United Kingdom in 1992 and then in Australia the following year. While benefits derive from the huge economies of scale available to a large company, the wine needed to be highly consistent with Penfolds red winemaking reputation. Both Koonunga Hill whites are well proportioned wines with distinctive primary fruit characters and good levels of intensity. They are a step up from the Rawson's Retreat whites, with more concentration and fruit power. The Semillon Chardonnay is an elegant style with lemony nuances and minerally flavours. The Chardonnay, which is matured for several months in small French oak barriques, is a richer style with plenty of varietal definition and creamy flavours.

Penfolds approaches the production of Koonunga Hill whites with the same diligence and attention to detail expected of a small volume, fine wine. Joseph Ward says, "Semillon Chardonnay is a convincing style. The wine has plenty of tropical fruit aromas and a good ripe palate. Compared to Rawson's Retreat, it's worth the extra couple of bucks". Huon Hooke says, "The Koonunga Hill Chardonnay at its best is an enjoyable quaffing wine with interesting barrel/lees complexity and a clean, soft, balanced palate".

The entire panel agrees that both the Koonunga Hill whites are early drinking styles. The Koonunga Hill Semillon Chardonnay and Chardonnay are considered by many to be amongst Australia's best value whites, delivering wine quality at an affordable pricepoint.

PENFOLDS
KOONUNGA HILL
SEMILLON
CHARDONNAY

First Vintage: 1996

Variety: Semillon (60-65%) Chardonnay (30-35%)

Origin: Multi-district blend from South Australia. Barossa Valley, Adelaide Hills. May vary considerably depending on vintage conditions.

Fermentation: Stainless steel tanks. Some components undergo malo-lactic fermentation.

Maturation: Primarily matured without the influence of oak.

PENFOLDS
KOONUNGA HILL
CHARDONNAY

First Vintage: 1991

Variety: Chardonnay

Origin: Multi-district blend often including: Barossa Valley, McLaren Vale, Langhorne Creek, Strathbogie Ranges. May vary considerably depending on vintage conditions.

Fermentation: Stainless steel tanks. Some components undergo malo-lactic fermentation.

Maturation: Some components are barrel fermented and oak matured for three to five months in French oak barriques.

PENFOLDS THOMAS HYLAND
CHARDONNAY

Penfolds

THOMAS HYLAND
SOUTH AUSTRALIA
CHARDONNAY
VINTAGE 2003

In 1863 Thomas Hyland met and married Georgina Penfold. His
stewardship of the company until 1914 saw the development of
what, in his lifetime, became Australia's most famous name in wine.

OVERVIEW: The Penfolds Thomas Hyland range, which includes a 100% Chardonnay, is named after Thomas Francis Hyland, an officer of the Victorian Civil Service, who married Christopher Rawson and Mary Penfolds' daughter, Georgina, in 1862. The new son-in-law initially helped market Penfolds wines to the emerging Victorian wine market. On the death of his father-in-law in 1870, Thomas Hyland moved to South Australia to help run the family business. His considerable administrative skills saw Penfolds emerge as a highly significant Australian wine producer, accounting for one-third of the South Australian vintage.

The Penfolds Thomas Hyland Chardonnay is an evolving Chardonnay style which seeks to express high quality Chardonnay fruit from the Adelaide Hills and other cool-climate South Australian sites. The wine is 100% barrel fermented to increase the complexity of aromas and flavours. After primary fermentation the wine is matured in new, one and two-year-old French oak barriques for seven to nine months. The wine is stirred regularly on lees to further enhance its palate texture and flavours. 100% malo-lactic fermentation is also encouraged to add creaminess and weight. Winemakers have adjusted down the level of new oak over recent vintages to bring out the clear fruit definition of Adelaide Hills Chardonnay. Minimal filtration is also employed to preserve the elegance of the fruit flavours. Although this is a modestly priced wine in the Penfolds portfolio, it includes relegated Yattarna fruit and embraces all the winemaking practices expected in an ultra-premium Chardonnay.

"Poor man's Yattarna perhaps?" suggests Oliver Crawford, Penfolds' white winemaker. Huon Hooke reports having a "good time" tasting through the "extremely consistent" Thomas Hyland Chardonnays. James Halliday goes further, saying that "these wines represent amazing value – one of the great benefits associated with a large organisation". He also notes that the style "steers away from the blood and thunder Chardonnay style".

PENFOLDS THOMAS HYLAND CHARDONNAY

First Vintage: 2001

Variety: Chardonnay

Origin: Primarily Adelaide Hills, with additional components from other premium viticultural regions including the Eden Valley and Robe.

Fermentation: 100% barrel fermented.

Maturation: Matured for seven to nine months in a combination of new (approximately 25%), one and two-year-old French oak.

Comments: Includes relegated Yattarna fruit. Minimal filtration, if any.

PENFOLDS THOMAS HYLAND
CHARDONNAY

2001 `Now`

Medium gold. Complex grilled cashew nut/melon aromas with some buttery notes. The palate is rich and smooth with plenty of sweet fruit and new oak. A good persistent finish.

2002 `Now` `2005`

Medium gold. Intense tropical/melon/grapefruit aromas with toasty/vanilla nuances. The palate is tight and intense with some new oak complexity.

2003 `Now` `2008`

Pale colour. A fragrant, elegant fruit-driven wine with grapefruit/nectarine aromas and subtle oak tones. Well-balanced palate with delicate melon/stone fruit characters, crisp acidity and medium length.

COMMENTARY: "These are all good generic Burgundy-style Chardonnays. The wines progressively become more fruit-driven and lightly oaked." (CPT) "The bracket begins with a rich, smooth, silky wine with plenty of smoky/charry/high-toast oak characters. It finishes with a fresh, rather undeveloped wine with barely noticeable oak and fine delicate flavours. Presumably it will build up with time." (HH) "These are amazing value wines when you consider the overall quality. You can see that the wines are evolving away from a blood and thunder style towards a more fruit-driven Chardonnay where oak plays a supporting role." (JH) "Oaky/100% malo-lactic/high alcohol Chardonnay styles are still very popular in the USA. The Thomas Hyland Chardonnay has become a refined style with medium weight fruit and nice tension." (JW)

(CPT) – CH'NG POH TIONG
(JH)   – JAMES HALLIDAY
(HH)   – HUON HOOKE
(JS)   – JOANNA SIMON
(JW)   – JOSEPH WARD

OVERVIEW: The Penfolds Aged Release Reserve Bin Riesling is either an Eden Valley or Clare Valley wine, depending on vintage conditions. Winemakers are looking for fruit of exceptional acid balance and flavour concentration. Such strict fruit selection means that the wine can be made only in special vintages. The Penfolds Clare Estate, Woodbury and High Eden vineyards are the principal sources of fruit, although a small percentage of independently grown fruit is used in the Clare Valley vintages.

The Penfolds Reserve Bin Riesling is a wine which must have sufficient structure to allow for medium to long term aging. Although it embraces house style winemaking, the wines produced can also show strong regional definition. Joseph Ward observes, "There is a distinct difference between the Clare Valley and Eden Valley Rieslings. The aged Clare Rieslings show plenty of toastiness and a structure and weight similar to Late Harvest Rieslings. The Eden Valley Rieslings, on the other hand, are more classically structured with honeyed aromas and fine crisp acidity". The wine is released after a period of maturation, usually about five years after vintage.

The Aged Release Reserve Bin Riesling is released purposely after five years to highlight the exquisite maturation characters of aged Riesling. When young, these wines are very aromatic, but lean in structure. During the aging process the floral/citrus characters of Riesling develop rich toasty honeyed aromas and flavours, balanced by the variety's naturally high acidity. White winemaker Oliver Crawford says, "We bottle these wines very early, relatively soon after fermentation. We seek to preserve freshness of fruit, but also a bead of very fine acidity. As the wine ages, it becomes more complex and develops very generous flavours on the palate".

PENFOLDS
RESERVE BIN RIESLING
AGED RELEASE

First Vintage: 1992

Variety: Riesling

Origin: Clare Valley (including independently grown fruit), Woodbury and High Eden Valley Vineyards. Regional sources depend on vintage conditions.

Fermentation: Stainless steel tanks.

Maturation: Maturation in bottle for five years before release.

PENFOLDS RESERVE BIN RIESLING
AGED RELEASE

1992 `Now` `2008`

Medium gold. Finely developed and classic Clare Valley style with buttered toast and some dried lemon/lime peel/honey aromas and flavours. The palate is rich and fleshy with fine tight mineral acidity.

1993 `Now` `2008`

Medium gold. An expressive and intense Clare Valley wine with toasty/lime/marmalade aromas. A soft palate with plenty of fruit richness, lemony acidity and flavour length.

1995 `Now` `2010`

Medium gold. A quintessential Eden Valley Riesling showing great balance and finesse. Intense grapefruit/lime/stone fruit aromas with some toasty/oilskin complexity. A very dry refined palate with lime/stone fruit flavours, plenty of mineral nuances and a very long finish. Great vintage.

1997 `Now` `2006`

Medium gold. A very rich generous wine with plenty of toasty/fruit compote aromas and touches of honey. The palate is already quite developed but retains classic Clare Valley structure with mid-palate richness and high-pitched acidity. Finishes with a minerally grip.

1998 `Now` `2018` ★

Medium gold. Highly aromatic distinctly Clare Valley wine with lemon/camomile/pear aromas and some spice/herb nuances. Tightly focused palate with richly concentrated lemony/mineral/spice flavours and fine indelible acidity. A wine with great mouth-feel and balance.

1999 `Now` `2006` ★

Medium yellow. An Eden Valley wine. Potent aromas of apricot, fig jam and lime juice followed by a fruit-laden, silky glycerol textured palate. Not a classic Riesling profile or structure but certainly a good drink now.

2000 `Now` `2020`

Medium yellow. An Eden Valley wine, with intense mineral/slate/fruit-sweet aromas with camomile/pear nuances. The palate is well-balanced and concentrated with lemon/lime flavours, crunchy acidity and plenty of length.

Outstanding vintages ★

COMMENTARY: "I find a distinct difference between the Clare Valley and Eden Valley Rieslings. The aged Clare Rieslings show plenty of toastiness as well as a structure and weight similar to Late Harvest Rieslings. The Eden Valley Rieslings, on the other hand, are more classically structured with honeyed aromas and fine crisp acidity. The 1992 Clare Valley vintage shows citrus/toast/honey aromas and a good acidic spine, but has very lush flavours for Riesling." (JW) "The wine has a lovely ripe palate with dried lemony aromas and toasty complexity." (CPT) "This is a classic Clare style with finely developed aged characters and a lean, tightly structured palate." (HH) "The bright golden colours from 1992 to 1997 are very consistent. The 1992 is rich, full and quite fleshy, but falls short at the finish. This wine needs to be drunk soon." (JH)

"The 1993 Clare Valley vintage has more toasty/honey characters and ripe fruit flavours. This is a very nice, soft ready-to-drink style." (JW) "It has plenty of toast and sweet spicy fruit with a very agreeable ripely textured palate." (CPT) "This is a broader style of wine with candied pineapple fruit characters, lovely richness, and fruit depth. It comes across a touch sweet, but that might be just rich fruit." (HH) "I find the wine has aromas reminiscent of buttered toast with a thin spread of marmalade. It has lovely lemony acidity and considerable length." (JH)

"The 1995 Eden Valley vintage shows different characters altogether, with mineral/lime/stone fruit aromas and some petrol nuances. It has a ripe citrus attack on the palate and some stonefruit/mineral flavours. It has a good finish, but isn't quite as long as I had expected." (JW) "This is a more refreshing wine, but I find it a little unbalanced and broad." (CPT) "The wine

has a glowing colour with lovely aged creamy/buttery/toast aromas. The palate is very dry and refined. I think this wine is a real cracker. It has real delicacy and finesse." (HH) "I like this wine too. It has a classic mix of toast and lime with some mineral/kerosene/petrol complexity. The palate is very lively with zesty acidity/minerality and a very extended finish." (JH)

"The 1997 vintage is a genuine Late Harvest style with ripe attack and soft fruit flavours." (JW) "The wine shows lovely ripe lemon/toasty fruit and delicious acidity. It has nice roundness and richness on the palate." (CPT) "This wine reflects a hot ripe year. It's very rich and generous with a big, developed toasty fruit compote nose. The palate is strongly flavoured, but lacks refinement and delicacy. This is a very good mouthful of wine, but it doesn't have the fine length of the best from this vintage." (HH) "While this wine shows classic aromas, structure and flavour it has a firm mineral finish. A slightly disappointing wine." (JH)

"The 1998 is the first of the Clare Valley Rieslings to show an apricot/pear profile. It has aromas similar to Californian Late Harvest Riesling, but the palate is soft and not quite as weighty." (JW) "The wine has developed petrol/floral aromas and tart acidity on the palate. I find it austere and not so balanced." (CPT) "I also find a high-acid palate, but it's a good wine. It has some candle wax/paraffin aromas, but the palate is tightly-packed and minerally with a drying finish. I think the wine is a little stripped." (HH) "I feel a bit like a shag on a rock here! I think the wine is a major surprise. It is bursting with aromatics and has great mouth-feel and balance." (JH)

"The 1999 Eden Valley vintage shows a crisp lime/petrol attack and a fresh blend of fruit and

PENFOLDS RESERVE BIN RIESLING
AGED RELEASE

acidity on the palate." (JW) "This is a charming light/medium bodied wine with mineral/honey (botrytis) aromas and plenty of freshness on the palate." (CPT) "I agree. I can see a whiff of apricot/botrytis characters, but it goes really well with those oily textures on the palate. I like the fig jam aromas and the sweet fruit entry. This wine does not have a classic Riesling profile or structure." (HH) "The wine shows strong lime juice/pineapple aromas, but the fruit laden palate is a touch flaccid, overwhelmed by botrytis characters." (JH)

"The 2000 Eden Valley vintage is a well focused wine with a fairly long life ahead of it. It has plenty of floral/citrus aromas and a crisp bright attack on the palate with citrus/pear flavours." (JW) "This is a very refined elegant wine with apple/floral aromas and lemony acidity." (CPT) "The wine shows fine fruit and delicacy, the more it sits in the glass. I find it unbalanced and slightly hot at first. It's locked away at the moment and needs time to reveal itself." (HH) "It has good structure, line and length. I find this wine very convincing with classic slate/lime aromas, a core of mineral/crunchy acidity and excellent length." (JH)

(CPT) – CH'NG POH TIONG
(JH)   – JAMES HALLIDAY
(HH) – HUON HOOKE
(JS)   – JOANNA SIMON
(JW) – JOSEPH WARD

> "The wine is delicious to drink young, yet has plenty of finesse and structure for medium to long term cellaring." – PETER GAGO

OVERVIEW: The Eden Valley Reserve Riesling is sourced from the mature Woodbury and High Eden Vineyards that were originally planted between 1940 and 1960. A sub-region of the Barossa, the Eden Valley lies about 450 metres above sea level. The soils are derived from schistic and sedimentary rock. They are mostly red clay soils and sandy, silty loams interspersed with schistic gravels. The Penfolds vineyards are located on particularly lean soil structures. The relatively higher altitude means a cooler growing season, ideal for aromatic grape varieties, especially Riesling. This is a definitive bone-dry Eden Valley Riesling style with 100% natural acidity and clear fruit aromas and flavours. Peter Gago comments, "The wine, with a bracing acid backbone and packed with fruit sweetness, is delicious to drink young, yet has plenty of finesse and structure for medium to long term cellaring". The wine is released in the vintage year and soon after bottling.

All bottlings of this wine since 2002 inclusive are sealed with a Stelvin, screwcap closure. Screwcap is not new to Penfolds' Rieslings – 1971 and 1972 Penfolds Autumn Rieslings and 1980 Penfolds Dalwood Riesling, for example, were all sealed under screwcap. This move proved to be ahead of its time, as consumers were not comfortable with the change. Today, consumer acceptance of this form of wine closure for many white wines has reached a level where Penfolds winemakers are confident of its acceptance.

Peter Gago is very clear in stating Penfolds' style objectives for this wine. "We are very much focused upon capturing the rose petal and summer blossom spectrum of aromatics, whilst a tightly defined acidity lends structure and length to the finish."

Ch'ng Poh Tiong describes the style as "particularly taut with plenty of mineral/floral/earthy aromas and nuanced fruit". Huon Hooke notes, "The 2002 is a glorious wine with seamless structure and generous flavours". James Halliday prefers the more recent vintages (2002/2003) because of their "clear lime aromas and stronger mineral tones".

The Eden Valley Reserve Riesling reflects both intense clear fruit definition and a strong sense of place. The floral lime/camomile aromas and flavours are intertwined with mineral nuances; the smell and flavours derive from the soil, with no oak or lees affects to mask its origins.

PENFOLDS
EDEN VALLEY
RESERVE RIESLING

First Vintage: 1999

Variety: Riesling

Origin: Woodbury and High Eden Vineyards, Eden Valley.

Fermentation: Stainless steel tanks. Bottling in July.

Maturation: Bottled early to retain freshness and released towards end of vintage year.

PENFOLDS RESERVE BIN RIESLING
EDEN VALLEY

1999 `Now` ★

Bright yellow gold. Intense honey/lime aromas with some toasty complexity. The palate is richly flavoured and fully developed with fine mineral acidity and drying finish.

2000 `Now` `2009`

Straw gold. Lime blossom aromas with some bottle development characters. Racy minerally palate with lemon/lime flavours, medium concentration and length.

2001 `Now` `2005`

Medium straw. A strongly aromatic wine with pear-skin/lime/citrus aromas and flavours. The palate is broad and well concentrated with a fine mineral backbone. A touch phenolic at the finish.

2002 `Now` `2012` ★

Medium straw. Classic Eden Valley wine with glorious lime blossom/pear/slatey aromas, hints of spice and flowing mouth-feel. Lovely juicy fruit and richness on the palate with high pitched mouthwatering acidity and plenty of flavour length. A refined, but generously concentrated wine with plenty of aging potential. Stelvin closure.

2003 `Now` `2012`

Pale straw. Very restrained delicate wine with dried wildflower/lime/camomile aromas. Tightly focused, tangy palate with minerally citrus/lime flavours and steely finish. Expected to age well. Stelvin closure.

Outstanding vintages ★

COMMENTARY: "The 1999 vintage is already showing quite a lot of age with plenty of buttered toasty characters, but it has lots of flavour, richness and balance." (HH) "It is prematurely developed, but I like the toast/honey/lime characters and the overall acidity, harmony, length and impact. Certainly it is a wine to drink soon." (JH) "The wine is showing some of those developed petrol nuances, but I like the compact structure and minerality." (JW) "This is a straightforward wine with over-ripe citrus fruit. I think it lacks the acidity for further aging." (CPT)

"The 2000 vintage is in a transition phase. It has plenty of lime blossom/mineral characters, but also some carbon dioxide lurking around. It will look very good when it comes out." (JH) "This wine is quite earthy/minerally, but lacks the high notes and concentration of a top notch Riesling. It has medium term aging potential." (HH) "This has the lowest acidity in the bracket. It has some good pear/lime aromas and citrusy flavours, but is sharp rather than crisp with some petrol nuances. The finish is short. I preferred the wines with stronger mineral tones." (JW) "I find the wine quite impressive – one of my favourites in this bracket. It is taut and perhaps a bit closed, but has the finesse and tight middle palate structure to age." (CPT)

"The 2001 is a powerful, robust wine with a strong mineral backbone and faint bitterness." (JH) "The fruit is at the fore with plenty of lime citrus characters. I find the palate quite soft and gentle – actually quite broad – finishing a touch coarsely." (HH) "The wine has nice weight and balance, although it is somewhat broader at the finish. It's an early drinking style." (JW) "There are some light petrol notes as well. The wine is forward and underpowered." (CPT)

"I love the glorious aromatics and flowing mouth-feel of the 2002 vintage. I enjoy those positive Eden Valley lime juice characters and long fine finish." (JH) "This is a wonderful wine; refined, seamless, rich and generous. This is an undeveloped but delicious wine with tremendous potential." (HH) "It's a glorious wine. I really like the bright lime/pear fruit characters, the overall weight and concentration of the wine. It has excellent flavour length." (JW) "This wine is very minerally and floral. It is ripe and round with wonderful nuanced fruit, intensity and length." (CPT)

"The 2003 has plenty of spicy minerality with crushed herb/blossom characters and a very tightly focused palate. It has a wonderful feather-touch vivacity." (JH) "This is a yeasty doughy, fresh fermented youngster with a bouquet of dried wildflowers. The palate is delicate with tangy, frisky acidity and good citrus flavours. This is a proper dry style with excellent structure and length." (HH) "This is a backward/restrained wine with very tight fruit and strong mineral notes. This is a classically structured Riesling with medium to long term cellaring." (JW) "The wine has a great core of steely acidity and plenty of floral/grapefruit/lime aromas and flavours." (CPT)

(CPT) – CH'NG POH TIONG
(JH)   – JAMES HALLIDAY
(HH) – HUON HOOKE
(JS)   – JOANNA SIMON
(JW) – JOSEPH WARD

The Reserve Bin A Series embraces a
tradition of experimentation at Penfolds –
a wine which reflects both house style
and individual winemaking skills.

Penfolds

RESERVE BIN
00A
2000 CHARDONNAY

OVERVIEW: The Reserve Bin A Series Chardonnay, a pathfinder wine, was first vintaged in 1994 and is a by-product of the Penfolds flagship white wine project. This is a style of Chardonnay that 'sits outside the square'. The wine is now made from 100% Adelaide Hills fruit sourced from up to 80 vineyards with core provenance from 10 cooler vineyard sites. Whilst acid balance and Baumé levels are important, winemakers are ultimately looking for flavour ripeness, particularly fruit with a guava/quince/grapefruit profile. The best vineyards are located around Birdwood, Balhannah, Morialta and Gumeracha. Invariably, yields are around three to four tonnes per hectare.

Each year the vines are aging, resulting in more consistent quality Chardonnay. Much of the fruit is sourced from independent growers, some of whom have gone to extraordinary lengths to ensure consistent fruit quality. The 1994, contained a touch of Sauvignon Blanc from Tumbarumba (in NSW) to add lift, but time has shown this component does not have the expected aging potential. The Reserve Bin A Series is a highly worked, multi-layered style. Winemakers are seeking to make a wine of heightened complexity through innovative, sometimes extreme winemaking practice. The wines are 100% barrel fermented in new French oak barriques and undergo 100% malo-lactic fermentation. Wild yeasts are increasingly used to impart interesting flavour profiles and textures. More recent vintages have been fermented on solids and purposely sulphide-influenced to further increase complexity. The Reserve Bin A Series embraces a tradition of experimentation at Penfolds', it is a wine which reflects both house style and individual winemaking skills.

Oliver Crawford comments, "Reserve Bin has evolved from a trial Bin wine to a wine that is an integral part of the Penfolds portfolio. The fruit is now sourced solely from the Adelaide Hills and the wine is made only in years with ideal growing conditions. The overall style combines full flavoured fruit with intensity and elegance, 100% wild fermentation in barrel in combination with high juice solids, provides the wine with complexity and structure".

In February 2004, the Reserve Bin 00A Chardonnay received resounding endorsement when it won three trophies, culminating in the Championship Perpetual Trophy for "Best Wine of the Competition" at the Sydney International Wine Competition.

PENFOLDS RESERVE BIN A CHARDONNAY

First Vintage: 1994

Variety: Chardonnay

Origin: Adelaide Hills, extending from Birdwood in the south to Gumeracha in the north. Earlier vintages comprise some Tumbarumba fruit.

Fermentation: 100% barrel fermented / 100% malo-lactic fermentation.

Maturation: Matured for 11 months in specially selected tightly-grained French oak barriques.

Comments: Originally a trial wine from the Penfolds flagship white wine project.

PENFOLDS RESERVE BIN A
CHARDONNAY

1994 `Now`
Bin 94A
Medium gold. Very developed nose with cashew/honey/toasted hazelnut aromas and flavours. The palate is well-concentrated and creamy with plenty of acidity and length.

1995 `Now` ★
Bin 95A
Medium gold. A well-developed fully mature wine with rich buttery/vanilla/roasted hazelnut aromas and some stone fruit characters. A richly flavoured, well-balanced palate with integrated vanilla oak and a spine of fine lively acidity.

1998 `Now` `2008` ★
Bin 98A
Medium straw gold. Fresh elegant wine with high-pitched grapefruit/fig aromas and toasted nut complexity. A soft creamy palate with stone fruit/grilled nut flavours, plenty of mid-palate richness, finishing crisp and long.

2000 `Now` `2010` ★
Bin 00A
Medium straw. Refined, delicate wine with flinty/lemon curd/tropical fruit aromas. The palate is fine and supple with flinty/stone fruit/lemon flavours, underlying savoury oak, followed by a long lingering finish.

2001 `Now` `2012`
Bin 01A
Pale straw. Fresh, undeveloped, well-focused wine with intense white peach/melon/tropical fruit aromas and some nougat/nutty complexity. A tightly structured palate with youthful lemony/tropical flavours, subtle oak and fine minerally acidity.

2002
Not made.

2003 `2006` `2014`
Bin 03A
Pale straw. Youthful, fresh grapefruit/mineral aromas with some grilled almond nuances. The palate is finely textured and creamy with ripe pear/grapefruit flavours, underlying savoury oak, plenty of leesy complexity and crisp acidity. Bottled 100% under screwcap.

Outstanding vintages ★

COMMENTARY: "The 1994 and 1995 vintages are fully mature and I don't recommend further cellaring. The 1994 shows plenty of hazelnut and rich aged characters, but I think the palate is quite lean and hollowing out. The 1995, on the other hand, is a marvellous wine. It has similar hazelnut/toasty aromas but more richness and finesse on the palate." (HH) "I agree. The 1994 and 1995s are looking quite elderly, but they still have plenty of line and length with remarkable acidity and intensity." (JH) "The 1995 vintage is my top wine of the tasting. It has lovely concentrated ripe fruit, wonderful grilled nut complexity and a persistent dry finish. I can see this wine keeping until 2009." (JW) "I find the 1994 austere and mealy with a short finish. The 1995 is a more evenly balanced wine with strong vanilla oak tones and very ripe fruit characters. It needs to be drunk soon." (CPT) "The Bin 94A was released before Yattarna and attracted plenty of interest. The Bin 95A is an 85% Adelaide Hills wine, whereas the 1995 Yattarna Chardonnay is an Adelaide Hills/Willunga (McLaren Vale) wine. Both were shown at the Sydney Wine Show. Len Evans was impressed by the Yattarna, saying he had never seen an Australian Chardonnay like this before. This persuasive remark led us to release the latter wine as Yattarna, but as winemakers we prefer the leaner, tighter Bin 95A style." (JD)

"The 1998 is a remarkably underdeveloped wine with plenty of toasted nut and sweet fruit characters. The palate is delicate, showing great finesse and length. I would imagine this has much to do with the three year vintage difference and refinement of style." (HH) "I particularly like the 1998 vintage as well. It is very complex with intense stone fruit/fig aromas and high-toast barrel ferment characters." (JH)

"I am less keen on the 1998. I find the wine quite compact and surprisingly firm. There is nothing about the palate structure which suggests that it will become more complex with time." (JW) "I find the 1998 in the same class as the 2000. It is fresh with lovely acidity and length, but I reserve judgement on whether it is a great wine." (CPT)

"The 2000 vintage is more refined and delicate than the 1998. The palate has lovely texture, but not quite the same length." (HH) "I think it's a glorious wine with almost perfect harmony between fruit oak and malo-lactic characters. The palate is fine and supple with excellent line and length." (JH) "The wine is very tight with tropical fruit/clove aromas and some candied notes on the palate. It finishes shorter than I expected but that might be the firmness of fruit." (JW) "I enjoyed this wine. It has a lovely balance of fruit, oak and acidity. Those wonderful flinty/smoky/mineral/vanilla aromas and flavours linger on like a great Meursault." (CPT)

"The oak is totally buried in the 2001 vintage. It's barely noticeable. The wine seems quite fruit driven compared to the other wines in this line-up. The palate is very subtle and refined, but with very long flavours." (HH) "The wild yeasts have almost added 'texture' to the aromas and certainly to the palate. The wine has great mouth-feel and intensity." (JH) "The 2001 is also very tight. I had trouble coaxing out the fruit at first, but it has the weight and structure to improve with age. I would leave it for a few years as it needs more time to show itself." (JW)

(CPT) – CH'NG POH TIONG
(JH) – JAMES HALLIDAY
(HH) – HUON HOOKE
(JS) – JOANNA SIMON
(JW) – JOSEPH WARD

"The Penfolds Organic Chardonnay is an elegant style with flowery aromas and lovely intensity of flavours". - CH'NG POH TIONG

Penfolds

ORGANIC
CLARE VALLEY
CHARDONNAY

OVERVIEW: Organic wine is simply wine from vineyards that are not exposed to man-made fertilisers, herbicides and pesticides. For a long time Penfolds has applied a philosophy of low-input viticulture. Achieving optimum fruit quality with minimal intervention is a priority. This is achieved through good vineyard management including vineyard design and trellising systems, bunch and leaf thinning, and maintaining low yields. It also helps if the vineyard is planted in the right place, with good natural drainage and aspect.

Penfolds adheres to a strict classification system at vintage. The whole idea of fruit quality is ultimately based on the condition of the fruit, its concentration and flavour profile. In some wine areas it is not practical to run an organically certified vineyard, particularly in the more maritime influenced regions where humidity can wreak havoc on developing grape bunches. However, in areas like the Clare Valley, where the climate is continental and the growing season is subject to long bursts of warm to hot weather, it is possible to apply strict organic principles without affecting the quality of the fruit.

Of the 218.99 hectares of Penfolds vineyard planted in the Clare Valley, 52.36 hectares are organically grown and have been certified by the National Association for Sustainable Agriculture Australia Limited (NASAA).

Sulphur dioxide has been used as a preservative in wine since Roman times. It is a natural product and organic wine must have minimal traces of this compound, just enough to ensure the wine remains fresh on the shelves for a while. To put this into context, the amount of sulphur used in a normal bottle of wine is about one-tenth the sulphite level used in the commercial production of dried fruits such as raisins and apricots. In a bottle of organic wine the level is further reduced. Peter Gago says, "The wines are not fined either. We adhere to a strict organic winemaking approach. We use separate hoses, pumps and tanks to make the wine". The Penfolds organic wines were released in response to growing worldwide demand for organic wines. Within their category they have already won many international accolades.

The Penfolds Organic Chardonnay aims to provide an organic equivalent to the classic Australian unoaked Chardonnay style. The wines are fresh and lively with plenty of peach/melon aromas

**PENFOLDS
CLARE VALLEY
ORGANIC
CHARDONNAY**

First Vintage: 1993

Variety: Chardonnay

Origin: Clare Valley Vineyard

Fermentation: Stainless steel tanks. Some components undergo malo-lactic fermentation.

Maturation: No oak maturation, no fining agents, minimal filtration.

**PENFOLDS
CLARE VALLEY
ORGANIC
CABERNET SHIRAZ
MERLOT**

First Vintage: 1993

Variety: Cabernet Sauvignon, Shiraz and Merlot

Origin: Clare Valley Vineyard

Fermentation: Stainless steel tanks.

Maturation: Eight months maturation in new and used French oak hogsheads, used for previous organic wines.

PENFOLDS CLARE VALLEY
ORGANIC WINES

and flavours. This is an early drinking style best drunk within 18 months of release. Ch'ng Poh Tiong says, "The Penfolds Organic Chardonnay is an elegant style with flowery aromas and lovely intensity of flavours". James Halliday observes, "The wine has good perfume, length and finesse, but it is important to stress that these are 'drink now' wines".

Penfolds Organic Cabernet Shiraz Merlot is also an early drinking style, but is a contemporary varietal blend with plenty of ripe berry fruit, flavour concentration and fine savoury tannins. Penfolds recommends that these wines be consumed within two years of release. Huon Hooke says, "The organic reds were a surprise package. They are bright, clean Cabernet-like wines which will easily keep for a few years".

PENFOLDS RED WINES

"Good wines don't just
happen. They are born
and bred in the minds of
the winemakers concerned."

– MAX SCHUBERT

EST 1844

OVERVIEW: Rawson's Retreat is named after Christopher Rawson Penfold's original stone cottage, which still stands among the vines at Magill Estate, in Adelaide, South Australia. The wine is an affordable, everyday, easy-drinking wine. Although the volume of production is significant, Penfolds still applies a rigorous selection and classification programme to ensure consistency of style and quality each year. The fruit is drawn from various South Australian wine regions, in particular, Padthaway, Langhorne Creek, Riverland and McLaren Vale. The wine is now a Shiraz-Cabernet blend, a classic Australian marriage of fruit power and structure.

The winemakers' objective is to produce a wine with pronounced fruit definition and vibrant flavours. The wines see a modicum of oak, but generally this is a fruit-driven wine which should be enjoyed within 18 months of release. Huon Hooke describes Rawson's Retreat as, "Bright attractive wines offering good value at this pricepoint". Joseph Ward says, "The wines are medium weighted with crisp fruit. It's a nice style for current drinking".

Penfolds Rawson's Retreat Shiraz Cabernet has recently been joined in all markets by a Merlot and a Cabernet Sauvignon. All these wines have enjoyed wide consumer acceptance and have successfully broadened the appeal of Penfolds' entry point red wine offering.

PENFOLDS RAWSON'S RETREAT SHIRAZ CABERNET

First Vintage: 1994

Variety: Shiraz and Cabernet, early vintages included Ruby Cabernet

Origin: Multi-district blend from South Australia. Padthaway, Langhorne Creek, McLaren Vale, Riverland. Sourcing may vary considerably depending on vintage conditions.

Fermentation: Stainless steel tanks. Components undergo malo-lactic fermentation.

Maturation: Some components are matured for three to six months in used oak.

PENFOLDS KOONUNGA HILL
CABERNET MERLOT

Penfolds

KOONUNGA HILL
CABERNET MERLOT

VINTAGE 2001

This wine combines the rich berry-like fruit flavours and firmness of
Cabernet Sauvignon with the plummy softness of Merlot. The result
is a full-bodied red, enjoyable now or with medium-term cellaring.

OVERVIEW: Koonunga Hill Cabernet Merlot was first vinified in 2001. The wine is a multi-district blend drawing fruit from several vineyards in South Australia including McLaren Vale, Barossa Valley, Padthaway, Langhorne Creek and Coonawarra. Named after the Penfolds Koonunga Hill Vineyard in the Barossa Valley, Koonunga Hill benefits from economies of scale and a highly focused approach to vineyard selection.

The overall selection of fruit follows a similar pattern to Penfolds Bin wines. Winemakers seek Cabernet Sauvignon and Merlot with clear fruit definition, optimum flavour development and tannin ripeness. After batch vinification in stainless steel, some components are matured in oak to enhance complexity. The individual components are then classified and trial-blended to achieve consistency and a characteristic style.

The release of Koonunga Hill Cabernet Merlot is built upon a tradition of rigorous fruit selection and skillful blending. It is a full flavoured but fruit driven wine, in contrast to the maturation style of the Shiraz Cabernet (which was first released in 1976). The Cabernet Merlot is an earlier drinking wine, which emphasises the clear, bright, fruit characters and fine grained tannins of Cabernet Sauvignon as well as the plummy flavours of Merlot. Peter Gago says, "The Koonunga Hill Cabernet Merlot is all about freshness and vivacity of fruit, with fine ripe tannins and plenty of flavour. It's a contemporary style, a perfect foil to the traditional Shiraz Cabernet, which was first released as a Selected Bin Claret".

James Halliday notes a strong Cabernet presence in the wine. Joseph Ward finds the Cabernet Merlot a good current consumption wine showing plenty of "bright fruit and a kick on the middle palate".

PENFOLDS KOONUNGA HILL CABERNET MERLOT

First Vintage: 2001

Variety: Cabernet Sauvignon and Merlot

Origin: Multi-district blend from South Australia. McLaren Vale, Barossa Valley, Padthaway, Langhorne Creek, Coonawarra. Sourcing may vary considerably depending on vintage conditions.

Fermentation: Stainless steel tanks.

Maturation: A moderate use of older oak.

Penfolds
KOONUNGA HILL
SHIRAZ CABERNET
SOUTH EASTERN AUSTRALIA

OVERVIEW: First produced in 1976, Koonunga Hill was named after the Koonunga Hill Vineyard planted a few years earlier in the Barossa Valley. The mid-1970s was a difficult period for the Australian wine industry. The red wine boom was over and cellars were full of surplus red wine. The export market was almost non-existent and marketers had to find new ways of moving excess volumes of allocated Penfolds Bin wine into a domestic market flush with stock. The winemakers came up with a robust barrel matured blend of Shiraz and Cabernet which at first release sold at under AUD$2 a bottle! The wine was an instant hit, and for many years was the entry point to Penfolds' portfolio of red wines.

Koonunga Hill, a multi-district blend based on Barossa, McLaren Vale and Coonawarra fruit, has since become a Penfolds classic with a reputation for over-delivery of quality at its pricepoint. The wine never sees new oak, but relies on the maturation effect – a red wine character that is central to the Penfolds house style. Winemakers seek to maintain its style, weight and concentration each year, regardless of vintage conditions. Shiraz usually leads the wine, varying from 50% to 65+% of the blend. Koonunga Hill has a reputation for medium, occasionally long-term cellaring potential, but has always been crafted for immediate enjoyment upon release.

The panel all agree that the quality of Koonunga Hill has improved over the years. Today incoming fruit is batched and classified prior to fermentation. The wine components are then earmarked for maturation in three to four-year-old 300 litre hogshead barrels. These wines are checked regularly and topped up over a twelve month period. A benchtop classification also takes place prior to blending to make sure that the wine is of Koonunga Hill standard.

Although the label has changed over the years, the style has remained true to its vintage origins. James Halliday says, "The Koonunga Hill Shiraz Cabernet is a remarkable wine showing strong Penfolds winemaking style. The wine reflects the vintage and in good years represents incredible value". While some of the older vintages are now past their prime, the panel was particularly impressed by the 1976, the first vintage, now considered a classic Penfolds year.

PENFOLDS
KOONUNGA HILL
SHIRAZ CABERNET

First Vintage: 1976

Variety: Shiraz and Cabernet. The proportions vary but Shiraz is always the dominant variety.

Origin: Multi-district blend from South Australia. Barossa Valley, McLaren Vale, Clare Valley, Coonawarra, Padthaway, Langhorne Creek and Bordertown. May vary considerably depending on vintage conditions.

Fermentation: Stainless steel tanks.

Maturation: 12 months' maturation in three to four-year-old oak hogsheads.

Comments: Labelled Koonunga Hill 'Claret' until 1991 vintage.

PENFOLDS KOONUNGA HILL
SHIRAZ CABERNET

Koonunga Hill has a reputation for medium, occasionally long-term cellaring potential, but has always been crafted for immediate enjoyment upon release.

Improved vineyard management has heightened the quality of top vintages, particularly the 1990s, many of which are likely to further improve for some years to come. Don Ditter, Penfolds former Chief Winemaker and the creator of Koonunga Hill, comments, "We used to make this wine from excess components, but always in the Penfolds style. The wine has evolved and improved. I don't think there's ever been such a thing as a crook Koonunga Hill. It's always a reliable drop, but in top years you can expect something out of the ordinary". At the 2001 International Wine Challenge in London, Penfolds Koonunga Hill won 'Great Value Red Wine of the Year'. In December 2003, the 2002 Koonunga Hill Shiraz Cabernet was listed as one of the top 50 New World wines by *Decanter* magazine.

93

PENFOLDS KOONUNGA HILL
SHIRAZ CABERNET

1976 `Now` `2006` ★

Brick red. Still holding up well with plenty of richness and ripeness. The wine is showing complex and inviting cigar box/mocha-berry aromas and some dried seaweed/leathery characters. The palate is rich and ripe with spicy/coffee/dark fruit flavours and balanced by fine chocolaty tannins, finishing dry and sinewy. In remarkable condition.

1977 `Now`

Dark brick red. A fading wine with earthy/chocolate aromas and some stemmy notes. The wine is still drinkable but the fruit is drying out and the tannins are quite leafy. It's past its best. Drink up.

1978 `Now`

Brick red. Hazelnut/minty/camphor aromas and flavours with some cedar/driftwood complexity and bitter chocolaty tannins. A lingering but drying finish.

1979 `Past – Now`

Brick red. Slightly over developed nose with savoury meaty/earthy/sandalwood aromas and some leafy notes. The palate is quite lean and dry with leafy, slightly aggressive tannins, but some cedar earthy flavours. Certainly past its best.

1980 `Past`

Brick red. Very evolved wine with earthy/stemmy/minty aromas and some mocha notes. The fruit has dried out leaving a palate dominated by leafy dry tannins. Past.

1981 `Now`

Brick red. Dried fruit/driftwood aromas with some porty/jammy nuances. The palate is quite rough with soupy dry tannins, but it still retains some sweet fruit and concentration. Drink now.

1982 `Now`

Brick red. A savoury, developed wine with meaty/gamy/leafy aromas and some dark choco-berry/cedar characters. A leanly structured palate with pronounced but not overtly assertive tannins, some prune/chocolate/leafy flavours.

Outstanding vintages ★

1983 `Now` `2006`

Brick red. Concentrated and developed dark choco-berry/cedar/briar/leafy aromas with a touch of leather. The palate is rich and sturdy with mocha/prune/herbal flavours, dense tannins building up chalky and dry at the finish. Drying out.

1984 `Now` `2006`

Brick red. Solid chunky wine with earthy/meaty/cherry fruit aromas and some minty/spicy nuances. The palate is still balanced with richness of fruit but the tannins are quite grippy. Will not improve further but should hold for a while.

1985 `Now` `2008`

Brick red. Aromatic small berry/dark chocolate/jammy aromas with hints of mint/spice. Rich concentrated meaty/choco-berry/dried cherry flavours and supple ripe tannins. Still a good drink.

1986 `Now` `2006`

Brick red. Elegant wine with developed dried red fruit/meaty/mushroom aromas. The palate is surprisingly lean for vintage, but shows some sweet fruit/mushroom/leather characters and fine chewy tannins. Holding but best drunk soon.

1987 `Now`

Brick red. Aromatic wine with plenty of chocolate/menthol/berry aromas and some polished leather nuances. A lean, sinewy, slightly underpowered palate with green tannins and fading fruit. Finishes short. Drink now.

1988 `Now` `2008`

Brick red. Intense black berry/chocolate aromas with some savoury notes. The palate is certainly at or beyond its peak, but it still has plenty of sweet fruit and loose-knit but firm tannin structure.

1989 `Now`

Brick red. Developed wine with savoury/earthy/leafy aromas and some green bean characters. The palate is quite austere with some stemmy/vegetal/jammy fruit characters and green soupy tannins. Best to drink now.

1990 `Now` `2012` ★

Brick red. A very impressive wine with rich complex cassis/plum/mocha fruit with some spicy notes. Extremely concentrated and well-balanced palate with ripe choco/berry fruit flavours and supple ripe tannins. A wine with great texture and structure. In a class of its own!

1991 `Now` `2010` ★

Brick red. Complex and savoury leather, vanilla, dark chocolate aromas. The palate is fleshy and concentrated with dark chocolate/dark cherry flavours and fine slinky tannins.

1992 `Now` `2006`

Deep Red. Aromatic leafy/red currant aromas with some camphor characters. Red currant/plum/earthy flavours are intertwined with fine slightly bitter tannins. Still holding up well but should be drunk before tannins take over.

1993 `Now` `2005`

Deep red. Intense plum/berry/briar/minty aromas and flavours. The palate is chocolaty but quite lean, with leafy tannins and only moderate concentration. Finishes tough and firm. Drink soon.

1994 `Now` `2010`

Medium red. Intense choco-berry/earthy aromas. A well concentrated palate with mocha/blackberry/earthy flavours and fine supple tannins. Finishes long and sweet.

1995 `Now`

Medium red. A light aromatic wine with some red currant/spicy/earthy aromas. A lightly structured palate with earthy/raspberry/mint flavours and fine brittle tannins. Needs to be drunk soon.

1996 `Now` `2015` ★

Deep red. Rich smooth dark choco-berry/plum aromas. A highly concentrated beautifully balanced wine with choco-berry/plum/sweet spice flavours and ripe chocolaty tannins. A superb wine of exemplary quality.

1997 `Now` `2007`

Medium red. More developed than the 1996 with cherry/menthol/briary/earthy aromas and flavours. The palate is medium concentrated with plenty of sweet fruit and fine slightly firm tannins. Builds up quite astringent at the finish. Drink soon.

1998 `Now` `2020` ★

Deep red. Substantial wine with intensely rich and ripe cassis/plum aromas. A plummy supple and well-concentrated palate with plenty of fine chocolaty tannins. A wine of exceptional structure, weight and balance.

1999 `Now` `2010`

Deep red-purple. Sweet juicy raspberry/blackberry Shiraz dominant aromas. The palate is very concentrated with plenty of sweet, jammy fruit and strong powerful tannins. This is probably a medium term wine and should be drunk before the tannins muscle in!

2000 `Now` `2010`

Deep red-purple. Aromatic raspberry/redcurrant/violet aromas. A lightly concentrated but elegantly proportioned and lively palate with plummy/raspberry flavours and leafy tannins. Remarkable for its vintage.

2001 `Now` `2010`

Deep red-purple. Intense raspberry/blackberry aromas and ripely structured palate with saturated blackberry fruit flavours and rich but strong tannins A very seductive sweet fruit style.

2002 `Now` `2012` ★

Deep red-purple. Crushed fruit/plum/mulberry/slightly herbal aromas and flavours. The palate is fresh and vibrant with plenty of sweet fruit and pronounced puckering tannins. Tannins are wrestling with fruit. Best to drink over next five years.

Outstanding vintages ★

PENFOLDS KOONUNGA HILL
SHIRAZ CABERNET

COMMENTARY: "The 1976 Koonunga Hill is a lovely old wine with baked fruit aromas and a soft ripe attack. There is still plenty of freshness and life." (JW) "I love the seaweed/leather/candied aromas and ripe chocolaty/mocha flavours. This is a ripe, rich, but well-balanced wine. It was made from the Year of the Dragon, which of course means it has staying power!" (CPT) "This is a freakish wine when you consider its sub AUD$2 release price. It's outlived a myriad other high quality wines from this vintage that sold at much higher prices." (JH) "It is a remarkable wine with a very mellow, inviting old wine nose and plenty of cigar box/mocha characters. And it's still living on." (HH)

"The 1977 to 1982 vintages should be consumed now, with most past their best. The 1977 is quite stemmy, the 1978 still shows some good fruit but the palate is certainly beginning to dry out. The 1979 is astringent, with fruit just hanging in there. The 1980 has some stalk/herb characters and is drying out. The 1981 is also stemmy and while I liked the 1982 at first, it has a sharp attack on the palate." (JW)

"The 1982 vintage has interesting Chinese prune aromas and some generosity on the palate, but the acidity is poking out." (CPT) "The fruit is rapidly dipping in many of these wines, leaving tannins to dominate. The 1978 is probably the best, with aromatic berry/herb aromas and a cedary palate. The 1981 is tending to roughness, but is concentrated and appears to have gained a second wind." (JH) "There's not much to add. I agree with James. The 1978 is the best from 1977–1982 with plenty of rich fruit and a firm and vigorous palate. The 1983 vintage is still holding, but is quite leathery and dry." (JW) "I find the wine shows coffee/prune fruit characters and is still drinking well. This is a much sturdier wine with blackberry/cedar/briar aromas and a rich and

powerful palate." (JH) "But it needs to be drunk soon. The tannins are puckery at the finish and I can see the fruit drying out." (HH)

"The 1984 – on reputation of vintage – is surprising. I can see hints of primary red fruit characters and some spicy notes. The Koonunga Hill starts getting interesting from here. The previous vintages are really curios." (JW) "The wine has a good healthy brick red colour and plenty of sweet red and black fruits. It has a good solid/chunky palate." (JH)

"The 1985 vintage has some nice candied fruit/leathery characters but becomes quite astringent at the finish." (JW) "I can see that austerity on the finish, but it has pleasant spice/dried cherry/kirsch-like aromas and flavours." (CPT) "The aromas are quite porty/jammy, but the palate is rich and meaty with abundant tannins. There is no pretence at elegance here." (HH)

"The 1986 is shy and unyielding with dried fruit characters and unbalanced tannins." (CPT) "This has been a curiously variable wine. I think the fruit is showing signs of departing." (JH) "It's a good drink but it's slightly dried out on the nose and the palate is ungenerous." (HH) "The 1987 is showing under-ripe fruit characters and is quite tart on the palate." (CPT) "It is showing meaty, old leather armchair aromas and hints of mint. The palate is lean and drying out." (HH) "I can see those leafy/minty characters, but I find the wine surprisingly aromatic with some chocolate/berry notes, while the palate is unexpectedly intense and long with savoury tannins." (JH)

"The 1988 is a straightforward wine with fruity red currant aromas and a dry palate." (CPT) "I think the wine is impressive with a complex aged nose and layer upon layer of flavours. The tannins are firm, but it's drinking well." (HH) "This wine was a near miss for me. I like the intense aromas

but the palate is jumpy and slightly aggressive." (JH) "I find a fair amount of fruit here. The palate would all be sorted out with a hearty dish." (JW)

"The 1989 might not be so representative, but I really like the peppery/blackcurrant/herbaceous aromas and the fresh crisp palate." (CPT) "I think this is a good wine too, but on the elegant side. It has some minty/green bean Cabernet characters and firm quite grippy tannins. It should be drunk soon." (HH) "I don't like this wine. It has too many jammy/confectionary/leafy characters." (JH) "I agree. It's no fun to drink." (JW)

"The 1990 has strong chocolate/plum aromas and flavours, but I still find the wine quite sharp on the finish." (CPT) "The wine is in a class of its own. It's still laden with sweet berry/cassis fruit and has a lovely texture and structure." (JH) "The wine is really fine and generous with red fruit/mocha/spice aromas and flavours. It has great persistency." (JW)

"The 1991 is a real surprise. It has complex leather/vanilla/dark chocolate aromas and a really good fleshy flavourful palate." (HH) "The 1992, reminiscent of some of the earlier vintages, is showing strong coffee/mocha characters and a drying palate." (CPT) "While this wine is still on the ascendancy, I find it rather rough with camphor/earthy/stalky characters." (HH) "I am quite impressed with this wine. The tannins are woven throughout the length of the palate." (JH) "It also shows some primary red fruit/plum characters. The finish is a bit of a let down." (JW)

"The 1993 is showing plenty of under-ripe characters and green tannins." (CPT) "It has a lean, firm, slightly astringent palate, but it has flavour and weight." (HH) "I like this wine more than the others. It still has plum/berry/briar aromas and a rich chocolaty and quite supple palate." (JH) "The 1995 has some nice red berry/raspberry/mint aromas, but the palate is quite lean and angular. The wine could improve." (HH) "I think the wine is pretty. It has some bright red fruits and very nice texture in the mouth. But it's a medium weight wine and needs drinking soon." (JW)

"The 1996 is a very striking wine and begins a very impressive bracket. The wine shows ripe red and dark berry aromas and a very fine, intense, beautifully balanced palate. The tannin quality is excellent." (HH) "This is a rich smooth wine with dark berry/plum/cassis aromas and wonderful texture and structure. I agree with Huon. Those tannins are exemplary. It is a sheer joy to taste a wine like this." (JH) "Yes this is really good stuff. It's hugely concentrated, intense and well-balanced – and it's still developing." (JW)

"The 1997 is showing more development. It's still a good wine, but the tannins are firm and unbalanced. Drink soon." (HH) "The wine is certainly more savoury than the 1996, but I find the palate quite supple and smooth. However it is close to its peak." (JH)

"The 1998 is another superb fruit-driven wine with Cabernet cassis/blackcurrant aromas and fine structure, focus and intensity. It has remarkable youth and promise for the future." (HH) "It has plenty of raspberry/red cherry fruit characters, but I also find some reductive characters." (CPT) "This is a substantial wine with plenty of chewy fruit and strong ripe tannins." (JW)

"The 1999 is a leaner and perhaps less fashionable style, but I like this wine. It has very positive Shiraz aromas of red currants, raspberries and plum. The palate has plenty of grip, but also very good flavour depth." (HH) "Those powerful tannins may well take over the wine one day, but it has plenty of sweet juicy fruit." (JH) "This is

PENFOLDS KOONUNGA HILL
SHIRAZ CABERNET

another good wine which needs more time. It's not as classic as the 1996 and 1998, but there's plenty of sweet ripe fruit." (JW)

"The 2000, a difficult year, has no sign of greenness. It's clean and tight with plenty of plummy/raspberry fruit characters." (HH) "At last – raspberries, violets and lovely sweet fruit and ripe tannins!" (CPT) "The 2001 vintage shows sweet raspberry/blackberry aromas and has a very ripe, seductive palate with sweet fruit galore!" (HH) "I can see very ripe shrivel characters in the wine and I think the tannins may ultimately defeat the fruit." (JH) "The wine is full of primary fruit with some floral notes. Needs a bit of time and patience." (JW) "I certainly find the wine more alcoholic and riper." (CPT)

"The 2002 vintage is a serious wine at a modest price. It has very youthful vibrant fruit and a well-structured balanced palate with ripe puckering tannins. Like all the later vintages, this is a nicely finished wine without the chippy oak of many of its competitors." (HH) "It is a very fresh wine with plenty of crushed fruit/floral characters and nice sweet fruit on the palate. The tannins may get the upper hand." (JW) "The Koonunga Hill wines follow the reputation of their vintage quite closely. In particularly good vintages like 1990, 1996, 1998 and 2002, these wines represent incredible value." (JH)

(CPT) – CH'NG POH TIONG
(JH)   – JAMES HALLIDAY
(HH)   – HUON HOOKE
(JS)   – JOANNA SIMON
(JW)   – JOSEPH WARD

PENFOLDS THOMAS HYLAND
SHIRAZ

THOMAS HYLAND

SOUTH AUSTRALIA

SHIRAZ

VINTAGE 2001

In 1861 Thomas Hyland met and married Georgina Penfold. His
stewardship of the company until 1914 saw the development of
what, in his lifetime, became Australia's most famous name in wine.

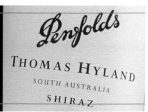

OVERVIEW: The Penfolds Thomas Hyland red wines, comprising a Shiraz and a Cabernet, are a recent addition to the Penfolds portfolio. The wines are named after Thomas Hyland, the son-in-law of Dr Christopher Rawson and Mary Penfold. In 1870 Penfolds & Co was formed, a new partnership of Mary Penfold, Thomas Hyland and cellar manager, Joseph Gillard. Thomas Hyland's considerable administrative skills and stewardship resulted in a rapid rise in fortune. By 1896 Penfolds accounted for one-third of South Australia's wine production, which was a remarkable achievement.

The Thomas Hyland Shiraz, a multi-district wine, draws fruit from South Australia's premium wine areas, particularly McLaren Vale, Coonawarra, Barossa Valley, Padthaway and Robe. The wine is a fruit-driven style underpinned by a touch of new oak to enhance overall complexity and freshness. The wine is matured for around 12 months in a combination of new (15%) and aged (85%) French and American oak.

While still evolving, the Thomas Hyland Shiraz shows all the hallmarks of the Penfolds house style with rich deep berry/mocha fruits, pronounced ripe chocolaty tannins and savoury oak nuances. The wine is an early drinking style, but can benefit from short to medium term cellaring. Ch'ng Poh Tiong says, "The wine has loads of Shiraz personality with plenty of ripe fruit and smooth tannins". Huon Hooke notes, "The Thomas Hyland Shiraz gets better with each succeeding vintage. The 2002 is a humdinger". Joseph Ward believes the wine style is perfect for the US market. "The wines, particularly the 2002, are beautifully made and well integrated," he says.

**PENFOLDS
THOMAS HYLAND
SHIRAZ**

First Vintage: 2000

Variety: Shiraz

Origin: Multi-district blend from South Australia. McLaren Vale, Coonawarra and Barossa Valley, Padthaway and Robe.

Fermentation: Stainless steel tanks.

Maturation: Approximately 12 months in new (15%) and aged (85%) French and American hogsheads.

Comments: Alternative Stelvin closure bottlings available in select markets.

PENFOLDS THOMAS HYLAND
SHIRAZ

2000 `Now`

Medium red. Blackcurrant/mulberry aromas with a touch of pepper. The palate is medium, concentrated with blackcurrant/mulberry aromas and fine ripe tannins.

2001 `Now` `2008`

Medium deep red. Smoky plum/berry aromas. Rich and flavoursome palate with plenty of plum/berry flavours and some spicy oak and ripe chocolaty tannins.

2002 `Now` `2015` ★

Medium deep red. Ripe perfumed plum/blackberry aromas and flavours. A supple but well concentrated palate with black plum/prune/liquorice flavours and ripe grainy tannins. A very appealing wine.

COMMENTARY: "The 2000 Thomas Hyland Shiraz is a surprisingly soft wine with some mint nuances. The wine just doesn't have enough stuffing. Drink now." (JH) "I thought the tannins poked out, but it has some pleasant red fruit characters." (JW) "It's certainly a short term wine. While it has some good blackberry/ mulberry aromas, the wine lacks fruit depth, clarity and vibrancy. The 2001, on the other hand, has a much better colour. It has some charry oak/smoky nuances and the palate is rich in flavour and extract. This is a more seriously weighted and structured wine." (HH) "The wine is quite forward with plum/cherry fruit and soft tannins." (JH)

"It shows plenty of ripe, blue fruits and nice balancing fresh tannins. The 2002 is the most convincing wine in the line up, with plenty of flesh, ripe smooth tannins and loads of Shiraz personality." (CPT) "The wine just gets better every succeeding vintage. The 2002 is a humdinger wine with lashings of sweet plum/blackberry fruit and a supple appealing palate." (HH) "The tannins are quite substantial here, but the wine has plenty of ripe fruit and a long persistent finish. The wines, particularly the 2002, are beautifully made and well integrated." (JW)

(CPT) – CH'NG POH TIONG
(JH)   – JAMES HALLIDAY
(HH) – HUON HOOKE
(JS)   – JOANNA SIMON
(JW) – JOSEPH WARD

Outstanding vintages ★

Penfolds

THOMAS HYLAND
SOUTH AUSTRALIA
CABERNET SAUVIGNON
VINTAGE 2001

In 1861 Thomas Hyland met and married Georgina Penfold. His stewardship of the company until 1914 saw the development of what, in his lifetime, became Australia's most famous name in wine.

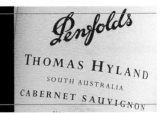

Penfolds

THOMAS HYLAND
SOUTH AUSTRALIA
CABERNET SAUVIGNON

OVERVIEW: The Penfolds Thomas Hyland Cabernet Sauvignon, a multi-district wine, draws fruit from Coonawarra, McLaren Vale and Robe. Whilst the style is essentially fruit-driven, Thomas Hyland Cabernet Sauvignon shows the classic varietal elements of ripe blackcurrant/cedar aromas and fine-grained tannins.

Coonawarra Cabernet Sauvignon features prominently in the wine, bringing perfume and generosity of flavour to the palate. Penfolds has access to several vineyards in Coonawarra, all located on highly-valued, well-drained terra rossa over limestone soils. This relatively isolated wine region, 400 kilometres south of Adelaide, is classified as a cool maritime region, despite the occasional searingly hot days during summer. While Coonawarra is some distance from the coast, cool afternoon sea breezes can have a beneficial moderating effect. Mild growing conditions during the Australian autumn allow optimum ripening and flavour development. Coonawarra Cabernet Sauvignon has a lovely inherent structure – even in average vintages – with pure varietal definition and fine chocolaty tannins.

The addition of ripe powerful McLaren Vale fruit and elegantly proportioned Robe Cabernet enhance the overall style. Vinification takes place in headed-down stainless steel vats and rotary fermenters, followed by maturation in a combination of new and aged French and American hogsheads for approximately 12 months before bottling. The wine illustrates the benefits of multi-district blending, the cornerstone of the Penfolds winemaking philosophy. The wine is an early to mid-term drinking wine. *The Rewards of Patience* panel agreed that the overall tannin structure of the Thomas Hyland Cabernet style would soften further with the benefit of a year or so of cellaring.

PENFOLDS THOMAS HYLAND CABERNET SAUVIGNON

First Vintage: 2001

Variety: Cabernet Sauvignon

Origin: Multi-district blend from South Australia. Coonawarra, McLaren Vale and Robe.

Fermentation: Stainless steel tanks.

Maturation: Approximately 12 months in new (15%) and aged (85%) French and American hogsheads.

Comments: Alternative Stelvin capsule bottlings available in select markets.

PENFOLDS THOMAS HYLAND
CABERNET SAUVIGNON

2001 `Now` `2007`
Medium red. Cassis/earthy/plum aromas and flavours. A very firm, dry style with pronounced gripping tannins, some subtle oak and good concentration and length. Tannins need to soften out.

2002 `Now` `2012` ★
Deep red-purple. Intense blackcurrant/blackberry aromas with powerful dark fruit/dark chocolate flavours and strong, but ripe tannins. A well-structured wine.

COMMENTARY: "The 2001 has clear cassis/blackcurrant fruit and subtle oak. The tannins are very firm and dry." (JH). "It has plenty of blackcurrant/plum/spice aromas and plenty of tannin and fruit on the palate." (JW). "It has very good depth and weight of fruit with big gripping tannins. It's worth cellaring for a while." (HH).

"The 2002 blackcurrant/blackberry fruit aromas and flavours have some bitter chocolate characters. The tannins are strong but balanced." (JH). "This is a very fragrant, clean wine with sweet ripe berry/cassis aromas. Like the 02 Shiraz, it has superb depth of rich, ripe, clean sweet fruit and abundant smooth ripe tannins – another good cellaring wine." (HH).

(CPT) – CH'NG POH TIONG
(JH)   – JAMES HALLIDAY
(HH) – HUON HOOKE
(JS)   – JOANNA SIMON
(JW) – JOSEPH WARD

PENFOLDS BIN WINES

"We needed wines made
in the image of Grange;
not the same, but similar."

– MAX SCHUBERT

> "Lots of personality and rustic charm with rich tannins and layers of flavour." – CH'NG POH TIONG

BIN 2
SHIRAZ MOURVÈDRE

OVERVIEW: Penfolds Bin 2 was first released in 1960, but was discontinued during the 1970s at the height of the white wine boom. It was reintroduced to the Australian wine market in the early 1980s, but again failed to find favour. The remaining stocks of the 1980 and 1981 vintage were redirected to the United Kingdom market where the wines attracted plenty of media attention and became an immediate commercial success. The original Bin 2 was a traditional 'Australian Burgundy' style – typically a soft, medium-bodied wine based on Shiraz. This blend was a precursor to the popular Rhône style wines found in the market today.

Bin 2 is a multi-regional blend drawing fruit from warmer vineyard sites including Barossa Valley, Clare Valley, McLaren Vale and Langhorne Creek. The wine is vinified in stainless steel and aged for a year in five to six-year-old hogsheads and larger vats. This 'maturation effect' allows the wine to further evolve and soften in structure.

The Bin 2 blend of Shiraz and Mourvèdre is relatively uncommon in Australian table wines. Also known as Mataro or Monastrell, Mourvèdre was introduced to Australia in the 1830s. Sometimes used in fortified wine production, this grape variety is widely planted in the Barossa Valley. It is greatly valued by winemakers for its blending attributes. It tones down the exuberant qualities of Shiraz, adding overall complexity and palate grip. Says Peter Gago, "Bin 2 is a relatively muscular wine. It embraces the ripe blackberry aromas, fleshiness and fruit sweetness of Shiraz and the lean earthy, savoury, even spicy, qualities of Mourvèdre. The two varieties compliment each other well, making an easy drinking wine which is not overtly concentrated, but has plenty of fruit, texture and flavour length."

Joseph Ward is 'pretty impressed' by the Bin 2 style, liking "the earthy tones, fruit concentration and good grip on the palate". Ch'ng Poh Tiong says the wines have "Lots of personality and rustic charm with rich tannins and layers of flavour".

PENFOLDS
BIN 2
SHIRAZ MOURVÈDRE

First Vintage: 1960

Variety: Shiraz and Mourvèdre

Origin: Multi-district blend from South Australia / Victoria. Barossa Valley, Clare Valley, McLaren Vale and Langhorne Creek.

Fermentation: Stainless steel tanks.

Maturation: 12 months' maturation in five to six-year-old oak hogsheads and larger vats.

Comments: Originally labelled Shiraz Mataro. Reintroduced to the Australian market in 2003.

"In the scheme of things Bin 28 may seem well below Grange, but when you consider the overall portfolio, the wine is quite high in the hierarchy." – JAMES HALLIDAY

BIN 28
KALIMNA SHIRAZ

OVERVIEW: Penfolds Bin 28 was originally a single vineyard Shiraz selection from the Kalimna Vineyard in the Barossa Valley. Introduced as one of the first Bin wines within the Penfolds portfolio, it has become an Australian classic. The wine can be found in the swishest restaurant in London and in a dusty outback pub in the Northern Territory. Indeed this wine style has universal appeal because of its intense fruit definition, ripe fleshy palate structure and generosity of flavour. The wine has a reputation (among single bottle buyers) for being an early drinking wine style, yet it is also highly valued by collectors for its aging potential on the secondary wine market. Indeed it has won "Red Wine of the Year" twice, in 1991 and 1995 at the International Wine Challenge, held each year in London.

During the late 1970s Bin 28 Shiraz became a multi-district blend. It made perfect sense to look further afield for high quality fruit as it was always a house style first, rather than a single vineyard wine expression. By European standards, the Kalimna Vineyard is large. Within its boundaries it has several vineyard blocks, each with its own particular nuances of place. With so much good quality Shiraz grown in the Barossa and elsewhere, Penfolds was able to increase the volume of production and improve the overall quality and maintain the generous warm climate style. James Halliday notes, "In the scheme of things Bin 28 may seem well below Grange, but when you consider the overall portfolio, the wine is quite high in the hierarchy. The grower will get a premium for his fruit if it's up to Bin 28 standard".

Joseph Ward remarks that recent vintages are "extremely fresh and exuberant with plenty of sweet fruit characters and plush tannins. I got a sense that this may have something to do with the quality of the vineyards". Certainly, Penfolds has improved its vineyard management and grower liaison practices. Steve Lienert says, "Our winemakers spend a lot of time assessing vineyards these days. They talk to the growers about the kind of fruit quality they need. The combination of better grower/winemaker teamwork, batch harvesting and improvements in viticulture and winemaking has paid us handsome dividends in quality".

The fruit is sourced from the Barossa Valley and McLaren Vale (including independent growers), Clare Valley, Langhorne Creek and even as far as Padthaway. Penfolds adheres to a very strict level

**PENFOLDS
BIN 28
KALIMNA SHIRAZ**

First Vintage: 1962

Variety: Shiraz

Origin: Multi-district blend from South Australia. Significant contributions from Barossa Valley, McLaren Vale, Clare Valley and Langhorne Creek.

Fermentation: Stainless steel tanks with wooden header boards.

Maturation: 15 months in one and two-year-old American oak hogsheads.

Comments: Originally a single vineyard wine, moving to a multi-regional blend in the late 1970s.

PENFOLDS BIN 28
KALIMNA SHIRAZ

Introduced as one of the first Bin wines within the Penfolds portfolio, it has become an Australian classic.

of fruit selection and the overall winemaking philosophy remains the same. It is foremost a showcase for warm climate Shiraz. During the 1980s the quality of pressing improved with the introduction of a membrane press. This has translated to better tannin structures, further improved by advances in tannin management during the 1990s. The wine is matured in one and two-year-old American and French oak barrels. Bin 28 has very clear ripe fruit definition when young, with plenty of concentration and fruit sweetness. Bin 28 contrasts with the more defined, cooler climate style of Bin 128. The wine has a reputation for improving with medium term cellaring and in exceptional vintages these wines are suitable for long term cellaring.

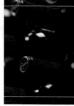

PENFOLDS BIN 28
KALIMNA SHIRAZ

1962 `Past – Now`
Brick red. Earthy/leather/meaty/vellum aromas. A fully developed wine with leafy tannins and some fruit sweetness. Beginning to dry out on the palate.

1963 `Now – Past`
Brick red. Meaty/earthy/apricot aromas. A rich sweet palate with meaty/prune/apricot flavours and fine tannins. Beginning to fade.

1964 `Now` ★
Brick red. A lovely mature red wine with meaty/mocha/earthy/bitumen aromas. Well-concentrated wine with sweet mocha/coffee/polished leather flavours, rich chocolaty tannins and a long finish. Drink now.

1967 `Now` ★
Brick red. Meaty/gamy/honeycomb aromas with some primary black plum nuances. Rich and satisfying wine with plenty of mocha/plum fruits and soft ripe tannins.

1970 `Now`
Brick red. Developed prune/meaty/earthy/leather aromas. The palate is rich and deep with ripe prune/chocolate/earthy fruit and ample tannins.

1971 `Now` ★
Brick red. Fully mature wine at the cusp of development with cedar/chocolate/mocha/cigar box aromas and flavours. The palate is deeply concentrated and fleshy with ripe/lacy/savoury tannins. Finishes firm. Excellent wine.

1975 `Now`
Brick red. Smoky/toffee/prune/chocolate aromas. A flavoursome wine with plenty of choco-berry/prune characters and fine bitter tannins. Grippy finish. Drink now.

1976 `Past`
Brick red. Tired, dusty, dried out wine with a sweet and sour, rather herbaceous palate. Neither bottle lived up to vintage expectations.

1977 `Now`   `2008`
Brick red. Intense prune/choco-mint/meaty aromas and some floral notes. Elegantly proportioned wine with complex bitter dark chocolate/prune flavours, and fine tannins. A major surprise.

1978 `Now`
Brick red. Mature briary/meaty/smoked oyster aromas. A lighter style wine with briary/meaty/earthy/walnutty flavours and dry grippy tannins.

1979 `Now`
Brick red. Chocolaty/earthy/seaweed/barnyard aromas and flavours. The palate has some fruit power and sweetness but the tannins are bitter and aggressive.

1980 `Now`
Brick red. Cedar/dark plum aromas with herb garden/mint nuances. Some rich sweet plum fruit/aniseed/mint flavours and persistent tannins. Much better than at 1999 ROP tasting.

1981 `Now`
Deep brick red. Prune/meaty, slightly barnyardy nose. A fully mature palate with ripe prune/mocha fruit and dusty/grippy tannins. Finishes firm and tight.

1982 `Past – Now`
Brick red. Bitumen/cherry/herbal aromas and flavours. The palate is soft and gentle with some fruit sweetness. An unfocused wine past its best.

1983 `Now`   `2008`
Deep red. A massive wine with earthy/meaty/prune/liquorice aromas. Immensely concentrated palate with thick/soupy tannins and some cedar/roasted meat/earthy fruit flavours.

1984 `Now – Past`
Medium red. Red cherry/herb garden aromas with some jammy/liquorice notes. A lighter bodied wine with some tangy cherry/mint/herb flavours and fine tannins. Not a wine for keeping.

Outstanding vintages ★

BIN 28
KALIMNA SHIRAZ

1985 `Now`

Deep red. Prune/black cherry/chocolate aromas/flavours and some leathery notes. The palate is quite austere with pronounced tannins and fading fruit.

1986 `Now` `2010` ★

Deep red. Complex classically mature wine with cedar/spice/choco-berry aromas. The palate is rich and flavoursome with plum/dark chocolate flavours and velvety/supple tannins.

1987 `Now` `2008`

Medium brick red. Developed colour with savoury leafy/mulch/earthy/cedar aromas. The palate is elegant with supple berry fruit and leafy tannins. A product of a cool vintage.

1988 `Now` `2008`

Deep red. Prune/choco-berry/liquorice aromas with some walnut characters. Medium concentrated palate with dark chocolate/plum flavours and dry/leafy/grippy tannins.

1989 `Now`

Medium red. Stewed fruit/jammy/herb garden aromas and flavours. Palate is quite herbal/vegetal with some confected jammy fruit. Tannins are leafy and green.

1990 `Now` `2020` ★

Deep red. A classic Penfolds vintage. Intense dark choco-berry/mocha/liquorice aromas. A rich and full flavoured wine with abundant ripe fruit and supple cedary tannins. Superb wine.

1991 `Now` `2020` ★

Deep red. Fresh Shiraz aromas of cherries/raspberries and scented plums. The palate is soft, ripe and concentrated with plum/prune/blackberry pastille flavours and fine grainy tannins. A really well-balanced wine.

1992 `Now` `2010`

Deep red-purple. Dark plum/black cherry aromas with some leafy/herb/mint characters. A plush well-concentrated palate with sweetly rich fruit and fine but firm tannins.

1993 `Now` `2008`

Deep red. Plum/blackberry/earthy aromas and flavours with some stewed fruit/herbal characters. The palate is dense but savoury with leafy tannin structure. Drink soon.

1994 `Now` `2015` ★

Deep red-purple. Intense potent wine with sweet plum/blackberry/mint aromas. The palate is opulently rich with deep-set plum/blackberry/flavours and ripe dense tannins.

1995 `Now`

Medium deep red. Berry/cedar/mint chocolate aromas. Loose-knit lighter style with red berry/cedar fruit and well-balanced fruit tannins.

1996 `Now` `2020` ★

Medium deep red. Smoky red plum/meaty/chocolate aromas. A dense, concentrated wine with ripe smoky/plum/choco-berry flavours and smooth satin tannins.

1997 `Now` `2008`

Deep red. Intense plum/red currant/leafy minty aromas and flavours. loose-knit savoury palate with redcurrant/sweet fruit, fine savoury tannins and long finish.

1998 `Now` `2025` ★

Deep red-purple. Intense ripe blackberry/plum/liquorice aromas with a touch of oak maturation character. The palate is immensely concentrated with opulent black fruit/choco-berry flavours and densely ripe tannins. A powerhouse.

Outstanding vintages ★

PENFOLDS BIN 28
KALIMNA SHIRAZ

1999 `Now` ········ `2015`

Deep red-purple. Fragrant spice/berry/leafy aromas. More leanly structured than the 1998 with dark berry/liquorice flavours and strong firm tannins. A muscular wine.

2000 `Now` ········ `2015`

Deep red-purple. Floral violet/raspberry/vanilla aromas. A well-concentrated wine with plenty of sweet mulch/raspberry/plum fruit and fine loose-knit tannins.

2001 `Now` ········ `2025` ★

Deep red-purple. Intense plum/berry/liquorice aromas. A very full bodied solid/dense wine with very ripe crushed plum/berry fruit and powerful chocolaty tannins. Very youthful exuberant wine.

Outstanding vintages ★

BIN 28
KALIMNA SHIRAZ

COMMENTARY: "I rate the first four wines from 1964 to 1971 fairly highly. They are all holding up well, but should be drunk soon. The second bottle of 1964 is a lovely old red wine which would go brilliantly with cheese at dinner." (HH) "It is a very appealing wine with earthy/polished leather/sweet mocha characters and a supple/satin texture. The 1967 is complex and ripe with liquorice, black plum spice aromas and a rich satisfying palate with lovely ripe dusty/mocha/plum flavours and soft tannins." (JH) "I saw plenty of mushroom/truffle/liquorice/mint aromas and lovely fruit sweetness on the palate." (CPT)

"The 1970 is a less glossy wine with fractionally angular tannins, but it has lots of character." (JH) "It's always nice when fruit triumphs in an old wine. There's plenty of sweet fruit on entry and good richness and balance." (JW) "The palate is deep and fleshy with ample tannins, chewy almost, but it's a ripe warm-grown style with crème brûlée characters. The 1971 has a fully mature but lovely old cigar box nose. Again it is deep, full and rich in the mouth with ample tannins and a fleshy texture. It finishes quite grippy. I found the wine did fade in the glass quite noticeably and I wondered whether there was a touch of 'Brett' (Brettanomyces)." (HH) "I thought it was beginning to fade too, but it does have great texture and mouth-feel." (JH) "I like the freshness and minerally tones in the wine. It is an elegant style with some attractive sandalwood characters." (CPT)

"The 1975 is quite tannic and packs a fair grip. The wine has become unbalanced, but it would still be a good drink with food." (HH) "It is quite pruny and spirity. It is sweeter than I expected on the palate, but the fruit is drying out." (JW) "The 1976 is tired, with some VA poking out. Both bottles look pretty ordinary." (HH)

"It isn't as I expected. It is a long and persistent wine, but very herbal and unattractive." (JH)

"The 1977 has liquorice/dried rose petal aromas and a very fruit sweet palate." (CPT) "It is a surprisingly powerful wine considering the vintage. It has a complex tapestry of flavours but it does demand food." (JH) "The 1978 is a meaty old thing with some smoked oyster characters. The palate is smooth, but it's lightly concentrated and dry and grippy at the finish." (HH) "There's some real heat on the mid palate, but it has some nice prune/spice/cedar notes and good fruit attack on the palate." (JW)

"The 1979 is very barnyardy with hard metallic tannins." (HH) "I agree; I have a faint suspicion that the wine has a touch of 'Brett' (Brettanomyces) bitterness." (JH) "The 1980 is a very nice wine, a lovely end to this bracket. It is just getting a bit old now, but it still has slabs of minty/sweet plum/aniseed fruit and a plush, rich palate." (HH) "It is a much better wine than at the 1999 *Rewards of Patience* tasting. It's a solid powerful wine with plenty of dark plum/liquorice/earthy aromas and persistent tannins." (JH) "I find the wine quite herbaceous and woody. It has good concentration but it finishes dry and tart." (CPT)

"The 1981 is meaty and fully mature with some barnyardy/animal nuances. The palate is very tannic." (HH) "The tannins have taken over and that baked plum/prune fruit is drying out. It needs to be drunk now." (JW) "It finishes short." (CPT) "The 1981 and 1983 vintages are drought years and this reflects in the wines. I actually quite like the 1981 with its prune/plum flavours and dusty tannins. The 1982, on the other hand, is showing those contrived DMS (dimethylsulphide) characters. The wine has sweet and sour flavours. I think it's past its best." (JH) "I can see

119

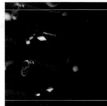

PENFOLDS BIN 28
KALIMNA SHIRAZ

the DMS but it's still a lovely old red wine." (HH) "The wine is very engaging with ripe sweet liquorice fruit and a soft palate." (CPT)

"The 1983 is a very powerful wine. It has plenty of tar/liquorice/prune/plum characters and mouth-puckering tannins, but I am not sure it has a long future. Those tannins may never come into balance, even though there is still plenty of fruit." (JH) "I agree. The wine is not for keeping but it has some good red fruit characters and some earthy tones." (JW)

"The 1984 is a big jammy, slightly porty wine with blackstrap liquorice aromas and a rather heavy/clumsy palate with thick chewy tannins." (HH) "I like this wine. It has lots of chocolate/spicy liquorice aromas and flavours." (CPT) "But I think it lacks conviction. Drink it now. The 1985 is a soft supple easy drinking wine, but it should be drunk soon as it is at its best now." (JH) "The tannins have elbowed the fruit aside with this wine. I agree the wine is ready now. The 1986, however, is a stand-out wine with sweet plummy fruit with plenty of concentration and flavour. It still seems to be developing." (JW) "At first the wine seems to be quite heavy and tannic, but it opens up as it sits in the glass." (HH) "This is a lovely wine with wonderful intensity and fruit definition. The palate is very velvety with plenty of sweet blueberry fruit characters. The 1987 is tired and tart." (CPT) "It has a greenish minty nose with mulch/crushed leaf nuances. The palate is very lean and lacks fruit and richness." (HH) "A product of a cool vintage, but still elegant and supple." (JH)

"The 1988 is a very savoury/lean wine with angular/tough tannins." (HH) "I like the wine more than that and rate it quite highly. It does have cooler spectrum fruit, but lovely fruit sweetness." (JW) "The 1989, on the other hand, is a very sweet and distinctly porty/jammy style of wine, but it's not unpleasant." (JH) "I find the wine is still very youthful and appealing, with clear cassis fruit and a ripe sweet palate." (CPT)

"The 1990 is a very intense and powerful wine with an abundance of lusciously ripe fruit, but never jammy. The wine quality goes beyond all its predecessors. There are plenty of baked fruits and spicy characters. The palate is sweet and ripe with a wonderful black fruit attack. It's intense and concentrated. The fruit is waiting its turn in the background." (JW) "The 1991 is also sensational stuff with lots of tannins but well-balanced with masses of fruit." (HH) "It's a great wine with textured velvety tannins and soft ripe plum fruits." (JH) "The 1992 is quite closed on the nose and the palate is oaky and dry." (CPT) "It's not particularly complex and the palate is dominated by tannins, but the wine has lots of ripe fruit." (HH) "I think the wine is really sensuous with its rich dark plum/prune/liquorice aromas and mouth-flooding sweetly rich fruit on the palate. It is something of a surprise." (JH)

"The 1993 is firm and savoury with blackberry/earthy characters and some leather/spice." (JH) "It does have some hints of herb and mint, but it's not badly green. The palate is a bit mono-dimensional and it finishes quite grippy." (HH) "I think it is very green too, especially on the finish." (CPT) "The 1994 is a potent, powerful and opulent wine with oscillating plum/blackberry fruit and ripe tannins." (JH) "I think this is a lovely vintage too. The wine has plum/red currant/mocha fruit and plenty of ripe fruit and chocolaty tannins on the palate. It has a fine future. The 1995, however is a light-weight and is completely outclassed by the 1994." (JW) "It looks and smells overdeveloped and the palate is lean and dry." (HH) "I find the wine to be complex with hints of gaminess and some berry/chocolate/mint characters. The palate is medium bodied but

well-balanced. The flavours are a touch unfocused/uncertain. The 1996, however, is perfectly weighted and balanced with perfect fruit ripeness and satin tannins. A wonderful wine." (JH) "It has simple, perhaps underdeveloped, red plum/cherry aromas and flavours with liberal but smooth tannins. A good vintage." (HH) "This is a huge wine with loads of plummy fruit and ripe chocolaty tannins." (JW)

"The 1997 has strong minty overtones. The pronounced savoury tannins are already threatening the balance." (JH) "This was a complete surprise for me. The wine is lean in this company, but it has a very ripe and spirity nose, like vintage port and an intense and long palate." (JH) "It achieves a very good balance between alcohol, sweet fruit and oak." (CPT)

"The 1998 is a very impressive wine with very fruity young Vintage Port characters including ripe raspberries and violets. The palate is soft, fruity and sweet." (CPT) "This is a very rich and opulent wine with dark plum/blackberry/cherry fruit. The palate is very complex with built-on tannins surrounded by canopies of black fruits." (JH) "It has a subdued nose at first, but the wine is a powerhouse. A very gutsy wine with some plum liquorice aromas and nutty oak nuances. The palate is deep, chewy, tannic and fleshy, but balanced by plenty of fruit and extract. This is a very impressive vibrant wine." (HH) "It doesn't have the sheer mass of the 1996, but is more perfumed and supple. This is a really fine wine." (JW)

"The 1999 is very fragrant with spice/leaf/berry/mint fruit and distinctly savoury tannins." (JH) "It's much leaner than the 1998 with plum/earthy aromas and a tight palate structure, it has some fleshiness and extract. I like this wine." (HH) "I like it too. It is in the more medium weighted style, but it had good sweet ripe fruit and fine but firm tannins." (JW)

"The 2000 has some Vintage Port characters again with plenty of violet/floral notes and nice background oak." (CPT) "It does have some of those mulchy 2000 characters, but the wine is remarkable for the vintage. It's slightly leaner than the 1998/1999, but it has very good flavour and ripeness." (HH) "The 2001 is very young but has great potential with crushed black fruits and some vanilla/spice nuances. It is very supple on the palate." (JW) "I am puzzled by this wine. It's quite exotic with powerful black fruit flavours and forbidding tannins." (JH) "This is a solid gutsy wine with great density and concentration on the palate. The wine has lovely sweet berry/liquorice/aniseed fruit with some violet/floral notes and some vanilla oak characters. The tannins are massive, but it has the dense richness of flavour to match." (HH)

"In the scheme of things, Bin 28 may seem well below Grange, but the wine is actually quite high in the hierarchy. The growers are paid a premium for this type of fruit." (JH) "I am really impressed by the 1998 and 2001 vintages. They have vibrant fruit and sweet dense plummy flavours." (HH) "The quality of these wines must have something to do with the vineyard. The wines from around 1994 show plenty of exuberant fruit and the palate structures have really improved." (JW) "Our winemakers are spending a lot more time in the vineyards with our growers, bringing a better understanding of fruit quality which extends to tannin ripeness and flavour concentration." (PG)

(CPT) – CH'NG POH TIONG
(JH)   – JAMES HALLIDAY
(HH) – HUON HOOKE
(JS)   – JOANNA SIMON
(JW) – JOSEPH WARD

PENFOLDS BIN 128
COONAWARRA SHIRAZ

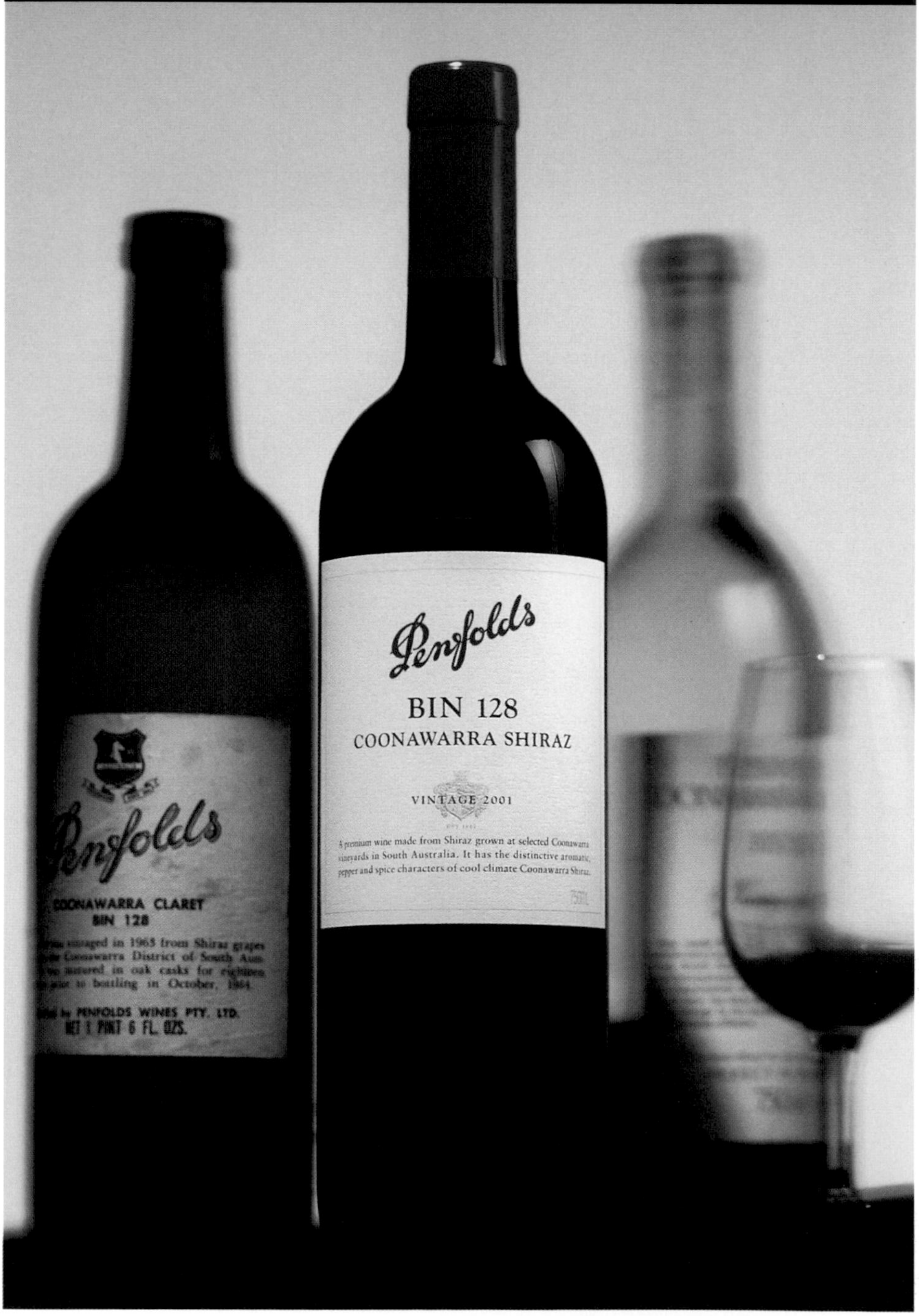

Penfolds

BIN 128
COONAWARRA SHIRAZ

OVERVIEW: The first vintage of Bin 128 Shiraz was produced in 1962 and it remains a regionally defined Bin wine. The fruit is almost entirely sourced from the extensive company vineyards in Coonawarra. This region was first established as the Coonawarra fruit colony in 1890. Winemaking followed, but was not a commercial success. Bill Redman, one of the early pioneers, once said, "From 1890 to 1945 you can write failure across the face of Coonawarra". By the 1950s, renewed enthusiasm and wine successes typified by the release of the now famed Woodley's Treasure Chest Series, attracted more investment capital. Penfolds was a later entrant, largely because of Max Schubert's preference for strongly flavoured and concentrated fruit. In 1960 he was persuaded by Bill Redman to purchase a parcel of Redman's vineyard called Sharam's Block.

Penfolds now draws fruit from a combination of company owned prime Coonawarra vineyard sites and selected independent growers. During the 1960s and early 1970s the fruit used to be crushed with the aid of an old car engine in a tin shed! The must was then transported by tanker up to Magill and later Nuriootpa for vinification. Investment in processing facilities during the late 1970s was enhanced by the parent company's acquisition of Wynns Coonawarra Estate.

The original release of Penfolds Bin 128 reflected the perceived view of the day that Shiraz was a more reliable performer. Certainly the wine has been made every year regardless of vintage conditions. While winemaking practice is essentially the same, between 1979 and 1983 Penfolds gradually changed its barrel maturation programme from American to French oak to enhance regional and varietal definition. James Halliday observes, "There is not only a seismic shift in oak handling around 1981, but the viticulture has improved out of sight over this period".

Vinification follows a traditional Penfolds house style of winemaking. The wine is matured in approximately 20% new, tightly grained one and two-year-old French oak for about 12 months prior to bottling. Joseph Ward notes, "There is a clear evolution happening with the Bin128s. It has a strong regional imprint with sweet black fruit character and firm tannin structures". Peter Gago comments, "The restrained and aromatic cool-climate Bin 128 is an excellent foil to the rich warm-climate Bin 28 style".

PENFOLDS
BIN 128
COONAWARRA
SHIRAZ

First Vintage: 1962

Variety: Shiraz

Origin: 100% Coonawarra, mostly from Penfolds vineyards.

Fermentation: Stainless steel tanks with wooden header boards.

Maturation: 12 months in new (20%) and aged (80%) French oak hogsheads. The often-noted changeover from American to French oak was progressive; it began in 1979 and was completed by the 1983 vintage.

Comments: In 1981 the wine changed name from Bin 128 Claret to Bin 128 Coonawarra Shiraz.

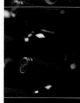

PENFOLDS BIN 128
COONAWARRA SHIRAZ

1962 `Past`
Brick red. Developed cedar/mocha/sous-bois aromas. The palate is still concentrated with dry cedar/mushroom/leather flavours and fine chalky tannins. Drying out. Drink now.

1963 `Past – Now` ★
Brick red. Fine elegant old wine with mocha/tobacco/leather/sandalwood aromas. A fine grained, supple palate with mocha/vanilla flavours and excellent flavour length. Drink now.

1964 `Past`
Brick red. Very developed wine with meaty/gamy/mushroom/leathery aromas. The palate has faded with some savoury chocolate/mushroom notes and leafy tannins.

1965 `Now`
Brick red. A mature old wine with coffee/chocolate/mushroom aromas and flavours. Plenty of freshness and sweet fruit on the palate, but it is beginning to dry out. Drink now.

1966 `Now` `2006` ★
Deep brick red. Rich ripe complex wine with berry/earth/mocha/autumnal aromas and rich chocolaty/mocha flavours. This is a multi-layered wine with lovely concentration and fine grainy tannins.

1967 `Now` `2007`
Deep brick red. An earthy/savoury wine with some smoky/sweet spicy nuances. The palate is rich and earthy with chocolaty loose-knit tannins. Fine old mellow wine.

1968 `Now`
Brick red. Aged, slightly tired wine with mushroom/fig-jam/caramel aromas and flavours. A mature/evolved palate with some savoury notes and richness. Beginning to fade.

1970 `Now`
Brick red. Honeycomb/chocolate/vanilla/meaty aromas. A mature well-balanced wine with a lovely array of mature plum/chocolate/honeycomb flavours and strong almost assertive tannins. At its peak.

1971 `Now` `2008`
Brick red. A fragrant wine with red cherry/prune/mocha/leather aromas. The palate is rich and complex with sweet leather/mocha/chocolate flavours and powdery loose-knit tannins.

1975 `Now`
Brick red. Menthol/cherry/tobacco aromas with hints of liquorice. A bittersweet but strongly flavoured palate with some solid gutsy fruit. Tannins build up a touch bitter and tight at the finish.

1976 `Now` `2007`
Dark brick red. Intense ripe jammy/mocha/liquorice almost vintage port aromas. Plenty of concentration and sweet fruit on the palate, but tannins become quite hard and green at the finish.

1978 `Now` `2006`
Medium brick red. Fresh redcurrant/vanilla/leafy aromas with some leather characters. Still holding up well with red fruits/chocolaty/herb flavours and fine tannins. Falls away at the finish. Drink soon.

1980 `Now` `2010`
Brick red. A rich meaty wine with some complex earthy/choco-berry aromas. Excellent richness on the palate with mature flavours and soft, savoury, drying finish.

1981 `Now – Past`
Brick red. Complex mocha/toffee/earthy aromas with hints of herb/mint. Mocha/chocolaty flavours on the palate with pronounced gritty tannins finishing a touch green.

Outstanding vintages ★

BIN 128
COONAWARRA SHIRAZ

1982 Now – Past
Medium brick red. A product of the vintage with leafy/prune/stewed aromas and flavours. The palate is tired with sinewy tannins and pronounced acidity.

1983 Now
Medium brick red. Aromatic prune/wintergreen/herb garden aromas. Moderately concentrated wine with bitter dark chocolate/leafy flavours and assertive tannins. Has lost much of its fruit.

1984 Past
Light brick red. Earthy over-developed aromas with some aromatic notes. A lean under-powered wine with a tough tannic finish.

1985 Now 2008
Medium red. Dark chocolate/earth/cedar/liquorice aromas. An unyielding but substantial palate with soft fruit flavours but overwhelmed by harsh green tannins.

1986 Now 2010 ★
Medium red. Intense blackberry/cedar aromas with some mocha nuances. The palate is well-concentrated with blackberry/cedar/mocha flavours and persistent but balanced tannins.

1987 Now
Medium red. Tobacco/leafy aromas. The palate has some vegetal/minty leafy flavours and a sweet and sour mouth-feel. Drink up.

1988 Now 2006
Medium red. Earthy/redcurrant/plummy aromas and flavours. The palate is austere with plenty of gritty tannins and fading fruit. Finishes lean.

1989 Now
Medium red. Stewed fruit/herbal/vellum aromas. A sweet and savoury wine with herbal/jammy characters and leafy dry tannins. A pleasant drink.

1990 Now 2020 ★
Medium deep red. A lovely refined wine with intense choco-berry/cedar/sandalwood aromas. A succulent, sweet fruited palate with plenty of choco-berry fruit flavours and fine ripe granular tannins. A wine showing elegance rather than power.

1991 Now 2010
Medium red. Blackberry/plum/mocha aromas. Richly flavoured palate with plenty of sweet fruit, fine tannins and a tangy finish.

1992 Now 2008
Medium red. A very tightly structured wine with some plummy/red fruit aromas and flavours. Leafy tannins build up to a very bitter finish. Fruit is under-powered.

1993 Now 2015
Medium red. Powerful wine with intense blackberry/earth/bitumen aromas. The palate is massively proportioned with dense ripe tannins and deep set fruit. Finishes quite grippy.

1994 Now 2008
Medium red. Complex earthy/meaty/chocolate aromas with some developed leather characters. Savoury palate with sweet earthy/choco-berry fruit and firm drying tannins. A good wine, maturing quickly.

1995 Now
Medium red-brick. A softer lighter style with red cherry/strawberry/cedar aromas and flavours. A lean palate with light fruit flavours and some chocolaty tannins. Drink soon.

1996 Now 2016 ★
Medium deep red. Intense blackberry/black cherry/plum/liquorice aromas. A rich but well-balanced wine with dark berry/liquorice flavours, fine but firm tannins and subtle oak.

Outstanding vintages ★

PENFOLDS BIN 128
COONAWARRA SHIRAZ

1997 `Now` `2008`

Medium red. Raspberry/blackberry aromas with some pepper/herbal nuances. A very concentrated tannic wine with plenty of sweet fruit flavours and some herbal/minty characters. Finishes very firm. Best enjoyed in the short term.

1998 `Now` `2018` ★

Deep red-purple. An opulently rich and seductive wine bursting with plum/blackberry/chocolate fruit. The palate is rich and round, with deep set choco-berry/aniseed flavours and supple ripe tannins. A lovely wine.

1999 `2005` `2018`

Deep red-purple. Fresh and intense blackberry/plum liquorice aromas. A well concentrated mouth-filling wine with plenty of ripe fruit, fine grained/savoury tannins and some new oak characters.

2000 `2006` `2015`

Medium red-purple. Cherry/plum/blackberry aromas with nutmeg/new oak nuances. Richly textured wine with plummy/blackberry/red cherry fruit and ripe persistent tannins.

2001 `2007` `2020` ★

Deep red-purple. Intense but very youthful wine with crushed blackberry/raspberry aromas and some new oak. Immensely concentrated palate with deep-set juicy blackberry/raspberry fruit and pronounced tannins.

Outstanding vintages ★

126

COMMENTARY: "This insightful tasting shows an interesting progression, an evolution of style. It not only covers a seismic shift in oak handling, but also the vast improvements in viticulture over the last 40 years. There are plenty of wines from the 1960s and 1970s with under-ripe green tannins. It seems that many of these wines have reached a plateau of indefinite period. Don't be surprised if you see wines with 'drink now' continuing further." (JH) "We are tasting these wines in old age with many showing faded fruit and astringent tannins, but there is enough evidence to show that these wines matured well for a long period." (JW)

"The 1963 vintage is a lovely old wine with plenty of mocha/caramel characters and a thread of honeycomb. It's smooth, elegant and drinking really well." (HH) "It is one of the highlights of the earlier vintages with plenty of coffee/malt/vanilla fruit and a finely grained supple palate." (JH) "It has aged very gracefully with plenty of evolved characters, but it should be drunk soon." (JW) "This is a very impressive start. The wine has complex and interesting camphor/sandalwood/leather/root-beer/liquorice characters." (CPT)

"The 1964 and 1965 are fading wines with some meaty/gamy aromas but lean, slightly hollow palates. The 1966, however, is a very stylish wine with burnished wood characters and multi-layered flavours." (HH) "It still has fine tannin structure and plenty of ripe fruit, but it should be drunk soon." (JH) "That intense ripe evolved fruit is held up by a lovely palate structure." (CPT)

"The 1967, 1968 and 1970 should all be consumed soon. The 1968 has some smoky bushfire notes but looks as though it is slightly maderised. The 1968 is tiring on the nose but still has richness and mature ripe flavours on the palate. The 1970 has an intriguing gunpowder nose and a lovely array of mature characters. The tannins are assertive, but the wine is still powering on. The 1971 is good, but not as great as I expected." (HH) "I liked the second bottle with its sweet leather/mocha/chocolate aromas and rich complex tapestry of multi flavours. You can see some nutty/vanilla American oak characters. The 1975 vintage shows very strong bitter tannins. I suspect the wine has a touch of 'Brett' (brettanonmyces)." (JH) "I agree. It has some dusty peppery notes. The fruit's falling away and the tannins are very grippy." (HH) "It has a camphor/joss-stick aroma and the fruit has dried out. I really like the 1976. It's ripe and fruity with an almost fortified richness. The palate is concentrated and ripe with a raisiny sweetness." (CPT) "I see those vintage port characters too. The wine is jammy and slightly bitter with aggressive and coarse tannins." (HH)

"The 1978 and 1980 vintages are drinking well now with soft spicy sweet fruit and nice texture. The 1978 is beginning to fade, but the 1980 is showing some life." (JW) "The 1980 is very complex with earthy/berry aromas and excellent richness and depth on the palate. The 1981, 1982, 1983 and 1984 vintages are all past their best. I don't like the 1982 at all. It has strong and off-putting DMS (dimethyl-sulphide) characters." (JH) "The 1981, however, is a compact wine with some sweet fruit. The tannins are quite hard on the finish." (JW) "The wine is quite impressive at first, but the tannins are dominating the wine. The 1982, 1983 and 1984 have seen better days and should be consumed now." (HH) "The 1985 is a very delicate wine with sandalwood aromas and light, charming fruit on the palate." (CPT) "Certainly it needs to be drunk soon. The tannins are quite bitter at the finish." (JW)

PENFOLDS BIN 128
COONAWARRA SHIRAZ

"I love the 1986. It is alive and sweet with plenty of blackberry/dark fruits and persistent but balanced tannins." (JH) "I see some herbaceous elements, plenty of cassis fruits and vivacious acidity." (CPT) "The tannins have completely conquered the fruit in the 1987." (JW) "The wine has some sweet and sour flavours/mouth-feel and the tannins are slightly green. The 1988, with ripe plum kirsch fruit, is supple and silky smooth." (JH) "There's a wrestling match happening in this wine. The tannins will win in the end, but there's still plenty of fruit. The wine should be drunk in the next three or four years. I don't like the 1989 vintage. It has a herbal edge which dominates the wine." (JW) "That's vintage character, but I find the wine pleasant enough. It has some sweet faintly jammy/cosmetic characters on the palate." (JH) "It has no future, but the wine is much better than I expected. It is surprisingly complex with interesting mature characters." (HH)

"The 1990 has plenty of fresh red cherry/red plum aromas and palate concentration." (CPT) "The second bottle reveals how good this vintage is. It's a lovely sweet, fresh, rich, ripe wine with stacks of concentration." (HH) "It shows more elegance than power with a supple/silky palate. The 1991 is richer and riper with very fine tannins and a pleasingly tangy finish, but it isn't quite in the same class as the 1990." (JH) "I like the mocha/coffee notes and the freshness of fruit and tannins." (CPT) "The 1992 vintage is more youthful in colour with a fresh but not particularly complex plummy nose. The palate is very tannic with a very straightforward fruit profile." (HH) "Those tannins are very aggressive and while the fruit gets through for the moment, I am not hopeful for the future. Best to drink soon." (JW)

"The 1993 is a very potent wine with powerful blackberry/earth aromas and abundant extract and fruit density. I find the tannins ripe. This is a long-lived style." (JH) "Those tannins are very big, once again, and I find the wine quite mono-dimensional and grippy. The 1994 is a slightly better wine with an attractive earthy/meaty/savoury nose and savoury palate. The tannins are quite pronounced and firm and drying at the finish." (HH) "I think those tannins are under control. It has a really nice fresh fruit attack and mouth-feel." (JW)

"The 1995 has some cherry/plummy/chocolaty fruit but I find the wine a little closed." (CPT) "It is a much softer lighter style – again a product of vintage – and while it lacks vinosity, it has some savoury tannins." (JH) "I agree with Poh Tiong. The fruit is really subdued. It's a gentle wine but should be drunk soon. The 1996 is a good wine with savoury/bacon fat aromas and some dark berry/raisiny notes. There's plenty of sweet fruit and some super-ripe liquorice characters but those tannins are very firm." (HH) "It has rich, but not in the least heavy, black cherry/plum/blackberry fruit. It has a fruit-driven structure with fine-boned tannins and underlying subtle oak. I think it lives up to vintage expectations." (JH)

"The 1997 is a very impressive wine with plenty of freshness and vivacity." (CPT) "I have no idea where this wine is going. Those tannins are muscling in, but the fruit is very lively and concentrated. I suggest drinking this wine sooner rather than later." (JW) "The 1998 vintage is powerful and opulently rich for Bin 128. It has some strong plum/blackberry characters and round supple tannins." (JH) "The wine has lots of lovely ripe sweet fruit with plenty of crushed red and black fruits and emerging plum characters. This is a very concentrated and well-proportioned wine with a heck of a future. There's a break in colour with the 1999 vintage. It looks more youthful. It's a fresh style with plenty of black fruits. The French oak has become a little more noticeable and the wine is a touch weightier and more alcoholic than the 1998." (JW) "I think it is quite alcoholic too, with blueberry fruits and an oaky palate." (CPT)

"The 2000 vintage has plenty of blackberry/ liquorice aromas and some spice. It's richly textured on the palate with ripe persistent tannins." (JH) "It has some nutmeg oak characters and rich, very ripe jammy characters on the palate. The 2001 has a very big colour with some walnut/dried banana (oak) notes. It is hugely concentrated and tannic and seems bigger bodied than usual. The wine style has put on a lot of weight during the 1990s." (HH) "It shows the characters of a cool vintage, but the wine is intensely concentrated." (JH) "This is an evolving wine style. From 1996 onwards the style has improved greatly. There's more richness and weight and the oak has become more noticeable. This is a good consistent performer." (HH)

(CPT) – CH'NG POH TIONG
(JH) – JAMES HALLIDAY
(HH) – HUON HOOKE
(JS) – JOANNA SIMON
(JW) – JOSEPH WARD

BIN 138
OLD VINE - BAROSSA VALLEY
SHIRAZ GRENACHE MOURVÈDRE

OVERVIEW: Penfolds Old Vine Barossa Valley Shiraz Grenache Mourvèdre (varietal mix variable, depending on vintage) was elevated to the Penfolds Bin range with the 1998 vintage. During the 1950s Penfolds experimented with blending Shiraz and the robust grape variety, Mataro (now referred to by the more lyrical French name, Mourvèdre) culminating in the release of the Bin 2 wines (first vintage 1960).

Considered at the time to be an inferior variety, Grenache was used mainly for fortified wine production. The Australian market, weaned on a culture of fortified wines, was slowly moving towards table wine. Recognising that this fledgling market was used to big flavours, Penfolds adopted a winemaking philosophy of house style and looked for grape varieties which showed intense colour, rich ripe fruit, strong flavours and tannins. This may explain why Penfolds experimented little with Grenache, preferring the more robust characters of Shiraz and Mourvèdre.

The introduction of Penfolds Bin 138 (first vintage 1992) was a natural response to a growing international market, increasingly interested in the highly perfumed and fleshy styles made famous by the wines of Chateauneuf du Pape. Curiously, the Barossa Valley, populated by Silesian and English settlers in the 1830s, was planted extensively with Shiraz (Syrah), Mataro (Mourvèdre) and Grenache from early on. Indeed, it represents some of the oldest genetic vine material in the world! It is ironic therefore that this style, now considered classic, was not made by Penfolds until the early 1990s. Fashion and taste largely account for both the lack of foresight and the immense international popularity of this wine today.

Penfolds sources much of the fruit for Bin 138 from low-yielding, independently grown grapes from around the Barossa Valley. Explaining the overall blend, Peter Gago notes, "The perfumed and seductive flavours of Grenache provide an essential element of the style. Shiraz brings colour, sweetness of fruit and palate richness. Mourvèdre provides some spicy top notes and plenty of savoury characteristics." Blended together, these varieties can make a sublime wine with great personality and structure. Interestingly, this is the only Penfolds wine that remains in component form during maturation, and is put together after several rackings just prior to bottling. Vintage conditions and ultimately the nature of the fruit determine the final blend.

**PENFOLDS
BIN 138
SHIRAZ GRENACHE
MOURVÈDRE**

First Vintage: 1992

Variety: Shiraz Grenache and Mourvèdre in varying proportions depending on vintage conditions.

Origin: Barossa Valley, South Australia.

Fermentation: Stainless steel tanks with wooden header boards.

Maturation: 12 months in older (often six years plus) oak hogsheads.

Comments: Sourced from several vineyards, with average vine age of 35 to 100+ years. Elevated to Bin range with 1998 vintage.

131

PENFOLDS BIN 138
SHIRAZ GRENACHE MOURVÈDRE

Blended together, these varieties can make a sublime wine with great personality and structure.

Hence each year the varietal make-up can vary accordingly. In more recent vintages the wine has been a Shiraz dominant blend, but both Grenache and Mourvèdre have led the wine in the past.

John Duval notes that "the early vintages from 1992 to 1997 reflected a fairly steep learning curve. By 1998 we had a better understanding of our fruit sources and the overall style we wanted to achieve". Bin 138 is a full-bodied style with an emphasis on musky plum fruit aromas and succulent sweet fruit. Peter Gago comments, "Unlike many Shiraz Grenache Mourvèdre blends, it is not of the fleshy/juicy high alcohol/extract style, nor does it rely on any new oak". After vinification the wine is matured in old hogsheads to enhance fruit aromas, promote integration of flavours and soften tannin structure. Bin 138 is a relatively early to medium drinking style which develops rich, complex, earthy nuances with age.

1992 `Now`

Brick red. Earthy/cedar/spice aromas with some mint/eucalypt notes. The palate is sinewy with some spicy/dark cherry fruit. Lean, austere wine.

1993 `Now` `2005`

Brick red. Exotic plum/spice/leatherwood/gamy aromas and flavours. A rich, fleshy wine with black fruit/gamy flavours and ripe tannins. Finishes quite dry.

1994 `Now` `2006`

Medium deep crimson. Intense earthy/plummy/liquorice aromas. Full-flavoured palate with plenty of dark chocolate/plum fruit and fine grippy tannins.

1995 `Now` `2006`

Red brick. Dark cherry/plum/spice aromas. The palate is well-balanced and generous with savoury/spicy characters and soft supple tannins.

1996 `Now` `2007`

Medium deep crimson. Intense aniseed/liquorice/choco-berry fruit. A solid wine with rich choco-berry flavours and ripe supple tannins. Builds up firm and tight at the finish.

1997 `Now` `2009`

Medium deep crimson. Restrained wine with plummy/floral/mint aromas. The palate is lean with spicy/plum flavours and chalky tannins.

1998 `Now` `2011` ★

Deep crimson. Rich ripe wine with spice/dark chocolate/plum aromas. A well-balanced palate with seductive chocolate/plum flavours and some peppery/spice nuances.

1999 `Now` `2010`

Deep crimson. Musky/black fruit/liquorice aromas. A very concentrated wine with musky/plum/spice flavours, plenty of fruit sweetness and fine leafy tannins. Finishes firm.

2000

Not made.

2001 `Now` `2010` ★

Deep crimson. Fresh plum/spice/rosehip/floral aromas. A really well-balanced wine with deep set plummy/currant/spicy fruit and smooth round tannins. A very fruit-driven wine.

2002 `Now` `2012`

Deep crimson. Intense liquorice/black cherry/musky/violet aromas. A well-concentrated palate with rich aniseed/musky/raspberry/black cherry fruit and firm sinewy/savoury tannins.

Outstanding vintages ★

PENFOLDS BIN 138
SHIRAZ GRENACHE MOURVÈDRE

COMMENTARY: "The 1992 has a pronounced gum leaf/eucalypt/earthy nose. It is quite lean and tart, lacking in flesh." (HH) "It smells of driftwood and mocha. The palate is sweetish with ripe tannins." (CPT) "Both the 1992 and 1993 vintages are fully developed with older multi-spice characters, leather/wood notes and minimal tannins." (JH)

"The 1993 is quite meaty and smoky with some red fruit characters and a slightly herbal cut. It finishes warm and dry, but I see no reason to keep this." (JW) "It is quite unusual with exotic, meaty and sweaty/gamy characters. The palate is soft and fleshy with balanced acidity. It has a very good palate, taste and texture. It is fresher on the nose with blackcurrant/mocha/chocolaty fruit and fresh acidity." (CPT)

"The 1994 is more youthful, with some aged, multi-spice aromas but plenty of dark chocolate/briary/berry notes. The palate is richer and there is more tannin structure." (JH) "This is a very complex, layered wine with meaty/earthy nuances and plum/dark chocolate/spicy aromas. It has serious tannin and weight on the palate with plenty of grip, richness, density, concentration and length." (HH)

"The 1995 is quite animal/gamy with some peppery/spicy fruit. It's a touch austere on the finish." (CPT) "It's much lighter than the 1994 with currants and blackberry fruit, but somewhat tired on the palate with significant tannins." (JW) "It's certainly more developed and advanced with a dusty/earthy aged nose and complex meaty/secondary characters that kick in later. The palate is soft and fleshy with savoury, dry tannins. It's a good wine, especially for the year." (HH)

"The 1996 is a more precise, focused wine than all the previous vintages, with fresh spice/plum aromas and a supple palate." (JH) "It is fresh and bright on the nose with plenty of blue fruits, balancing acidity and a nice grip of fresh, crisp tannins on the finish." (CPT) "It smells brambly with some smoky/cherry/blackberry fruit. The wine has plenty of concentration, but the tannins are significant." (JW)

"The 1997 has a shy, subdued nose with some nutmeg/clove/dry spice aromas. The palate is rather lean and tough; the acid and tannin dominate." (HH) "It's a very closed wine, very taut." (CPT) "Interestingly, it doesn't show the cool climate characteristics as much as the other 1997 wines." (JH)

"The 1998 is a massive colour shift in both density and hue. It has beautiful liquorice/spice/satsuma/plum/dark chocolate fruit. The wine is in another dimension with tremendous fruit richness, fine tannins and great balance." (JH) "The fruit really builds nicely through the mid palate; it has excellent flavour length." (JW)

"The 1999 smells of liquorice and blue fruits. There's some early roundness, but it finishes with crisp tannins." (CPT) "It is a big wine with rustic, grippy tannins and lots of earthy, savoury, secondary flavours." (HH) "It's a nice wine with exotic leather/black fruit aromas and a savoury but sweet palate." (JH)

In 2000 the wine was not made.

"The 2001 has excellent potential with crushed berry/spicy aromas and powerful ripe/round fruit." (JW) "It's a complex, inviting wine with fresh nutty/dry spice aromas and floral/violet notes. There's plenty of fruit sweetness early and then lots of tannins – smooth, round, sweet tannins." (HH) "It has a smooth even flow of aromas, a well-balanced palate and sweet plum/spice core of fruit. It just needs more time." (JH)

"It is a very similar wine to the 1998. The 2002 has intense, ripe cherry/raspberry/musky aromas with hints of liquorice. The palate is rich and juicy with plummy/red berry/musky fruit, fine firm tannins and plenty of flavour length." (AC)

"We have a much better understanding of fruit source and wine style. As a result the wines are getting richer, fleshier and more seductive." (JD)

(CPT) – CH'NG POH TIONG
(JH)   – JAMES HALLIDAY
(HH) – HUON HOOKE
(JS)   – JOANNA SIMON
(JW) – JOSEPH WARD

BIN 407
CABERNET SAUVIGNON

OVERVIEW: The Penfolds Bin 407 Cabernet Sauvignon is a multi-district blend largely from the south east of South Australia – specifically, the Limestone Coast (including Coonawarra and Robe) and Bordertown. In some years the wine may contain a parcel of Western Australian Cabernet Sauvignon. The wine was first released in 1993 with the superb 1990 vintage. The wine was developed by John Duval, Penfolds former Chief Winemaker, in response to the increasing availability of high quality Cabernet Sauvignon fruit. Although the style embraces the Penfolds multi-district blending philosophy, Bin 407 has become a definitive cool climate Australian Cabernet. After vinification 30% of the wine is matured for 12 months in a combination of new French and American oak. The remainder is aged in one and two-year-old French and American oak.

The name of this wine, Bin 407, does suggest a family resemblance to the Penfolds flagship Bin 707 Cabernet Sauvignon. Although Bin 407 draws fruit from similar wine regions and is vinified using the Penfolds winemaking method, the wine is a more restrained, elegant style with very clear varietal blackcurrant/cassis fruit definition, fine grained tannins and cedary oak. The wine greatly benefits from both new oak and the maturation effect. The oak never overwhelms the fruit, placing the Cabernet fruit at centre stage. Penfolds winemakers like to describe the oak in this context as 'framing' the wine.

Generally Bin 407 stands out in the classic Penfolds years of 1990, 1996 and 1998. Ch'ng Poh Tiong notes, "The Bin 407 style is quite masculine and reminiscent of the Bordeaux wines of Moulis in the Medoc." James Halliday notes the wines are generally very structured styles, "When the fruit is of the appropriate ripeness in the cassis/blackcurrant/chocolate spectrum, the wine seems to carry those pronounced tannins very well. In leaner vintages the tannins seem to outlive the fruit, even though they are very much part of the Penfolds style". The upshot of this is, of course, that optimum drinking also varies according to vintage. 1995, 1997 and 2000 are all good examples of early drinking styles and should be drunk relatively soon. On the other hand, several vintages have much longer drinking windows. Inevitably these vintages show more fruit definition, concentration and tannin ripeness. While Bin 407 is a multi-district blend, it does largely reflect the conditions of the south east South Australian vintage. In years like 1994, 1996, 1998 and 2001 Bin 407 can outperform within its price category. Certainly the wine is a lovely contrast to the more opulent and powerful Bin 707.

PENFOLDS
BIN 407
CABERNET
SAUVIGNON

First Vintage: 1990

Variety: Cabernet Sauvignon

Origin: Multi-district blend from South Australia's Bordertown, Padthaway, Coonawarra, Robe, McLaren Vale, Clare Valley, Barossa Valley.

Fermentation: Stainless steel tanks with wooden header boards. Some components complete fermentation in barrel.

Maturation: 12 months in new French and American (30%) oak. Also one and two-year-old hogsheads, some of which have been used for previous vintages of Bin 707.

PENFOLDS BIN 407
CABERNET SAUVIGNON

1990 `Now` `2010` ★
Medium deep red. Complex cedar/cigar box/mocha aromas. A lovely aged wine with tobacco/chocolaty flavours, fine soft/supple tannins and some savoury nuances. A fully mature wine which will hold.

1991 `Now` `2011` ★
Medium deep red. A very savoury wine with some mushroom/blackcurrant/sandalwood/earthy aromas. A dry, well concentrated palate with a core of choco-berry fruit, puckering tannins and firm finish. Tannins poke out. Probably best now.

1992 `Now` `2010`
Medium deep red. A tightly knit very tannic wine with earthy/cedarwood/blackcurrant/herb aromas and flavours. Lovely fruit but tannins are very muscular. Will hold.

1993 `Now` `2008`
Medium deep red. Fragrant dark chocolate/prune/herb aromas. A firm grippy palate with some blackcurrant/earthy flavours, but the fruit is beginning to dry out. Best drunk soon.

1994 `Now` `2015`
Medium deep red. Powerful blackcurrant/mulberry/plummy aromas with some leafy nuances. A big ripe wine with sweet blackcurrant/mocha fruit, some savoury spice/cedar characters and solid but ripe tannins. Still developing.

1995 `Now`
Medium deep red. A loose-knit early drinking style which needs to be drunk soon. The wine still has some leafy/cassis/minty aromas and flavours but is quite earthy and dry on the palate.

1996 `Now` `2016` ★
Deep red. Very ripe sweet blackcurrant/cedar aromas. The palate is elegantly structured with choco-berry/liquorice fruit flavours and ripe grainy tannins. Excellent length and balance.

1997 `Now`
Medium red-purple. Prune/black olive/vegemite/marmite aromas with a touch of mint. The palate is big and tough with compost/leafy flavours. Looks slightly over-developed. Drink soon.

1998 `Now` `2018` ★
Deep red-purple. Rich and concentrated wine with intense blackcurrant/black olive/chocolate aromas. Deep set flavoursome palate with choco-berry fruit and fine grained slightly grippy tannins. A beautifully focused and poised wine.

1999 `Now` `2015`
Deep red-purple. Cassis/leafy aromas with some menthol/spice notes. The palate is well concentrated with cassis/leafy/meaty flavours and fine slightly drying tannins. Not as powerful as the 1998.

2000 `Now` `2010`
Deep red-purple. Fragrant cassis/redcurrant aromas with some floral notes. Full ripe balanced wine with blackcurrant/cedar/vanilla flavours and smooth tannins. Builds up to a grippy finish. A medium term wine.

2001 `Now` `2016`
Medium deep red-purple. Scented spice/blackcurrant/plum aromas. The palate is ripe and concentrated with plenty of sweet blackcurrant/chocolate fruit and fine supple ripe tannins. Still very young/elemental.

Outstanding vintages ★

Penfolds

BIN 407
CABERNET SAUVIGNON

COMMENTARY: "The 1990 has quite a penetrating nose of cassis/black olives and tar and a touch of dark chocolate. It has some nutty development, but the wine remains fresh, rich, supple and sweet on the palate with plenty of spicy/tobacco/cedar/cassis." (JS) "The wine is maturing reasonably quickly, but it is very scented, elegant, fine and long." (JH) "It gets better and better in the glass, but it's close to fully mature. The tannins have softened off very nicely. The 1991 is pretty earthy and aged with some raisiny characters. The palate is savoury and dry with some puckering tannins. The wine needs cheese, and it will go further out of balance with age." (HH) "It is a really perfumed wine. I liked the cassis/sandalwood aromas and the soft fruit and fresh crisp acidity on the palate. This is a very enjoyable wine." (CPT)

"The 1992 shows some beguiling fruit characters. It has gently ripe fruit on the palate, but the tannins really kick in at the finish." (JH) "Those tannins are quite substantial and the fruit leans towards green. I just don't see the fruit triumphing." (JW) "It has some pleasant dusty/plum/chocolate characters, but the palate is rather dry and slightly parched." (JS)

"The 1993 is very developed and earthy with hints of cigar box, prune and raisin. The fruit's drying out." (HH) "I find the wine has good balance with some fragrant mint/herb lift and intense blackcurrant/bitter chocolate/herb flavours." (JH) "The 1994 is a really good style with some smoky/meaty/blackfruit aromas and nice sweet fruit on entry. I like the texture and the tannins are well integrated." (JW) "It has marginally more depth than the 1993 and a ripe, open, plummy, full-fruited nose. It has plenty of blackcurrant ripeness and savoury spice/cedar notes. This is a big, ripe, developing wine." (JS) "I like the overall structure of this wine. It has some attractive leafy/dusty but ripe Cabernet flavours and chunky tannins." (HH)

"The 1995 is a lighter, more leafy/minty style with pleasant fruit on the palate and dusty tannins on the finish." (JH) "It has a light cassis fragrance, but the palate is short on fruit and quite dry. It should be drunk soon." (CPT) "The 1996 is a very stylish wine with elegant blackcurrant cedar characters. The tannins are quite evident on the palate." (JH) "This wine has a much deeper, more penetrating nose with very ripe sweet fruit and a touch of mint, but is not herbaceous. The palate is deep and full with chocolaty ripe fruit, but matched by strong tannins." (JS) "It has plenty of chocolate, liquorice and ripe blackcurrant fruits, but I find the oak slightly heavy." (CPT)

"The 1997 is quite forward with developed earthy/sump oil/black olive aromas. It's big, tough and tannic. It might go on for a while, but I can't see age improving this." (HH) "The tannins linger ominously." (JH) "I find quite a lot of eucalyptus, a touch of oak and plenty of marmite characters. It is correctly varietal but not a very exciting wine." (JS) "There's fruit here, but the wine is doomed. The tannins are getting the upper hand." (JW)

"The 1998 is a beautifully focused and poised Cabernet with rich luscious cassis fruit and all the classic flavours." (JH) "It has ripe sweet plum/blackcurrant notes and some black olive/spice nuances. It's full and well-balanced with fine tannins." (JS) "This is a brute of a wine with cassis/plum/grilled meat aromas, a huge fresh dried fruit attack and ripe tannins. The 1999 is a bit of a lack lustre wine after the 1998! But it has good sweet fruit and balance. It's got plenty of blackcurrant/spice fruit and decent length." (JW)

PENFOLDS BIN 407
CABERNET SAUVIGNON

"The 2000 has lots of primary cassis/ blackberry/currant fruit. The wine is full of charm and is fresh and alive. This is a surprise package! I am really impressed by this wine." (HH) "It's richly aromatic on the nose and full of black plums and cassis together with cedar/ tobacco and a touch of vanilla. The palate is full, ripe and balanced with smooth tannins." (JH) "The wine is brighter, more brilliant and fruitier than the others with blueberry/dark chocolate characters. The palate is fleshy and ripe with round tannins and acidity. The 2001 is a less fruity wine with more oak, but is still enjoyable." (CPT) "The wine is still a baby. It's not as rich as the 2000 and the tannins are almost too much." (JW) "I agree with its being a baby, but I found the wine had some nice berry fruit and some serious depth and firm structure. The tannins are supple and ripe. This is the only vintage to show obvious oak, but the wine should power on." (HH) "It is a well-shaped wine. It has slight dustiness on the nose with very sweet plum fruit on the palate, some sandalwood spiciness and fine tannins." (JS)

"I am generally surprised by the structure of the wines. Some of the early vintages are particularly tannic, the fruit losing out in the end. The 1991, 1992 and 1993 are good examples." (HH) "I commented on the tannins too, but rarely mentioned oak. Certainly there are structural issues, but wines like the 1990, 1996 and 1998 are gorgeous. It's difficult to assign drinking windows. In some vintages the tannins seem to be outliving the fruit. When the wines show strong Cabernet fruit of the appropriate ripeness, the tannins appear to be well-covered." (JH) "The three most outstanding wines are the 1990, 1996 and 1998. The 1990 was pretty spectacular and I also liked the 1994." (JW)

(CPT) – CH'NG POH TIONG
(JH) – JAMES HALLIDAY
(HH) – HUON HOOKE
(JS) – JOANNA SIMON
(JW) – JOSEPH WARD

PENFOLDS BIN 389
CABERNET SHIRAZ

BIN 389
CABERNET SHIRAZ

OVERVIEW: Penfolds Bin 389 Cabernet Shiraz has earned a reputation among wine consumers and collectors as an Australian classic. Doug Crittenden, a Melbourne wine merchant, was an early supporter of Bin 389 and used to transport the wine over from Adelaide in barrels. Originally Bin 389 (first vintage 1960) was a single vineyard wine, drawing fruit from the now defunct Auldana Vineyard near Magill Estate. Predominantly a Barossa Valley wine at one point, the Bin 389 is now a multi-district South Australian blend with fruit sourced from the Barossa Valley, Coonawarra, Padthaway, McLaren Vale, Langhorne Creek and Clare Valley, and more recently, Penfolds' new vineyards in Robe and Bordertown.

Over the last 40 years Bin 389 has developed a strong identity for its consistency, reliability and value. Notwithstanding the vagaries and character of each vintage, the wine has universal appeal among buyers. Wine consumers buy it because it's delicious to drink, even when first released. Collectors appreciate it because the wine over-delivers on quality – especially in classic vintages such as 1976, 1986, 1990, 1996 and 1998. And, as a blend of Cabernet Sauvignon and Shiraz, it's a very Australian style of wine.

Max Schubert recognised that blending Cabernet and Shiraz could bring something extra to both aroma and palate. Although there have been major improvements in viticulture and winemaking, the basic idea holds true today. Cabernet Sauvignon is a highly perfumed grape variety with a firm structure and fine grainy tannins. Shiraz is more opulent and fleshy with both power and generosity of fruit. Combined, they produce a wine which can show richness, finesse and longevity.

Penfolds Bin 389 epitomises the Penfolds winemaking philosophy and the art of multi-regional blending. While regional characters are intertwined, it is ultimately the personality and the structure of the fruit that really matters. Bin 389 is vinified in a traditional Penfolds manner. The wine is fermented in headed down, stainless steel tanks. Some components of the blend complete fermentation in barrel to enhance complexity, richness and integration of new oak. The wine is then matured in a combination of new (20-30%) and one and two-year-old American hogsheads for 18 months prior to bottling, with many of the older barrels having been used for the previous vintage of Grange.

PENFOLDS
BIN 389
CABERNET SHIRAZ

First Vintage: 1960

Variety: Cabernet Sauvignon and Shiraz

Origin: Multi-district blend from South Australia's Barossa Valley, Coonawarra, Padthaway, Robe, Bordertown, McLaren Vale, Langhorne Creek and Clare Valley.

Fermentation: 10 and 20 tonne stainless steel fermenters with wax lined, wooden header boards. Some components complete fermentation in barrel.

Maturation: 18 months in American oak hogsheads (300 litres). 20-30% new, 70-80% one and two-year-old oak, including barrels used for previous vintage of Grange.

143

PENFOLDS BIN 389
CABERNET SHIRAZ

In some respects Bin 389 bathes in reflected glory, although one might argue to the contrary that an otherwise classic wine in its own right is overshadowed by its higher profile siblings. In Australia Bin 389 is often referred to as 'Poor Man's Grange'. In America some people call it 'Baby Grange'. However the proof is in the pudding. With all its ripe fruit, richness and generosity, the wine has been much loved over several generations of wine drinkers. James Halliday calls the older vintages "an army of lovely old wines" and Joanna Simon describes the 1961 vintage as "magnificent". Huon Hooke is impressed by the 1970 vintage, "A stand-out wine reminiscent of dusty old barrels, earthy old cellars, forest floors and barnyards."

Penfolds Bin 389 epitomises the Penfolds winemaking philosophy and the art of multi-regional blending.

With the compelling virtues of drinkability and cellaring potential, Bin 389 is one of the stalwarts of the secondary wine market. The best vintages are eagerly sought after by collectors – and for good reason. Vintages such as 1986, 1988, 1990, 1991, 1994, 1996 and 1998 were all stand-out wines in this tasting, delivering on their reputation. The panel agreed that there had been "meaningful progress" over the years, largely because of the improvement in vineyard management. Words such as "harmonious", "seamless" and "glorious" are used increasingly to describe the better and more recent vintages. James Halliday says, "The last bracket from 1989 to 2001 is very even – reflecting an impressive discipline in fruit selection and winemaking – especially in such difficult vintages as 2000".

Joanna Simon says of Bin 389, "This is the archetypal Australian wine – it comprises all the very best elements of Australian wine". James Halliday agrees, "Bin 389 is a blend of Cabernet and Shiraz from warm and hot climates. The result is a mix of complimentary aromas and flavours. It just can't work with cool climate fruit".

Along with the other Bin range wines of the 1960s (except Bin 707), Bin 389 derived its name from a compartment, or 'Bin', in the Penfolds cellars at Magill. When experimental wines were bottled, and before they were labelled, they were known by the number of the 'Bin' in which they were stored. When Bin 389 became an ongoing member of the Penfolds portfolio it simply adopted the name of its original storage 'home'.

145

PENFOLDS BIN 389
CABERNET SHIRAZ

1961 `Now` ★

Deep brick red. Mature gamy/leather/walnut aromas with some sweet dried fruit/minty characters. A complex, layered palate with plenty of sweet fruit and fine tannins. Becomes dry at the finish. A lovely old wine but drink soon.

1964 `Now` ★

Brick red. Mocha/cedar/meaty aromas with some vanilla notes. Still showing plenty of fruit sweetness on the palate with fine chocolaty/smooth tannins. Holding up well but drink now.

1966 `Now`

Deep brick red. Well concentrated wine with complex mushroom/barnyard/liquorice/camphor aromas. The palate is well developed and sweet-fruited with mushroom/meaty/minty flavours and fine powdery/grainy tannins. Finishes grippy and tight. A Cabernet-driven wine.

1967 `Now`

Brick red. A mellow wine with sweet meaty/spice/leather aromas. The palate is fully developed with sweet ripe fruit and savoury tannins. Slightly drying finish.

1970 `Now`

Brick red. A lovely old wine with dusty/cedar/earthy/leather/barnyard aromas and a rich mellow chocolaty palate. The tannins are quite drying at the finish.

1971 `Now`

Brick red. A very aromatic complex sweet fruited wine. Mocha/berry/leather aromas and plenty of savoury nuances. The palate is well concentrated with sweet leather/mocha flavours and grainy/chalky tannins.

1975 `Now`

Brick red. Complex earth/cedar/leafy/herb aromas with some sweet berry aromas. The palate is mature with earth/cedar/mushroom/miso soup flavours and grainy, slightly hard tannins. Still holding up well.

1976 `Now` `2011` ★

Brick red. A powerful wine with sweet ripe notes of liquorice, black fruits, mocha and tar. A slightly oaky but superbly concentrated palate with mocha/liquorice/chocolaty flavours and ripe (but pronounced) tannins. A classic Bin 389 vintage.

1977 `Now` `2007`

Medium brick. A sweet and savoury wine with herb garden/floral/minty aromas and some leathery nuances. The palate is solid showing some dark chocolate/berry flavours and strong tannin structure.

1978 `Now` `2008`

Medium brick. Old leather/honeycomb/mocha/malt aromas with some leafy characters. A loose-knit wine with mocha/vanilla/sweet earthy flavours and firm tannins.

1979 `Now`

Brick red. Aromatic mocha/leafy/minty Cabernet aromas. A fresh mature palate with some rich gamy/mocha fruit and fine slinky tannins. Finishes dry and a touch minty. Cool vintage.

1980 `Now – Past`

Brick red. Fragrant herb garden/cassis aromas and flavours. A medium concentrated palate with some sweet fruit and pronounced drying tannins. Finishes hard and tight. Drink up.

1981 `Now – Past`

Brick red. Earthy/liquorice/meaty aromas. A firmly structured wine with earthy/liquorice/minty flavours and fine grippy tannins. Leafy and dry at the finish.

1982 `Now`

Brick red. Complex coffee/crème brûlée/mulberry/tomato leaf aromas. The palate is ripe and supple with fine leafy tannins. Drink soon.

Outstanding vintages ★

1983 `Now` 2010

Brick red. Massive wine with complex cigar box/ sweet leather/dark chocolate aromas. Immensely concentrated palate with paneforte/chocolaty flavours and monumental tannins.

1984 `Now` 2008

Medium deep red. Attractive sweet cherry/plum/ cassis aromas with leather/spicy notes. The palate is medium bodied but fresh and fleshy with plenty of ripe fruit. Finishes firm. A surprise considering vintage reputation and past ROP form!

1985 `Now` 2010

Medium deep red. Cedar/earth/sweet berry aromas. Well concentrated wine with black cherry/cedar/ sweet blackberry flavours, strong gravelly tannins and grippy finish.

1986 `Now` 2012 ★

Medium deep red. Intense prune/blackberry/ liquorice/allspice aromas. Richly concentrated multi-layered palate with prune/blackberry/mocha fruit and ripe chocolaty tannins. An immensely proportioned wine.

1987 `Now`

Medium deep red. Redcurrant leafy aromas and flavours. Elegantly structured wine with some sweet fruit and chalky tannins. Won't get any better.

1988 `Now` 2013

Medium deep red. Intense dark chocolate/coffee/ meaty aromas. The palate is rich and ripe with mocha/berry fruit, pronounced tannins, spicy oak and plenty of flavour length.

1989 `Now` 2008

Medium deep red. Liquorice/redcurrant/herb garden aromas. Generously proportioned palate with fleshy redcurrant/leafy fruit and chocolaty tannins. Build up is savoury and it is grippy at the finish.

1990 `Now` 2025 ★

Deep red. Lovely complex wine with plum/cassis/ mocha aromas and some earthy/autumnal notes. A richly concentrated palate with masses of sweet fruit and chocolate/plummy flavours intertwined with ripe slinky tannins and mocha oak. The fruit, tannin and oak are in perfect alignment. A great vintage.

1991 `Now` 2020 ★

Medium deep red. Intense cassis/plum/anise aromas with some malty oak characters. A beautifully concentrated and balanced wine with deep-set ripe cassis/plum fruit, fine ripe tannins and classy new oak. An excellent foil to the 1990.

1992 `Now` 2012

Medium deep red. Earthy/blackberry/liquorice aromas. The palate is well concentrated and solid with black fruit/chocolate flavours and strong, almost monumental tannins. A powerful but tough structure.

1993 `Now` 2012

Deep red. Stewed prune/dark chocolate/sour cherry aromas. A strongly flavoured palate with choco-berry/sour cherry/herbal flavours and pronounced tannins.

1994 `Now` 2025 ★

Deep red. Profoundly deep wine with intense mocha/berry/meaty/paneforte aromas. The palate is richly concentrated and balanced with plenty of sweet blackberry chocolate/coffee fruit and a massive fine grained tannin structure. A superb wine.

1995 `Now` 2015

Medium deep red. Dark cherry, earthy aromas with some minerally notes. A medium bodied loose-knit palate with cherry/earthy/wet stone flavours and chalky firm tannins. An elegant style.

Outstanding vintages ★

PENFOLDS BIN 389
CABERNET SHIRAZ

1996 `Now` ──────── `2020` ★

Medium deep red. Intense pure liquorice/ blackcurrant/plummy aromas with some underlying malty oak. A lovely sweet rich ripe wine with plenty of choco-berry fruit flavours, ripe slinky tannins and underlying malt/vanillin oak. Superb flavour length.

1997 `Now` ──── `2008`

Medium deep red. Meaty/plum/raspberry aromas with some leafy/herbal tones. An elegantly structured palate with sweet plum/raspberry flavours and fine leafy/chewy tannins. Drink earlier rather than later.

1998 `2006` ──────── `2030` ★

Deep red. A huge ethereal wine with intense blackberry/liquorice/spice/malt aromas. The palate is richly concentrated with deep-set blackberry/ mocha fruit and ripe velvety/chocolaty tannins. A blockbuster!

1999 `Now` ──────── `2020`

Deep red-purple. Ripe plum/blackberry aromas with some meaty nuances. A fleshy wine with plum/ blackberry flavours and malt/vanillin oak. The tannins build up firm and grippy towards the finish. A well-balanced wine.

2000 `Now` ──── `2010`

Medium red. Red cherry/redcurrant/aniseed aromas with some vegetal/compost notes. A loose-knit early drinking style with attractive red/blackberry flavours and fine tannins.

2001 `2006` ──────── `2020` ★

Deep colour. Intense blackberry spicy/nutmeg/ aniseed aromas. The palate is well concentrated with dark chocolate/blackberry flavours and supple ripe tannins. Finishes firm and tight. Still in adolescence.

Outstanding vintages ★

148

BIN 389
CABERNET SHIRAZ

COMMENTARY: "The first bracket, 1961-1978, is very strong – an army of lovely old wines. Amazingly, some of these wines, which five years ago, we thought should be drunk soon, are still holding up beautifully and showing no signs of fading!" (JH) "The 1961 is a magnificent wine – and a highlight of the entire tasting. It has a mature, gamy, leathery nose with some dried fruits and touches of peppermint/eucalyptus. The palate is complex and sweet with layers of flavours." (JS) "I give it two extra stars for bravery! It is a lovely old wine with sweet fruit still at its core." (JH)

"The 1964 has a rich meaty old nose. It's a nice old wine, but it's leaning out now." (HH) "It's more closed on the nose, but the fruit is more persistent than the 1961 with plenty of sweet spices and leather. The 1966 has plenty of sandalwood/camphor aromas and sweet prune/leather fruit on the palate. It has good length and some clove-like nuances." (CPT) "I think the wine is beginning to dry out at the finish, but the second bottle has some cedar/meaty/baked aromas and good sweet fruit on the palate." (JW) "It has a tight structure, probably driven by the Cabernet component." (JH)

"The 1967 is meaty and mellow as well. The palate is quite tannic – again that Cabernet structure – but it has delicious sweet ripe fruit. A lovely, harmonious wine. The 1970 is a stand-out wine reminiscent of dusty old barrels, earthy old cellars, forest floors and barnyards." (HH) "The wine is much richer and more chocolaty than the bouquet suggests, and it's still holding its structure." (JH) "It has very strong farmyard characters on the nose and palate – overpoweringly so. The 1971 is dry and grainy." (JS) "The wine still has lovely sweet rich fruit but it's definitely in graceful decline now." (HH)

"I think they are both slightly disappointing bottles – considering the reputation of the vintage – but it's still complex and savoury with sweet fruit on entry, then tannins. The 1975 is a moderately intense wine with herb/earth/spice/berry aromas and distinct tannins, but happily on the mid-palate rather than on the finish." (JH) "The wine smells of old driftwood and tastes jammy and then dry at the finish." (CPT) "It's beginning to tire and dry out now. It's lean and short." (HH)

"The 1976, on the other hand, is a powerful wine with masses of fruit and tannins. I would drink the wine now, before the tannins take over." (JW) "It's still majestically rich and powerful with abundant style, presence and character." (JH) "I find it very big and concentrated with plenty of chocolaty/spicy/oaky notes. It's impressive, but in the end it's a chunky rather than charming wine." (JS)

"The 1977 is just an old decent red with dusty/earthy/honey aromas and a solid gripping/tannic palate. It needs food." (HH) "It's quite austere and sinewy on the palate." (CPT) "The 1978 has a lovely old leather/honey/sweet earthy nose, but it's got a very firm grip on the palate." (HH) "I found some farmyard characters and a touch of mint. The palate is rather dry-parched and leathery." (JS) "The 1979 has a sweet, leafy, aged Cabernet nose and is quite sweet, fleshy and lush on the palate. It's a nice drink." (HH) "I found it very fresh and attractive with smoky/tobacco/leather aromas and flavours." (CPT) "The nose is gamy, sweet and mellow with some leather/matchstick notes. The palate is rich and gamy with some farmyard characters, but not overwhelmingly so – yet!" (JS)

"The 1980 has dried out completely." (JW) "It has youthful sweet fruit characters together with

149

PENFOLDS BIN 389
CABERNET SHIRAZ

lots of rich/developed gamy spicy notes." (JS) "I think the wine is past its best now. Those tannins are very pronounced and the palate is drying." (HH) "The 1981 is another austere wine with tobacco aromas and flavours." (CPT) "It has less tannin than the 1980, but it's beginning to hollow out on the back palate." (JH) "It's got an earthy/dusty/dry nose but the palate is too firm now. Drink up!" (HH)

"The 1982 is a spicy/savoury wine. It has ripe fruit which flows on to the palate and some smoky notes." (JH) "The nose is very different with ripe, sweet, blackberry/vanilla/creamy characters and an exotic spicy note. It's ripe and supple with very sweet/dried fruits and touches of Port/mint/milk chocolate. The 1983 has a dark brooding nose with plenty of dark chocolate characters and a dark, sweet spicy/gamy palate. It's a very big, concentrated wine with a lot of oak, but there's enough fruit to take it!" (JS) "There's a vinous arm wrestle happening here. It even smells tannic! But after sitting in the glass for a while, it reveals a lovely cedar/cigar box complexity. The 1984 has plenty of Cabernet character. It's a really stylish wine with lots of depth/concentration and fruit weight. The tannins are there, but it's deliciously ripe." (HH)

"The 1985 has meaty/dried red fruit aromas. It's mid-weighted and fruit ripe but those tannins are getting the upper hand." (JW) "I think the wine is well-balanced with sweet ripe black cherry/plum/cassis aromas and a medium bodied palate." (JH) "It's not particularly complex, though it's still drinking nicely." (HH) "The 1986 is a lovely wine with perfect balance and structure. It has fresh cedar/earth/sweet berry aromas with an elegant fine palate. It's at the peak of its power." (JH)

"The 1987 is chocolaty and peppery, but the palate lacks fruit power." (CPT) "It's slightly green with leafy tobacco characters and a lean, angular (rather tough) palate." (HH) "The 1988 has plenty of dark chocolate and vanilla on the nose. It's a big, concentrated wine with lots of warmth and spice, if not a bit oak dominated." (JS) "It's a monster with rich meaty/barbecued aromas and a very ripe, rich, concentrated (but hugely tannic) palate." (HH)

"The 1989 shows a significant colour shift away from the brick towards purple. It has an abundant mix of blackcurrant/blackberry/plum and liquorice with luscious fruit on the palate." (JH) "There are some minty notes on the nose too. The palate is chocolaty with spicy oak. The wine shows clean, pure flavours, if not huge richness. The 1990 is a lovely rich, sweet wine showing autumnal fruit development. The palate is very succulent and mouth-filling with very rich, ripe fruit and tannins and great length." (JS) "This is a very youthful, lively beauty with sweet ripe meaty/plum aromas and perfect balance." (JW) "The wine is fresh and vivacious with ripe cassis fruit and a supple concentrated palate." (CPT) "It's got masses of sweet fruit, perfect ripeness and superb balance. I think it's slightly shaded by the 1991, which is sheer class. The Cabernet shows through with cassis/plum slight anise aromas and ample smooth tannins. This is a really lovely wine (worth waiting for) with glorious balance and structure. A wine for the long haul." (HH)

"The 1992 is quite extracted and porty with a coarse palate." (JS) "The palate is drying and it really lacks the balance of fruit for the long term. It's a very walnutty/earthy wine with a tough after-palate." (HH) "I am less critical. Those tannins are slightly tough, but I think it's a solid four-square wine with lots of fruit

structure and surprising strength. The 1993 is a rich, powerful wine with some blackberry/blackcurrant aromas. The tannins are very firm, maybe too much so." (JH) "Yes, those tannins are ferocious." (HH) "I find the wine stewy and dusty. The 1994, however, is a dense, substantial wine with a deep penetrating nose of black fruits/sandalwood/beeswax polish. It promises so much and the palate lives up to it. The wine has great richness with ripe, sweet blackfruits/dark chocolate flavours and fine-grained tannins." (JS) "That oak is big time, but the wine is immensely concentrated and ripe, with plenty of chocolaty fruit." (CPT)

"The 1995 shows a cooler spectrum of fruit aromas and I see more of a Shiraz influence in the wine. This is not a blockbuster, but the wine has sweet attack, and is developing nicely." (JW) "It's an elegant and long wine with a smooth mix of red and black fruits and deft oak. The palate is supple and polished. The 1996 is a really well constructed and balanced wine with fresh fragrant, juicy berry fruit and mint aromas. There's lots of blackcurrant on the palate with long lingering tannins. The tannins off-set the juicy fruit very well." (JH) "Yes. It's a big, sweet, ripe, plummy wine with plenty of generosity and richness on the palate. Those big tannins are well-balanced. Exceptional!" (HH)

"The 1996 is a great wine with mouth-coating fruit, ripe tannins and great length. It's got the whole enchilada! The 1997 is a more compact wine with blackcurrant/plum aromas. It's possible that the wine suffers from coming after the 1996, but I just don't see this wine developing for the long term. It doesn't have enough concentration." (JW) "I tend to agree. It has developed surprisingly quickly. It's an elegantly proportioned wine with good length and finesse, but should be drunk sooner rather

than later. The 1998, however, is an abundantly ripe wine with sweet black fruits and good oak to complement. The palate is just an explosion of flavour with solid tannins." (JH)

"It's a real blockbuster. The wine is closed up on the nose, but the palate is hugely concentrated with mouth-crippling tannins and loads of extract. This wine needs forever!" (HH) "There's no over-ripeness or jam in the wine. The palate is deep, rounded and chocolaty/velvety with a very long finish." (JS) "The 1999 is very Cabernet-driven. It's got plenty of cassis/plummy fruit and big oak." (CPT) "It's a well-balanced wine which should guarantee it a fairly, long, graceful life." (JW) "The wine has lovely, big ripe plum/blackberry aromas. It's a solid wine without being too oaky with ripe smooth tannins. The 2000 is more lightly structured, however, with spicy/plum aromas and a soft easygoing palate. It's slightly composty/vegetal but there's plenty of tannin and flavour." (HH) "It's not a wine of great complexity, but it has some intense sweet blackberry fruit and a fairly concentrated, chunky palate with chewy blackberry fruit and some spice/oak." (JS)

"The 2001 is a rich, ripe oaky wine." (CPT) "The oak is very well handled." (JH) "It's a very good wine, but may lack the extra concentration of the greats. It's not a massive wine but it shows plenty of Eastern spices and anise character." (HH) "It has an impressive nose with masses of cherries and aromatic spices. The palate is lush and concentrated with chocolaty fine tannins and underlying oak. Promises well." (JS)

(CPT) – CH'NG POH TIONG
(JH) – JAMES HALLIDAY
(HH) – HUON HOOKE
(JS) – JOANNA SIMON
(JW) – JOSEPH WARD

OVERVIEW: The tradition of innovation and experimentation is central to the philosophy of the limited production Penfolds Cellar Reserve wines. These wines do not necessarily fit into any particular genre. In many respects the whole winemaking process is a voyage of discovery. Without the expectation of making a wine to a housestyle, winemakers are allowed to play with the fruit and make something that is different. Largely available only through Penfolds Cellar Doors and the Magill Estate Restaurant, these are effectively experimental wines. The first of this line, the 1993 Penfolds Cabernet Shiraz is perhaps the most 'Penfolds' in style. Primarily drawn from Coonawarra Cabernet Sauvignon and Clare Valley Shiraz, this wine is described by James Halliday as "rich, dense and opulent".

Very well received, the 2002 **Cellar Reserve Grenache** is one of the highlights of *The Rewards of Patience* tasting. Huon Hooke says, "This is a very impressive wine with lovely ripe floral Grenache aromas and full, yet beautifully rounded tannins". Ch'ng Poh Tiong says, "The 2002 Grenache has a wonderful perfume of violets and loads of ripe red fruits". Joanna Simon is also impressed, "This is textbook Grenache with exuberant fruit and chocolaty, round, mouthfilling flavours. The wine is sourced from mature Grenache bush vines in the Barossa Valley including the Seppeltsfield Vineyard". Peter Gago says, "This type of Grenache vintage comes around only two or three times in a decade". James Halliday comments, "The wine has fantastic structure. It is reminiscent of the Rayas structure. Mark Shield (an Australian wine writer who died far too early in life) would have loved this style".

The **Cellar Reserve Pinot Noir** has been an ongoing project. The fruit derives primarily from the Adelaide Hills and the Barossa Ranges,

and the wine is made at Magill Estate. Penfolds purchases fruit of varying clonal types from up to 14 different vineyards. Typically, the fruit is cold soaked for up to a week and vinified (up to 30% whole bunch) using natural yeasts. During fermentation the grape skin cap is 'pigeaged' (punched down) regularly to optimise flavours and texture. The wine is matured in about 50-60% new French Dargaud, Seguin Moreau and Jaegle oak for a period of about 12 months on lees without SO_2. It is bottled unfiltered. Winemakers are continuously refining and experimenting with this grape variety. Huon Hooke describes the wines as "very impressive". James Halliday says, "The 2001 Pinot Noir shows plenty of generous varietal fruit, but the 2002 is still locked up – a monster!".

The **Cellar Reserve Sangiovese**, first vintage 1998, uses fruit from the Penfolds 8 row block in the Kalimna Vineyard. Planted in 1984, this variety is relatively new to Australia. Winemaking is intuitive to vintage conditions rather than a set piece. Over the last few vintages winemakers have encouraged natural wild ferments and post-fermentation macerations to enhance flavours and textures. The wine is matured in five to six year old French oak (on lees). This is largely a fruit-driven style. Huon Hooke says the more recent vintages show "better clarity and definition". Certainly Penfolds is still working out this most compelling variety. The tannins are generally quite pronounced, but Sangiovese has plenty of fruit sweetness and flavour. The panel thought the 2001 and 2002 were generally the most successful vintages, with plenty of varietal definition and savoury palate structures. The Cellar Reserve range remains a project in progress. Zinfandel and Tempranillo wines are currently under trial.

PENFOLDS SUPER PREMIUM WINES

"The greatest wines have
implanted in them the
ideas of the winemaker as
to what they should be.
Their character is part
of the wine."

– MAX SCHUBERT

EST 1844

PENFOLDS YATTARNA
BIN 144 CHARDONNAY

> **"This is a top class Chardonnay with all the style and finesse of a Grand Cru Burgundy."** – CH'NG POH TIONG

OVERVIEW: When first produced in 1995, Penfolds Yattarna attracted great interest from Australian wine drinkers and the media, winning front page news. The wine adds a new chapter to Penfolds' history, as Yattarna is the end product of Penfolds flagship white wine project, which the media termed the 'White Grange' Project.

For several years Penfolds had been interested in making a high quality white wine that would be a counterpart to Penfolds Grange, Australia's most famous red wine. The research and development of this wine was reminiscent of the experimental red winemaking climate of the 1950s and 1960s. The Reserve Bin A Series was one spin-off of this project. The high expectations of wine drinkers and the wine press made for a long period of trial and error.

The name, Yattarna, is a local indigenous word meaning 'little by little' or 'gradually', reflecting the overall time and refinement required before Penfolds felt ready to release the wine to a highly expectant and critical wine market. Indeed, the Bin number – 144 – is derived from the total number of wine trials undertaken in the wine's development!

The great success of a 1995 Adelaide Hills/McLaren Vale Chardonnay at the Sydney Wine Show convinced Penfolds that a multi-regional blend was the way forward. It embraced the Penfolds philosophy of house style and a non-compromising approach to winemaking. The style has evolved further since its first release, as winemakers seek to refine and perfect Yattarna Chardonnay. Almost every element of winemaking practice has been fine-tuned. Improvements in vineyard management, batch harvesting and initial classification have led to a heightened level of fruit quality at vintage time.

Unconstrained, Penfolds is able to source fruit from the Adelaide Hills and the cooler sites of South Australia as well as from the high altitude vineyard of Tumbarumba in New South Wales and Henty in the far south of Victoria. Penfolds may also soon begin sourcing cool climate fruit from the island state, Tasmania.

Winemakers are looking for specific ripe fruit characteristics, usually well-concentrated grapes which possess an apple/white peach/melon flavour profile and natural, minerally acidity.

PENFOLDS YATTARNA BIN 144 CHARDONNAY

First Vintage: 1995

Variety: Chardonnay

Origin: Multi-district blend, primarily Adelaide Hills but contributions from the Snowy Mountains region of Tumbarumba, New South Wales and Henty, Victoria.

Fermentation: 100% barrel fermented in new (50-100%) and one-year-old French oak barriques.

Maturation: 18 months in 50-100% new French oak barriques.

Comments: Packaged in laser-etched bottles since 1995.

PENFOLDS YATTARNA
BIN 144 CHARDONNAY

For several years Penfolds had been interested in making a high quality white wine that would be a counterpart to Penfolds Grange.

Barrel fermentation, malo-lactic fermentation and yeast stirring (battonage) bring important elements to the Yattarna style. The experimentation, innovation and ongoing consumer feedback from the pathfinding Reserve Bin A Series Chardonnay may point Yattarna in new directions.

Partial wild yeast fermentation is just one example of change. Penfolds has refined the use of oak dramatically since the 1995 vintage. Early vintages saw 100% new oak maturation. While it added a strong savoury component, winemakers believed that it over-seasoned the wine, masking overall fruit quality and broadening the palate. In recent vintages Penfolds has moved towards tightly grained, lightly toasted oak from coopers including Dargaud and Jaegle, Seguin Moreau and Louis Latour. Yattarna is now matured in French oak, some of it new, for approximately 18 months prior to bottling. The contemporary Yattarna style aims to be elegantly complex and exquisitely proportioned with no component overwhelming another.

Peter Gago notes, "We seek minerality, texture, layering and longevity. The results so far are extremely pleasing but the journey continues and the style is still evolving."

Huon Hooke comments, "With cooler climates Penfolds is seeking higher natural acidity, finer structure, a different spectrum of flavours, longer, tighter palate structure and potentially greater longevity. The target is to make a fine, long-aging style like the great French Burgundies, whereas to date even the best Australian Chardonnays have generally been relatively short-aging wines".

Joseph Ward notes, "The Yattarna style is heading away from the vernacular Aussie style. The wines have immense concentration and flavour intensity with Burgundian complexity and elegance".

1995 `Now`
Medium gold. Rich complex, fully developed wine with toasted/dried fruit aromas and crème brûlée nuances. The palate is rich, ripe and broad with yellow peach/caramel flavours, pronounced nutty/savoury oak. A massively proportioned wine which needs to be drunk soon.

1996 `Now`   ★
Medium gold. Mellow mature nose with layers of hazelnut/dried flowers/vanilla and toast. A fully developed but beautifully balanced palate with rich round hazelnut/peach/buttery fruit and charry/toasty oak. Finishes long and fruit sweet. Great drinking now.

1997 `Now`   2007
Medium straw gold. Complex lanolin/melon aromas with toasty/candied fruit nuances. A well-balanced, intensely concentrated palate with smooth tropical fruit/buttery flavours and malty/vanilla oak characters. The wine finishes dry and long. Still holding up well.

1998 `Now`   2010   ★
Medium straw gold. A very stylish subtle wine with fruit compote/stone fruit/cashew nut aromas and underlying savoury oak. The palate is superbly balanced with supple, concentrated stone fruit/grilled nut flavours, fine long acidity and underlying oak. A wine with tremendous mouth-feel and flavour length.

1999 `Now`   2008
Pale medium straw. Classically proportioned Chardonnay with tropical fruit/lemon curd/baked apple aromas and touches of honey. A very tightly structured but textured wine with layer upon layer of flavour, a strong spine of fine acidity, and plenty of length.

2000 `2005`   2012   ★
Pale straw. Fresh and intense citrus/stone fruit aromas with some lanolin/vanilla complexity. The palate is tangy and concentrated with stone fruit/citrus flavours, zesty acidity and subtle oak. Finishes tight.

2001 `2005`   2012   ★
Pale straw. A wine with strong personality. Intense tropical/lemon fruit aromas with charry/burnt match/barrel ferment nuances. A rich mouth-filling, well-structured wine with tropical fruit/lemon flavours, some complex buttery characters, fine flinty acidity and integrated oak.

2002 `2006`   2015
Pale straw. Very youthful wine with baked apple/butter/tropical fruit aromas. The palate is very refined and concentrated with subtle tropical/lemony fruit, underlying savoury oak and a very long finish. Lovely balance and flavour.

Outstanding vintages ★

PENFOLDS YATTARNA
BIN 144 CHARDONNAY

COMMENTARY: "There's a logical progression in this bracket. While there are some ups and downs, winemakers are clearly coming to grips with the Yattarna style. The 1995 has a massively proportioned palate. Drink soon. The 1996 vintage is also fully developed, but still has plenty of life with nice sweet fruit flavours and sufficient acidity to keep for a while." (JH) "I can also see the progression of Yattarna. The style is heading out of Australia and becoming more Burgundian in structure. The 1995, the starting point, has plenty of stuffing, but quite frankly, the wine is fading and is best drunk now. The 1996, on the other hand, is more impressive with a ripe tropical fruit attack and a rich buttery mid-palate." (JW) "The 1995 is soft, round and smooth with lots of crème brûlée and nutty oak characters. The 1996 wasn't as complex or convincing, with ripe pineapple aromas and overly-sweet exotic fruit on the palate." (CPT) "The 1995 is very rich and developed and much broader and fatter than Bin 95A. It is a big mouthful of a wine with lots of flavour, but ultimately lacks the finesse of its sister wine. The 1996, however, has remarkable colour with layers of hazelnut, dried flowers, vanilla and toast aromas and flavours. The palate is fine and long with impeccable balance." (HH)

"The fruit and oak battle for supremacy in the 1997 vintage. The wine shows potent complex bottle development which includes some vegetal Burgundian cabbage characters." (JH) "I can see plenty of barrel-ferment/lees characters in the wine, together with mango/citrus flavours. I find the wine quite firm, but more focused than the earlier vintages. Ultimately it's the least interesting wine in the flight." (JW) "The wine shows vanilla/mealy aromas and some charred/toasty/buttery characters. The oak dominates the fruit." (CPT) "It is quite similar, but a little less nuanced than the 1996. I can see those cabbage characters too, also candied fruits, toasted nuts and candle wax. The palate is very smooth and nicely textured, perhaps slightly hot on the mid-palate, but still well-balanced and flavourful." (HH)

"The 1998 vintage is very stylish and subtle with an excellent interplay between fruit, oak and malo-lactic characters. The wine has very good mouth-feel from entry to finish." (JH "I picked up a touch of sulphur. The wine is youthful and complex with vanilla/toast characters and some mineral/grilled nut undertones. It has a very tightly structured palate with prominent oak, but I can see the wine beginning to yield. The wine will still improve." (JW)

"This is a top class Chardonnay with all the style and finesse of a Grand Cru Burgundy. It has wonderful intensity of fruit, acidity and balancing oak." (CPT) "I agree. The wine is impressive with great intensity and finesse. It's still very taut and youthful." (HH) "I think the 1999 vintage is still in transition. The oak is still quite obvious and the palate is big, ripe and mouth-filling." (JH) "There's a lot happening in this wine. It has cooler fruit aromas and a ripe attack on the palate. The fruit needs to be coaxed out, but it's there. That strong spine of acidity suggests that the wine needs more time to reveal itself." (JW) "It is an elegant charmer with vanilla/caramel/toast characters and medium bodied palate." (CPT) "This is a refined, intense and tightly structured wine with great layers of flavours and wonderful finesse and texture. This is a long keeper." (HH)

"The 2000 vintage is a very youthful wine with citrus/stone fruit characters and a tight restrained palate." (JH) "The wine is more open and expressive than the 1999 vintage with some very good ripe fruit flavours, but it is still very young and should be cellared for a while longer." (JW) "I find the wine quite closed as well, but it is soft and round on the palate." (CPT) "I like the zestiness and citrus jumpiness of the wine. It's a very tangy exuberant wine and still in its ascendancy." (HH)

"The 2001 is the most complex of the Yattarnas to date. It has a very strong personality. It is an in-your-face wine with plenty of charry/barrel ferment and burnt match characters. It follows precisely down the same track on the palate." (JH) "I wouldn't touch this wine for a while. It's completely different to preceding wines. It's very tightly structured with subtle oak and should develop well." (JW) "It's a very stylish flinty wine with lovely integration of ripe fruit, oak and acidity." (CPT) "The 2001 has a remarkably young colour. The wine is very delicate and subtle with some offbeat wild ferment characters and complex malo-lactic characters. It has tremendous intensity and focus and should build up over time." (HH)

"The 2002 is a very tight wine with very good integration and balance and delicate use of oak." (JH) "It has a ripe citrus/tropical fruit attack and mouth-coating flavours. There is still a firm spine of acidity, but it has the texture and persistence for a great future." (JW) "This wine is so very young, it's almost unfair to taste it now! But you can see that it has excellent potential." (CPT) "This wine has incredible length of flavour and very subtle, almost imperceptible, oak. It's a fine-boned vintage which will be a ripper with time." (HH)

(CPT) – CH'NG POH TIONG
(JH)   – JAMES HALLIDAY
(HH) – HUON HOOKE
(JS)   – JOANNA SIMON
(JW) – JOSEPH WARD

St HENRI SHIRAZ

OVERVIEW: Auldana Cellars, adjacent to Magill Estate, was established in 1853 by Thomas Auld, an early South Australian settler. In 1842, he purchased the land in two sections comprising a total of 460 acres at the usual price charged by the Crown of £1 an acre. He planted a small vineyard, but went into commercial wine growing only in 1853 after being impressed by the quality of the fruit on his return from England. In 1861 he floated the South Auldana Vineyard Association with a market capitalisation of £12,000. In 1862 the Association's first vintage produced 3,000 gallons of white and red wine.

The property was subsequently taken over by Josiah Symon, a prominent Adelaide identity who was a vocal advocate of Federation. The fledgling South Australian wine industry had much to benefit from the colony's becoming a part of the new Australian nation. Until 1901 trade tariffs between the colonies had created artificial trade barriers resulting in localised wine markets. After Federation, South Australia experienced a substantial increase in vineyard plantings. The Auldana Vineyard, now defunct because of urban pressure, was once one of the most important and well known vineyards in South Australia. There are plenty of early reviews of the wine by keen wine enthusiasts and critics. At Auldana, the winemaker was a Frenchman, Leon Edmond Mazure, who is credited with being the creator of the famous and unique style of Australian Sparkling Burgundy. Mazure was also responsible for the creation of the St. Henri label which is believed to be named after Mazure's son. Curiously, a few bottles from this era have survived. A bottle of 1896 Auldana Cellars St. Henri Claret, found in the cellar of a Tasmanian collector, surfaced in the late 1980s. A bottle of 1911 appeared at a Penfolds Red Wine Re-corking Clinic in Hobart in 1996.

The Auldana Vineyard was acquired by Penfolds in 1944. The St. Henri label, which replicates the original, was revived by John Davoren, a brilliant Penfolds winemaker, in the early 1950s. Davoren had a strong family background in wine; both his grandfather and father worked at Dalwood, a famous Hunter Valley vineyard. Originally owned by the Wyndham family, it was subsequently split in half, with one portion of 52 hectares sold to Penfolds in 1904. John Davoren's father Harold, a winemaker of considerable note, became manager. By the 1930s, John Davoren was making wine at Penfolds Dalwood, subsequently becoming

PENFOLDS St HENRI SHIRAZ

First Vintage:
1953-1956 experimental
1957 commercial

Variety: Shiraz and Cabernet Sauvignon

Origin: Multi-district blend from South Australia. Significant contributions of Shiraz from Barossa Valley, Eden Valley, Clare Valley, McLaren Vale, Langhorne Creek and Bordertown; Cabernet Sauvignon from Coonawarra and Barossa Valley.

Fermentation: 10 and 20 tonne stainless steel tanks with wax lined, wooden header boards.

Maturation: 18 months in large (1460 litre), 50+ year-old oak vats.

Comments: Labelled Claret until 1989 vintage, Cabernet Sauvignon plays a secondary role to the dominant Shiraz. There is some controversy over the first vintage. At one of the 2003 Penfolds Red Wine Re-corking Clinics a bottle of 1955 was discovered. There are indications of developmental work from 1953. Packaged in laser-etched bottles since the 1996 vintage.

PENFOLDS ST. HENRI
SHIRAZ

manager of the now defunct Penfolds Minchinbury Vineyards at Rooty Hill in Sydney. After serving in the RAAF in the South Pacific, John Davoren returned to Australia. A brief stint managing the newly purchased Kalimna Vineyard in the Barossa Valley was followed by his appointment in 1947 as manager of Penfolds Auldana Cellars adjacent to Magill Estate. With such a long family association with Penfolds and a deep sense of history, it is perhaps unsurprising that John Davoren's vision was to draw inspiration from the past. While Max Schubert was already experimenting with Grange during the early 1950s, John Davoren was keen to develop a traditional style of wine based on the original work of Leon Edmond Mazure. John Bird, a retired Penfolds winemaker, observes, "There is a definite feel about St. Henri and Grange. They began life together in friendly rivalry, offering contrasting styles for an emerging and inquisitive Australian table wine market."

> While Grange is now seen as the quintessential Australian wine, John Davoren's work with St. Henri is of equal importance. Indeed both these wines set new standards for their day.

While Grange is now seen as the quintessential Australian wine, John Davoren's work with St. Henri is of equal importance. Indeed both these wines set new standards for their day. St. Henri established an elegant, perfumed style based on fruit definition and maturation in old oak. Grange established a blockbuster barrel fermented style (in American oak) with a richness and fullness 'that few people initially cared for'. Indeed Penfolds St. Henri was the preferred style. Contemporary reports refer to St. Henri as "one of the only true Claret (sic) styles in Australia". Don Ditter, a former Penfolds Chief Winemaker, recalls, "There was a strong following for St. Henri from the very outset. Initially both Grange and St. Henri were priced at the same level. The demand for each of the wines was quite similar, some preferring the large old-wooded maturation style of St. Henri over the more strongly flavoured, barrel fermented and new oak matured style of Grange". John Bird observes, "Curiously there is some kind of similarity between St. Henri and Grange between 10 and 15 years of age. There is no doubt about which stable they come from".

Originally St. Henri, first experimental vintage 1953, was made from Auldana, Magill Estate, Morphett Vale, Paracombe and Adelaide Hills fruit – mostly Shiraz but with a proportion of Cabernet Sauvignon. Sometimes a touch of Kalimna or Modbury Vineyard Cabernet Sauvignon was used in the blend. The original

wines were called 'Penfolds St. Henri Claret', but since 1991, with the release of the 1989 vintage, St. Henri has been labelled varietally. Like Grange, the wines have always been Shiraz driven, with small varying percentages of Cabernet Sauvignon. The 1994 and 1995 labels in fact acknowledge the increased Cabernet Sauvignon component of these vintages. While the Auldana Vineyard ceased providing fruit in 1975 and the Modbury Vineyard followed suit in 1983, new vineyards have come into production. Nowadays St. Henri is a multi-district blend drawing Shiraz from the Barossa Valley, Eden Valley, McLaren Vale, Clare Valley, the foothills of the Adelaide Hills, and Langhorne Creek. Cabernet Sauvignon, which provides firmness and structure to the St. Henri style, is sourced from the Barossa Valley, Coonawarra and Bordertown.

Original vintages of St. Henri were foot crushed and a relatively high percentage of stalks was retained in the vinification. James Halliday once noted that "stalk retention (a common practice in Burgundy) partially explained the distinctive character of St. Henri" in some earlier vintages. The style and source of fruit, however, has evolved over the years. "It is interesting to look through the eras of St. Henri. You can see an evolutionary progression where things unfold and fade; a reflection of the vintage and the times. Each wine has its own story to tell," says John Bird.

Winemakers have worked on improving the St. Henri style over the past decade, but without compromising John Davoren's original intent. Peter Gago says, "More recent vintages of St. Henri reflect a substantial leap in viticultural management. We are able to identify and batch potential parcels of fruit which have the desired aromatics, concentration and structure in the vineyard. Winemaking has also been tweaked, the wine shows enhanced fruit definition and riper tannins". After batch vinification in stainless steel tanks, the wine components are classified. Increasingly, Penfolds is using a larger proportion of Barossa and McLaren Vale fruit to achieve more fruit sweetness on the mid-palate. The young wines which make 'the cut' are then matured for 15 to 18 months in large (1460 litre), old oak casks. During this maturation period the fruit becomes more complex and the tannins soften, such that the St. Henri style produces a unique Shiraz textural impression unlike any other Penfolds Shiraz.

Some call it old fashioned. Certainly it is a wine based on fruit definition and flavour, but the absence of new oak – so prevalent in contemporary Australian Shiraz – sets it apart.

PENFOLDS ST HENRI
SHIRAZ

Penfolds St. Henri is often referred to as a 'maturation' style. Some call it old fashioned. Certainly it is a wine based on fruit definition and flavour, but the absence of new oak – so prevalent in contemporary Australian Shiraz – sets it apart. Winemakers seek a ripe, perfumed expression of Shiraz, pure concentration and fine chocolaty tannin structures, certainly textually different. Cabernet Sauvignon provides aromatic top notes of violets/cassis and firm grainy tannins. The maturation effect brings these components together into a harmonious whole.

Huon Hooke describes *The Rewards of Patience* tasting of St. Henri (the most comprehensive ever held) as a "rare privilege". Joanna Simon says, "It is an amazing bracket – the top vintages are substantial wines packed with fruit sweetness and balanced with ripe tannins. I have never before tasted 41 consecutive vintages of a single wine in one sitting".

The older vintages of the 1950s and early 1960s are now extremely rare. Occasionally they can be found at auction and often at relatively inexpensive prices. The best vintages, usually the most powerful and concentrated, will evolve for up to 30 years and sometimes even further. But generally these wines are best consumed after 10 years of age. St. Henri has had a very strong and devoted following among collectors and wine enthusiasts. Today it is considered an Australian classic with a wonderful heritage of its own thanks to the vision of its creator, John Davoren.

1956 `Now`

Brick red. Sweet leather/mocha/sandalwood aromas with some burnt sugar notes. The palate is soft with some rich fruit/cedar flavours and supple/silky tannins. Drinking well but some bottles may be past.

1958 `Now – Past`

Brick red. A lifted earthy old red with some liquorice/chocolate/caramel notes. The wine is fading with some earthy/walnutty flavours and chalky tannins.

1959 `Now – Past`

Brick red. Sweet earthy/dusty/leafy/vegetal aromas. A cedary dry palate with some vegetal notes and fine brittle tannins.

1961 `Now`

Medium deep brick red. Intense liquorice/prune/dark fruit/mocha aromas and flavours. A substantial palate with some prune/coffee flavours and thick fine slightly grippy tannins.

1962 `Now`

Deep brick red. Dusty earthy old nose with some walnut/meaty/leather aromas. A very tannic big-boned wine with plenty of redcurrant/earthy flavours and concentration.

1963 `Now`

Deep brick red. Sweet ripe mocha/blackberry fruit with some leather/earthy nuances. The palate is rich, sweet and concentrated with ripe berry fruits and mocha/chocolaty flavours. The tannins are sappy and build up firm at the finish.

1964 `Now`

Deep brick red. A very solid muscular wine with some savoury black berry fruits and some leafy notes. The palate is sinewy and dry. A fading wine.

1965 `Now`

Deep brick red. Chocolate/mocha/spice aromas with some meaty complexity. A substantial palate with rich ripe concentrated fruit and soft grainy tannins.

1966 `Now`

Deep brick red. Earthy/chocolate/meaty aromas. The palate is solid and powerful with plenty of fruit richness and strong grippy tannins.

1967 `Now`

Medium brick red. A leathery/dusty/spicy old nose with some leafy characters. Plenty of fruit sweetness on the palate, with fine grippy tannins and good flavour length.

1968 `Past`

Medium brick red. A fading wine with vegetal/earthy aromas and fine brittle tannins. Underpowered and over the hill. A remnant of former days.

1969 `Now – Past`

Medium brick red. Spicy/leafy/mocha/orange marmalade aromas. The palate is slightly over-developed with sweet spicy/leafy/mocha/marmalade fruit and grippy tannins.

1970 `Now`

Medium brick red. Earthy/cedar/dark chocolate aromas. A refined smooth completely mature wine with plenty of fruit sweetness, cedar complexity and silky tannins.

1971 `Now`   `2010`

Medium brick red. Intense fresh mocha/dark chocolate/paneforte aromas. Lovely rich dark berry/chocolate/liquorice flavours balanced by firm tannins. A multi-layered wine with great complexity.

1972 `Now`

Deep brick red. A well-concentrated wine with sappy chocolate/cedar/cigar box aromas and flavours. The palate is fleshy and sweet with fine leafy tannins and good flavour length.

1973 `Now`

Medium deep brick red. Leather/earth/spice/dried fig aromas with some meaty nuances. A developed medium bodied wine with cedar/earth/spice flavours and fine but grippy tannins. Finishes firm and tight.

Outstanding vintages ★

PENFOLDS S^{T.} HENRI

SHIRAZ

1974 `Now`

Deep brick red. Developed hazelnut/chocolate/burnt coffee aromas. The palate is rich and chalky with some chocolate/leather flavours and grippy tannins. Still holding up. A pleasant surprise for such a difficult vintage.

1975 `Now`

Medium brick red. Complex mushroom/earthy/leather aromas with some mocha characters. An elegantly structured wine with mushroom/gamy/mocha flavours and lingering dry tannins.

1976 `Now` ▬▬▬▬ `2012` ★

Deep brick crimson red. A very powerful beautifully balanced wine with liquorice/gamy/dark fruit aromas. The palate is fresh and complex with rich chocolate/dark berry flavours, plenty of sweet fruit and fine lacy tannins. A dense and opulent wine with superb fruit definition. Quintessential St. Henri.

1977 `Now`

Deep brick red. Intense walnut/dusty/earthy aromas with some prune characters. A very dense, rich wine with prune/earthy flavours and pronounced tannins. Finishes grippy and dry.

1978 `Now`

Medium deep brick red. Aromatic wine with redcurrant/mocha fruit and some dusty/earthy notes. The palate is elegantly structured and medium concentrated with redcurrant/earthy flavours and fine leafy tannins.

1979 `Now – Past`

Medium brick red. Herb garden/spicy/sandalwood/balsamic aromas with some meaty nuances. A lighter bodied wine with some vegetal/meaty/minty flavours and fine chalky tannins. Finishes lean and short.

1980 `Now`

Deep brick red. Intense developed prune/mushroom/herbal/eucalypt aromas. A well-concentrated wine with prune/mushroom/bitumen flavours and strong tannin structures. Finishes dry and tight. A substantial wine.

1981 `Now`

Medium crimson. A compact solid wine with sweet earthy/black fruit aromas and flavours. There is plenty of sweet fruit on the palate, but the tannins are very muscular and drying.

1982 `Now`

Medium crimson. A lighter bodied wine with raspberry/cherry aromas and vegetal notes. The palate is soft, balanced and elegant. Drink soon. Expected better from the vintage.

1983 `Now`

Medium crimson. Dark chocolate/prune/plum aromas with some liquorice/mocha nuances. A refined, balanced wine with prune/chocolate flavours and supple tannins. A savoury, dry finish.

1984 `Now`

Medium crimson. Intense leafy/chocolate/mocha/prune aromas. The wine is rich and dense with plenty of sweet fruit and leafy firm tannins.

1985 `Now` ▬▬▬▬ `2008`

Medium crimson. A soft mellow wine with sweet coffee/mocha/plum fruit and fine grainy tannins. The palate finishes savoury and long. A lovely wine.

1986 `Now` ▬▬▬▬ `2015` ★

Deep crimson. Intense blackberry/liquorice/dark chocolate aromas. The palate is textbook St. Henri with succulent blackberry/dark chocolate flavours and ripe grainy tannins. A superbly concentrated and balanced wine.

1987 `Now`

Medium deep crimson. An elegant style with leafy/cedar/dark liquorice aromas. The palate is lean and firm with some leafy/bitter chocolate flavours and muscular tannins.

Outstanding vintages ★

ST HENRI
SHIRAZ

1988 `Now`
Deep crimson. Intense blackberry/cassis/gamy aromas. A generously flavoured wine with plenty of blackberry fruit and ripe chocolaty tannins. Drink soon to enjoy fruit flavours.

1989 `Now`
Deep crimson. Vegetal/herb garden/dark chocolate aromas. The palate is sweet and rich with jammy/chocolate/vegetal flavours and chalky tannins. A difficult vintage.

1990 `Now` `2020` ★
Deep crimson. A very powerful wine with abundant sweet plum/blackberry fruit. A superbly concentrated palate with perfectly ripe plum/blackberry flavours and fine grained tannins. Finishes long and sweet. A classic vintage.

1991 `Now` `2015` ★
Deep crimson. Fragrant spicy/blackberry/mocha aromas. The palate is very concentrated but quite muscular with plenty of fruit sweetness, some cedar/mocha complexity and velvety tannins. A compact beautifully balanced wine.

1992 `Now` `2010`
Deep crimson. Sweet plum/cherry aromas with leather/gamy nuances. A strongly flavoured, robustly structured wine with sweet plum/dark chocolate/leather flavours, but stern, slightly aggressive tannins.

1993 `Now` `2008`
Deep crimson. Perfumed crushed leaf/herb/raspberry aromas. An earlier drinking style with herb/raspberry flavours and firm tannins. Builds up chalky and dry at the finish. Drink soon.

1994 `Now` `2014`
Deep crimson. Lovely concentrated and balanced wine with dark cherry/blackberry/violet/aniseed aromas. Plenty of juicy blackberry/chocolate/aniseed flavours balanced by firm balanced tannins.

1995 `Now` `2010`
Medium deep crimson. Herbal/blackberry/red currant aromas with some stewy notes. Medium concentrated wine with red currant/stewy flavours and firm sinewy tannins. Finishes short.

1996 `2006` `2025` ★
Deep crimson. Opulent wine with rich sweet plum/black berry/spicy/liquorice aromas. A richly concentrated, powerful palate with plenty of prune/black plum/blackberry fruit, ripe grainy tannins and superb flavour length.

1997 `Now` `2015`
Deep crimson-purple. Intense sweet plum/red berry/spice aromas with some herbal tones. The wine is quite firm and tight with exuberant red currant/raspberry flavours and fine gritty tannins.

1998 `2006` `2028` ★
Deep crimson-purple. The wine is beautifully opulent with ripe blackberry/plum/violet aromas. A solid, dense, but richly concentrated palate with plenty of blackberry/plum/dark chocolate flavours and ripe slinky tannins. A great St. Henri vintage.

1999 `2008` `2018`
Deep crimson-purple. An elegantly structured but very balanced wine with pure blackberry/dark cherry liquorice aromas and flavours and fine chocolaty tannins.

2000 `Now` `2010`
Medium crimson-purple. Leafy/redcurrant/spicy aromas. The palate is medium-bodied with redcurrant/leafy flavours and fine loose-knit tannins. An early drinking style.

2001 `2008` `2025` ★
Deep crimson-purple. Intensely perfumed plum/raspberry/blackberry aromas. A superbly concentrated but elemental wine with deep-set, pure raspberry/blackberry fruit and pronounced but rounded tannins. A long future ahead.

Outstanding vintages ★

169

PENFOLDS Sͭ HENRI
SHIRAZ

COMMENTARY: "This is a wonderful review of St. Henri, a rare privilege. The first bracket from 1956 to 1967 is really a class of curios. The 1956 has a sublime old wine nose with meaty/burnt sugar aromas. The palate is still soft and silky, but it's beginning to fade now." (HH) "It smells like Chinese joss sticks with hints of leather, old coffee beans and sandalwood." (CPT) "The wine still has freshness. It has a sweet gamy/cedary nose with complex, mature autumn flavours. The acidity is beginning to poke through. Drink soon." (JS) "The 1958 is showing touches of liquorice and sweet earth. The palate is firm and a touch acidic." (HH) "These wines are reminiscent of old ladies' handbags!" (JS) "The 1958 and 1959 have both lost their fruit." (JW) "The 1959 is past drinking now. It's very dry and tannic." (HH)

"The 1961 is surprisingly rich, with plenty of dark fruit aromas. The structure is still holding with some mocha/coffee and residual berry flavours." (JH) "I find the wine less attractive. The palate is thick and chewy with lots of tannins but precious little fruit." (HH) "The 1962 is quite a substantial wine with grassy sweetness and even some red fruits on the palate. It has a long and drying finish." (JS) "It's quite a powerful wine with earth/spice/polished leather characters and residual tannins." (JH)

"The wine is big-boned with very grippy tannins and plenty of guts. It's past its prime. The 1963 smells like an old leather Chesterfield sofa, with some dusty/meaty nuances and a rich, deep, fleshy palate." (HH) "It's significantly sweeter and richer than preceding vintages, with distinct chocolate/mocha flavours and good balance." (JH) "It's a touch rustic on the nose, but in the mouth the fruit, acidity and tannins are in complete harmony. The 1964 is very dry and sinewy." (CPT) "The wine is quite maderised

and drying but there's still a trace of sweet concentrated fruit." (JS) "But it fades into the acid and tannin. Drink up! The 1965 smells of dried fruits, herbs and spices. The fruit is now overwhelmed by the tannins." (JW)

"The 1966 is a lovely old wine with plenty of dried figs, dates and vegemite characters." (CPT) "This vintage has a great reputation, but the wine falls slightly short of expectations. It has ripe developed fruit and a strong structure." (JH) "I think the aroma is strange, perhaps slightly maderised. It smells of stewed apples and dusty old attics! The palate is more impressive with sweet powerful fruit and drying tannins at the finish." (JS) "The 1967 is leafy and herbal with sharp acidity." (JH) "The fruit has really faded." (CPT)

"The 1968 is also a remnant of former days." (JH) "It's still a good drink though, with gamy/animal/chocolaty aromas and a fleshy but tannic palate. The 1969 is short with very herbal/leafy characters and domineering tannins." (HH) "The 1970 has some good fruit sweetness and a gentle warm soft palate." (JW) "It still has some attractive cedar sweetness on the palate with a mature mellow structure. It needs drinking soon." (JS) "The 1971 has a much deeper colour than the previous wines. It has quite powerful black fruit/aromas. The palate has plenty of rich dark chocolate/blackberry/leather flavours with tannins in the background." (JH) "It has layers of complex and mature flavours. The tannins are firm rather than aggressive. A lovely wine." (JS)

"The 1972 is a gem with plenty of cedar/tobacco/cigar box complexity. The palate is soft and smooth with fleshy/succulent fruit." (HH) "I sloshed this one around a bit and while it's clearly past it, the wine's still OK." (JW) "I think

ST HENRI
SHIRAZ

it has an attractive sweet 'bourbon' nose with lots of delicious sweet fruit on the palate." (CPT) "The 1973 is quite aromatic with some leather/earth/spicy notes and a touch of volatile acidity."(JH) "The palate is quite substantial with cedar/spice/dried fruit flavours and a touch of game. I can see the volatile acidity – but there's no harm done. The tannins become dry and chalky at the finish but overall it's a powerful wine." (JS)

"The 1974 is very tannic and starting to dry out." (HH) "There are some nice dried fig/smoky/toffee aromas. The palate starts out fresh, but the tannins take over the wine on the back palate." (JW) "The 1975 is a solid wine with leathery/earthy/chocolaty fruit and lingering tannins." (JH) "It's rich, smooth and ripe, but those tannins become quite grippy. The 1976 is a sumptuous, multi-layered and profound wine with tremendous fruit concentration and flavour." (HH) "It has a very strong, deep, dark, brick red colour with powerful liquorice/gamy/black fruit aromas and flavours." (JH) "The palate is big and powerful and is packed with sweet cedary fruit, dried plums and blackcurrants and ripe tannins. This is a very substantial St. Henri. The 1977 is very dusty and pruny with plenty of sweet fruit on the palate. It has almost a creamy texture." (JS) "This is a very potent and powerful wine with pervasive tannins." (JH)

"The 1978 is a very enjoyable wine with minty/capsicum/flinty aromas and a fresh light fruity palate." (CPT) "It seems to have plenty of cool Cabernet characters. I find similar aromas, but the palate is lean and short. Not a great year." (HH) "The 1979 is a very meaty wine with some redcurrant fruit. It has a pronounced tannin attack and pushes the fruit aside." (JW) "It has some earthy/spicy notes and a slight VA (volatile acidity) lift. The palate is drying out. The 1980 is dusty and herbal on the nose, but the palate is

richer than expected with some aged mulberry fruit characters and hard tannins." (HH)

"The 1981 is also fairly dusty on the nose and pretty tannic. There's sweet fruit, but not enough to take on the tannins." (JS) "It's a compact and solid wine with earthy/black fruit aromas. The palate begins with some fruit sweetness, then moves into a wild ride of tannins and then acidity." (JH) "The 1982 is a soft, balanced, elegant and finely textured wine." (HH) "It smells like candied fruit, but it is a good medium weighted wine." (JW) "I think it's green and acidic!" (JH)

"The 1983 has sweet prune and blackcurrant on the nose. The palate is ripe and supple with mellow blackcurrant flavours and lots of ripe tannins. At the same time it seems to be developing mature cedary characters." (JS) "The 1984 has nice slurpy fruit on the palate but I found the nose quite closed." (CPT) "It has pruny/porty aromas with a very rich, almost super ripe sweet fruit palate. It's a big fleshy wine with plenty of fruit opulence." (HH)

"The 1985 smells of fresh baked red fruits and spices. It has a very ripe fruit attack with some spicey/peppery notes and fairly tough tannins." (JW) "The wine has held its ground very well. It has some sweeter plum and mint aromas which track through to the palate." (JH)

"The 1986 is a substantial wine with luscious blackcurrant fruit and lots of ripe tannins." (JS) "It's a very fresh wine with wonderful cassis aromas. The palate is loaded with fruit and grainy tannins." (CPT) "At last I can see elegant sweet fruit, fine tannins and life. This is a very substantial wine with a core of dark berry/blackberry fruit." (JH)

"The 1987 is a sweetly aged mellow wine with some leafy/cigar box characters. The palate is

lean and firm and somewhat tight in structure (HH). It's a bit lacking in sweetness and breadth of flavour." (JS)

"The 1988 is a well-balanced wine with plenty of ripe dried red fruits and some spice. The palate is ripe, but not overtly rich." (JW) "This wine has excellent harmony with mint/cassis aromas and plenty of youthful, primary fruit for a 15 year old." (CPT)

"The 1989 is a sweet, generous wine but a touch jammy." (HH) "I find the fruit quite stewy/herbal. The wine is not for me." (JW) "I violently object to the wine. It has very strong DMS characters, more apparent than at the last *Rewards of Patience* tasting." (JH)

"I found the wines were pretty consistent throughout the 1980s, considering vintage conditions. The 1983 and 1986 were the best wines of that decade." (JB)

"The 1990 has an abundance of sweet plum and blackberry fruit. It has a very powerful compact structure with fruit and tannins in very good balance." (JH) "The colour is fantastic for its age. I can still see purple. The wine is remarkably fresh and firm, with plenty of plummy fruit and fine grained tannins – all in perfect harmony. The 1991 is an excellent follow up with clean, plummy/herb fruit and a seductively fruit sweet palate." (HH) "I saw some damson fruitiness in the wine. It's not as showy as the 1990, but it has an excellent tight structure and concentration." (JS)

"The 1992 is a touch unfocused. The tannins completely dominate the palate. It's so disjointed now, I wonder whether it will ever come into balance?" (JW) "I am not sure either. It has some gamy/leathery aspects but it finishes quite bitter." (JH) "I find this wine something

of a surprise. It has very good colour, sweet plum/dark cherry aromas and stern tannins." (HH)

"The 1993 is slightly minty with some weedy notes. It lacks freshness on the mid-palate." (JS) "I find the wine a fraction stewy, but the tannins are in control." (HH) "The 1994 is developing extremely well. It has plenty of crushed red berry/plum/black berry fruits and chocolaty tannins." (JW) "The wine is quite gamy on the nose and has substantial tannins and acidity on the palate." (CPT) "The wine does have a certain raciness, but it has firm blackberry/anise/chocolate flavours and balanced tannins. It's a powerful wine with plenty of length. The 1995 is slightly stewy. The fruit shortens dramatically on the palate into tannin and acid." (JH) "It has an oddly sweet nose with a bitter sweet palate. Although there's fruit concentration, those tannins are a bit out of balance. The 1996 has an immensely sweet nose with black cherry/blackberry/black olive fruit and liquorice aromas. The palate is densely packed with fruit, making those grainy tannins barely noticeable." (JS)

"It's an intense, focused, powerful wine with rich, sweet, plummy fruit and liberal tannins. It's still too young to drink." (HH) "I am not entirely convinced that this is a great St. Henri vintage, but all the same it has rich opulent prune/black plum/blackberry fruit. The palate is chock full of flavours." (JH) "I think it's a very fine wine with a wonderful persistent finish. Those big ripe tannins are babysitting exuberant primary blackberry/cassis fruit! The wine has a great future. The 1997 is also very nice with plenty of fruit sweetness and chocolaty tannins." (JW). "It has sweet plum/vanilla, slightly jammy aromas. There's a herbal/mint undertone especially on the palate. The tannins are quite astringent and become very tight and unyielding at the finish." (HH)

"The 1998 has incredible concentration with very ripe cassis/dark berry fruit and big ripe tannins." (CPT) "It has penetrating ripe black fruits with a dark chocolaty richness and very ripe tannins on the palate. This is a great wine." (JS) "It's an ultra-ripe, exotic, hedonistic wine with a big, solid, dense palate crammed with fruit. This will be a great wine in time." (HH)

"The 1999 is quite concentrated, with a classic blackberry fruit profile. The palate has plenty of blackberry fruit and chocolaty tannins. Another impressive 1999." (JH) "It has lovely cassis/ curranty fruit and great palate structure. There's plenty of fruit sweetness at the finish." (JW)

"The 2000 has plenty of blackberry/vanilla fruit on the palate with fine grainy tannins. It's not nearly as powerful or concentrated as the 1998 and 1999, but it will cellar and improve." (JS) "It's eccentric in this line-up. It has a vegetal spiciness, typical of the year." (HH) "While there's plenty of flavour, a mix of leafy/spicy, slightly porty fruit, I suspect that the overall structure is quite fragile. Probably best to drink early." (JH)

"The 2001 is a beauty. It is completely hedonistic with sweet overripe plum/prune aromas and hints of jam, violets and eau-de-vie. The palate is opulent and spicy with lovely fruit sweetness. Those gripping tannins are well under control considering the sheer opulence of fruit." (HH) "It's a well-balanced wine with ripe blackcurrant/blueberry fruit and some floral notes." (CPT) "This is a terrific ending to an amazing range of wines. The 2001 has lovely ripe raspberry/blackberry cordial aromas. The palate is really exuberant and almost Grenache-like with musky/raspberry flavours and ripe tannins." (JS)

"I think the last three vintages are absolutely spot on, showing an excellent balance between fruit and tannins. From my perspective, the 1997 and 1998 are atypical wines with tremendous fruit power, but not the elegance associated with the St. Henri style. Interestingly, I notice that St. Henri performs really well in lesser vintages. This is largely because of the overall structure and elegance of the wine." (JB) "In more recent vintages St. Henri also reflects the focused approach to vineyard selection." (SL)

(CPT) – CH'NG POH TIONG
(JH) – JAMES HALLIDAY
(HH) – HUON HOOKE
(JS) – JOANNA SIMON
(JW) – JOSEPH WARD

OVERVIEW: The historic and heritage-protected Penfolds Magill Estate is one of the few single vineyards in the world located within city boundaries (8 kms from the Adelaide Town Hall). It was here that Dr Christopher Rawson Penfold and his wife Mary settled in 1844, just eight years after the founding of Adelaide. Today the vineyard comprises only 5.2 hectares (12 acres), but it remains a highly evocative piece of South Australian winemaking history. The original cottage, built in 1845, still stands among the vines. Penfolds' turn-of-the-century bluestone cellar complex is an important landmark. The cellar door, located in what was once Penfolds 'Still House' (distillery), and the critically acclaimed contemporary Magill Estate Restaurant (2003 South Australian Restaurant of the Year), are both important drawcards for all wine lovers. Max Schubert, Penfolds Chief Winemaker from 1948 to 1973, worked at Magill Estate and lived nearby. This is where the experimental and early Granges were first made. In 2001, the South Australian Heritage Council recognised Grange as a heritage icon of South Australia. Penfolds decided to return the winemaking and maturation of Grange to the Magill Estate winery and cellars from the 2002 vintage onwards.

Penfolds Magill Estate Shiraz was developed after the vineyard was saved from being engulfed by urban development. Magill fruit had always been used for premium Penfolds table wines including Grange, but a single estate wine was a compelling justification for the continued use of this vineyard (by then, just 5.2 hectares of the 120 hectares which once covered an entire hillside). Max Schubert, who remained a director of Penfolds and kept an office at Magill, and Don Ditter, Penfolds current Chief Winemaker, wanted to make a wine which showed the character of the vineyard but was more elegant in style than most Penfolds reds. Don Ditter comments, "Magill Estate needed to be something completely different from Grange, almost the complete opposite in style. While Grange has plenty of opulence and power, Magill Estate would show elegance, finesse and restraint".

The Magill Estate style has evolved over the years. The early vintages were quite lean and tight. From the early 1990s the wine shows greater fruit definition and palate vitality. The leaps and bounds in viticulture have also helped. Winemakers are particularly interested in flavour development and tannin ripeness, resulting in wines with supple structures and more fruit richness.

PENFOLDS MAGILL ESTATE SHIRAZ

First Vintage: 1983

Variety: Shiraz

Origin: Single vineyard wine using selected parcels of fruit from the 5.2 hectare (12 acre) Magill Estate, Adelaide, South Australia.

Fermentation: Wax-lined, open cement fermenters with wooden header boards. Components complete fermentation in barrel, following a traditional basket pressing.

Maturation: 12-14 months in two thirds new French and one third American oak.

Comments: Approximately 1500-3000 cases. Packaged in laser-etched bottles since the 1997 vintage.

PENFOLDS MAGILL ESTATE
SHIRAZ

Penfolds Magill Estate is vinified in open, wax-lined concrete tanks at low temperatures. Towards the very end of fermentation the wine is drained and gently basket pressed. Once fermentation is complete, the wine is now matured in a combination of two thirds new French and one third new American oak for a period of 12 to 14 months. It is a medium-to-long term cellaring wine which builds up further complexity over time. In exceptional vintages like 1996, 1998 and 2002, the optimum cellaring potential is around 15 years. In a lesser vintage the wines develop more quickly and should be consumed earlier.

> One part of the vineyard will bring perfume and structure, another concentration and ripeness, and a third complexity and finesse. When it comes to assembling the wine, we can blend the best of these characteristics...

James Halliday says, "The Magill Estate style turned a corner in 1990 with riper fruit and better tannin structures. The early-picked low alcohol strategy of the 1980s did not pay long term dividends. Since the 1998 vintage the style seems to have moved in another direction completely, with more intense, powerful fruit and persistent tannins". Joseph Ward describes the 1996 and 1998 vintages as "truly outstanding" and Huon Hooke says the 2002 has "beautiful modulated ripeness".

Retired Penfolds winemaker, John Bird, who still plays a role in the classification and blending of the wine, comments, "For a single estate wine we have to employ a very focused approach to winemaking. It is not dissimilar to the way a Bordeaux Grand Cru Classe is produced. We batch vinify to optimise our blending options. One part of the vineyard will bring perfume and structure, another concentration and ripeness, and a third complexity and finesse. When it comes to assembling the wine, we can blend the best of these characteristics to make a wine in the Magill Estate style, within the constraints of the vintage".

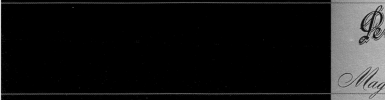

1983 `Now - Past`
Brick red. Cedar/cigar box aromas and some old leather nuances. The palate is smooth and mature with some sweet mocha fruit. Finishes a touch short. Beginning to dry out.

1984 `Past`
Medium brick red. Leather/gamy aromas, but a very lean austere palate.

1985 `Now - Past`
Brick red. A fading, overdeveloped wine with leather/chocolate/mushroom aromas and flavours. The fruit has dried out and the tannins are firm and chalky.

1986 `Now`
Brick red. Gamy/chocolate/cedar aromas. The palate is medium concentrated with gamy/cedar flavours and fine grainy tannins. Still holding up.

1987 `Now`
Medium red. Leafy/dusty/leather aromas with some minty notes. The palate is quite austere and builds up tannic and firm at the finish. Drink up.

1988 `Now`
Medium red. Meaty/leather/earthy/driftwood aromas. A well concentrated palate with some dark fruit/meaty/leather flavours and firm tannin structure.

1989 `Now`
Medium red. Cherry/blackberry/tobacco aromas with some stewed characters. A leanly structured wine with some ripe cherry stone/tobacco fruit and fine tannins. Finishes chalky dry.

1990 `Now`
Medium red. Plum black cherry aromas. The palate is sinewy and dry with some spicy characters. A very muscular wine.

1991 `Now` `2010` ★
Medium deep red. A stark contrast to 1990. Meaty/chocolate/blackberry/plum aromas with some liquorice/leather notes. A rich mellow wine with plum/leather/cigar box flavours and fine savoury tannins.

1992 `Now` `2006`
Medium red. Paneforte/mulberry/gamy aromas. The palate is rich and ripe with paneforte/red fruit flavours, fine grained tannins and good length. Drink soon.

1993 `Now` `2008`
Medium red. Dried herb/raspberry aromas with some cedar/vanilla notes. Well concentrated, slightly soupy palate with some plum/berry flavours but firm grippy tannins. Unlikely to improve.

1994 `Now` `2014` ★
Medium deep red. A classic Magill Estate with cedar/dark plum/chocolate aromas and flavours. The palate is smooth and concentrated with plenty of fruit sweetness and fine soft tannins.

1995 `Now` `2012`
Medium deep red. A surprising wine. Intense dark cherry/plum/blackberry aromas. A fresh, well-balanced palate with plenty of ripe cherry/plum/mocha fruit, fine tannins and excellent flavour length. Finishes a touch bitter.

1996 `Now` `2015` ★
Medium deep red. Smooth supple stylish wine with blackberry/plum/meaty aromas. A beautifully proportioned palate with concentrated plum/chocolate fruit, ripe slinky tannins and superb flavour length. A great vintage.

1997 `Now` `2008`
Medium deep colour. Restrained wine with blackberry/raspberry aromas and some dusty/earthy complexity. The palate is rich and deep with red berry/chocolaty fruit and plenty of savoury/leafy tannins. A medium term wine.

Outstanding vintages ★

177

PENFOLDS MAGILL ESTATE
SHIRAZ

1998 `2005` `2025` ★
Deep red-purple. Intense blackberry/smoky/meaty aromas. A powerful, concentrated palate with dense dark cherry/blackberry/dark chocolate flavours and ripe ample smooth tannins. A wine with layers of fruit and tannins. A long lived creature.

1999 `2005` `2015`
Deep red. Deeply concentrated wine with plenty of blackberry comfit/vanilla aromas and some spicy/earth nuances. The palate is very powerful and concentrated with plenty of juicy fruit and mocha oak. The tannins are firm and bristling but well-integrated into the wine at this stage.

2000 `Now` `2010`
Medium red. A very Rhône-like style with raspberry/pepper aromas and savoury/nutty oak. A lean medium-bodied wine with sweet ripe fruit and savoury tannins. An early drinking style.

2001 `2005` `2015`
Deep red-purple. Intense youthful perfumed wine with black cherry/plum/liquorice/violet aromas and some savoury/malty oak. The wine is rich and deep with plenty of plum/dark fruit flavours and chocolaty tannins. Finishes long and flavourful.

2002 `2005` `2018`
Deep red-purple. A fresh intense elemental wine with plum/dark cherry fruit, plenty of underlying malty oak and persistent chocolaty tannins. An elegant style with balance and charm.

Outstanding vintages ★

COMMENTARY: "The 1983 Magill Estate is a deep mature wine with leather/spice/marmite on the nose and palate. It's slightly mushroomy, but still has some fruit sweetness. The wine is beginning to dry." (JS) "I think it's past it now. It was a better wine a decade ago." (JW) "This is a nice old red with lovely old leathery/toasty/nutty aged Shiraz characters and a smooth, light-medium bodied palate. It needs to be drunk soon though." (HH)

"The 1984 is stewy and mawkish and really well past its best." (JH) "The 1985 has some liquorice, sweet cloves and some leather notes. There's a singed fruit character that makes the wine appear tired." (CPT) "The wine is pleasant with some leather/chocolate/berry fruit aromas. It has much better structure and presence than the above wines, but should be drunk soon. The 1986 vintage is starting to dry out and has left the tannins exposed." (JH) "It's probably best to drink this wine within the next four years. It has a meaty, barbecued nose, but is lean and lacks concentration. The finish is very tannic." (HH) "It has a very hard middle and finish, but it has some good fruit. The 1987, however, quickly withers in the face of those harsh tannins." (JW) "It has a very bitter finish and smells old rather than mature on the nose. There is something slightly dirty on the palate." (JS) "The wine is dry, woody and austere." (CPT)

"The 1988 is a very savoury wine with some earthy edges. The palate shows solid dark fruit characters, but the tannins are a real concern." (JH) "This is a very good wine. It has a leather/meaty/animal-hide bouquet and a fresh vibrant palate. The 1989 is lean and drying out. It lacks richness and fruit." (HH) "I am more positive about this wine. It doesn't have much richness on the nose and shows some herbaceous characters, but it holds up well on the palate with ripe blackberry/smoky flavours. It is drying but there's still sweetness of fruit." (JS)

"The 1990 is disappointing considering the vintage." (HH) "You can see a definite style change here. The fruit is a touch riper with plum black cherry characters, but those tannins are starting to creep up." (JH) "I found the wine quite enjoyable with tobacco, wood, figs, liquorice and spices." (CPT)

"The 1991 is a very 'Penfoldian' tasting wine. It has a rich nose and is fuller on the palate. It has plenty of cigar box/leather characters and is soft, mellow and savoury. It's a pleasant oldie – but needs to be drunk soon." (HH) "The wine has good depth and length with greater ripeness and richness than the preceding wines." (JS) "It's a wine with fully ripe flavours and tannins. I like the consistent fruit characters, in all the Penfolds 1992s. The 1992 Magill Estate has an understated softness and ripeness, without worrying tannins." (JH) "The nose is perfumed with some mulberry fruit and the palate is attractively spicy." (JS) "I saw some peppery notes in the wine, but it has good depth, weight and richness in the mouth." (HH)

"The 1993 is at or near its best with a sweet berry/cedar/vanilla bouquet and a ripe fleshy palate." (JH) "I can see the sweet fruit, but the wine is neither very concentrated nor substantial. It has a slightly mushroomy character which I don't particularly like. The wine is also likely to dry soon." (JS) "It's an unbalanced wine with slightly weedy/asparagus notes and firm grippy tannins dominate the palate." (HH)

"The 1994 is a very stylish wine with cedar/cigar box/spice/dark plum aromas. The palate has perfectly ripened fruit with elegant flavours and fine soft tannins." (JH) "It's a nice old red with a leather/dusty bouquet and a sniff of bacon fat. The palate is mellow and savoury but finishes lean and somewhat firm. A nice old red, but it lacks distinction." (HH) "The wine shows plenty of freshness with some light plummy fruit, but there's an absence of a greater fruit quality." (CPT) "I really liked this wine and gave it a good+ grade in my notes. This was the first wine which I felt was still developing. It has plenty of sweet fruit, substantial tannins and a very persistent finish." (JW) "This is a well integrated and rounded wine with a blackcurrant/prune even Vintage Port-like aroma on the nose and deep, sweet fruit characters and nutty oak on the palate. The 1995 is supple but not nearly as concentrated. It has a scented cassis/nutty oak nose with some milk chocolate/cassis flavours and ripe tannins on the palate." (JS)

"There's an amazing colour shift here. The wine performs entirely against the reputation of the vintage. It has abundant/luscious blackberry/plum aromas and is stacked with flavour structure. The 1996 is a beautifully poised and balanced wine. It has been superbly handled with lovely black cherry/plum balanced with sympathetic oak. I would be happy to drink it quietly in a corner!" (JH) "The wine has much more flesh and intensity than previous Magill Estates. It's got plenty of meaty/bacon characters and gripping tannins, but there's plenty of flavour and concentration. This is a lovely balanced wine." (HH) "Those 'Incredible Hulk' tannins really dominate the wine!" (CPT)

"The 1997 is a gentle balanced wine with a scented blackberry/apple-pie/nectarine nose and a soft, round, ripe, spicy/chocolaty palate." (JS) "There are plenty of fresh, ripe red fruits, but those tannins haven't intertwined. For the sake of the fruit, it should be drunk soon." (JW) "It's a good wine with liberal oak flavour and some Shiraz spice. It has structure and length, albeit in the leanish Magill style. The 1998, however, is an outstanding wine with plum/red berry/cherry/spice fruit and hints of earth and oak. It has great flavour and structure." (HH) "It's a massively powerful wine with very ripe intense blackberry fruit and barrel-ferment oak characters. It has layers of fruit and tannin on the palate; it is difficult to recognise as Magill Estate." (JH) "Those rich silky tannins weave and hold together the wine." (CPT) "It's a wine for the long haul with plenty of creaminess, dark chocolate and smoky bacon oak. It's concentrated and oaky on the palate with substantial but fine grained tannins." (JS)

"The 2000 is floral and fruity with a rich, ripe fleshy palate. It has plenty of sweet fruit and oak with excellent balance." (CPT) "I would be drinking the wine sooner rather than later. It could go each way, but the tannins could catch hold in the middle." (JW) "It's very Rhône-like in structure with red berry/aniseed aromas and some new nutty/banana oak. The palate is leaner and lighter than many of the others, but the flavours are intense and forceful. It has lovely sweet ripe lush fruit and a gentle savoury structure. It's an oddball wine and already good to drink." (HH) "It is a very idiosyncratic vintage." (JD)

"The 2001 is a clean smooth wine with plum/blackberry fruit and integrated oak. It has a nice range of sweet red/dark fruits and chocolate on the palate with nice tannin structure." (HH) "The wine is still very youthful, but integrating nicely with a perfumed cassis/spice nose and a round chocolaty palate with ripe tannins." (JS) "The fruit is in control here with plum/cherry aromas and some oak spiciness. The tannins are there but covered by sweet black fruits." (JW)

"The 2002 is an even fresher version of the last two with lean red berry/dried spice aromas and banana oak. It's a very elegant stylish wine with beautifully modulated ripeness." (HH) "It has a piercing blackcurrant nose. The palate shows sweeter blackberry/plum fruit and some liquorice notes. It's not a really ripe/rich wine, but there's plenty of concentration and lots of tannins." (JS) "Overall there have been some substantial improvements with the style, the more recent vintages showing more freshness, fleshiness and riper fruit quality." (HH)

"The 1996 and 1998 vintages are truly outstanding wines. I am not so sure about the 1997, and 2000, but this is probably a vintage character." (JW) "There is a 'wait and see' element about the 2000 vintage, but you can see the style evolving away from the lean structures of the past. My top wines of the last decade were 1994, 1995, 1996 and 1998. The 1998 has so much stuffing I feel it is something of an aberration. The 2002 is an intense wine with black fruits and persistent tannins." (JH)

(CPT) – CH'NG POH TIONG
(JH)   – JAMES HALLIDAY
(HH)   – HUON HOOKE
(JS)   – JOANNA SIMON
(JW)   – JOSEPH WARD

RWT

OVERVIEW: Penfolds RWT Barossa Valley Shiraz was released largely in response to Penfolds' increased access to outstanding Barossa Valley Shiraz fruit and emerging recognition of regional provenance among collectors and wine enthusiasts.

In many respects the wheel has turned full circle. During the early 1960s Penfolds released its highly regarded Bin 28 Kalimna Shiraz, a 100% Barossa Shiraz. While this was originally a single vineyard wine, the winemaking emphasis was on the house style absolutely central to the Penfolds winemaking philosophy. Increasing demand and finite resources in the Barossa resulted in this wine becoming a multi-regional blend.

Since the Nuriootpa winery was established in 1911, the Barossa has featured in many Penfolds wines. Barossa Shiraz is a fundamental component of Bin 28, Bin 389, St. Henri and, of course, Bin 95 Grange. The idea of making a 100% Barossa Shiraz once again, reflected growing interest and enthusiasm for regional definition and individual vineyard sites. Certainly the Barossa Valley is considered one of the classic wine regions of the world. Barossa Shiraz is quintessentially Australian with some of the world's oldest genetic Shiraz vine material. Settled by both English and Silesian immigrants during the mid 19th century, the region also has a unique heritage.

The development of Penfolds Red Winemaking Trial (RWT) reflects extraordinary progress in viticulture and winemaking. The two disciplines are increasingly intertwined, as growers and winemakers work together in search of optimum balance, ripeness and flavour. Identifying the best vineyard sites around the Barossa Valley, securing a regular supply of independently grown fruit, and establishing a clear idea of winemaking philosophy, are the key elements to Penfolds RWT.

RWT draws fruit from 20 to 100 year-old vineyards arcing across the west and north-west of the Barossa Valley, mostly independently grown. The dry, hot northern district, which centres around Kalimna, Moppa and Ebenezer, is largely open, sweeping country of alluvial plains, with red loam and red brown clay soils dissected by gullies and rivulets. Stands of eucalypt trees and scrub provide natural windbreaks.

PENFOLDS RWT BAROSSA VALLEY SHIRAZ

First Vintage: 1997

Variety: Shiraz

Origin: Barossa Valley, South Australia.

Fermentation: 10 tonne stainless steel tanks with wax lined, wooden header boards. Fermentation completed in barrel.

Maturation: 12-15 months in 50-70% new French oak hogsheads (300 litres).

Comments: Packaged in laser-etched bottles.

PENFOLDS RWT
BAROSSA VALLEY SHIRAZ

Most of the Shiraz is dry grown. The best vineyards produce fruit of voluptuous intensity, ripe tannins, and juicy flavours. The central west district around Stonewell, Marananga and Seppeltsfield is an undulating landscape, a rumpled patchwork of vineyards, many planted several generations ago. At vintage time the fruit is batch vinified and then classified according to intensity, texture and concentration. Each parcel is like a jigsaw piece.

> The best vineyards produce fruit of voluptuous intensity, ripe tannins, and juicy flavours.

Ultimately winemakers seek fruit with strong aromatic qualities, fine textures and overall opulence. The RWT Shiraz has a very seductive style with a plum/blueberry fruit profile and fine ripe tannins underpinned by savoury French oak. Peter Gago observes, "The RWT wine style is an excellent foil to Penfolds Grange. While vinification is followed along similar lines, including partial barrel fermentation, RWT differs because of its more fleshy, regionally distinctive fruit selection, and the use of French rather than American oak".

Since its first vintage in 1997, collectors have recognised the sheer class of RWT. Already the wine has a strong secondary market following, illustrating its collectability and cellaring potential. Joanna Simon says of RWT "All the vintages are outstanding. The wines are very consistent with lovely succulent fruit and concentration. The 1998 stands out, but the 2001 could well equal it". James Halliday notes, "This wonderfully consistent group of wines rises above the vagaries of vintage – a very classy display of fruit framed by supple tannins".

PENFOLDS RWT

BAROSSA VALLEY SHIRAZ

1997 `Now`   `2011`
Medium red-purple. A fragrant wine with blackberry/plum aromas and traces of mint. The palate is supple and round with fleshy rich concentrated blackberry/plum fruit, fine tannins and subtle oak. Outstanding for vintage.

1998 `Now`   `2020` ★
Deep red-purple. A powerfully concentrated wine with luscious blackberry/spice/chocolate aromas and savoury oak. A rich, beautifully proportioned palate with opulent raspberry/blueberry/blackberry/chocolate flavours and ripe slinky tannins. A wine with enormous depth and persistence.

1999 `2006`   `2020` ★
Deep purple-red. Intense blackberry/plum aromas with nutmeg/malt oak. The palate is densely packed with lovely fruit sweetness, plenty of savoury oak and ample fine tannins. A top Barossa vintage.

2000 `Now`   `2015`
Medium red-purple. An earlier drinking style with spicy/raspberry/minty aromas and some grilled nut/oak complexity. The palate is medium concentrated and supple with some raspberry/chocolate fruit, plenty of savoury oak and loose-knit tannins.

2001 `2008`   `2023` ★
Medium purple-red. A rich intense wine with potent blackberry/blueberry/plum fruit and savoury oak. A beautifully concentrated fleshy wine with deep-set black fruit flavours, abundant ripe tannins and integrated oak. A wonderful wine.

Outstanding vintages ★

RWT

COMMENTARY: "This wonderfully consistent group of wines rises above the vagaries of vintage – a very classy display of fruit framed by supple tannins. The 1997 is a very clear, elegant wine with subtle oak and blackberry fruits. The palate is round and supple – totally delicious." (JH) "It has some minty nuances, but the wine is very clean and fresh, with fleshy rich concentrated fruit and chewy/sandy tannins." (HH)

"It's a very solid wine with plenty of succulent blackberry fruit and marked oak without being over assertive. The 1998 is a powerfully concentrated wine. It has plenty of sweet fruit and a rich textured mouth-feel." (JS) "It shows plenty of liquorice, chocolate and cherry characters. This is an incredibly complex wine with rich fruit and ripe tannins." (CPT) "This is a wonderful wine – potentially a great vintage. The wine has a huge amount of blackberry/spice fruit on entry with some mocha/vanilla oak tones. The tannins are ripe and the finish is very persistent." (JW)

"The 1999 is multi-faceted with lovely fruit and elegant fine tannins." (JH) "The oak pokes through, but it is a very thick, dense wine with lots of tannin and extract. It needs time to meld." (HH) "It smells of blueberries/blackberries and spice. There's plenty of sweet fruit, ample tannins and flavour length. The wine has more structure but it's extremely well-balanced. This could turn out to be a classic." (JW)

"The 2000 is a ripe, rich, sweet fruited wine with plenty of violets and blue fruits, fresh tannins and smoky oak." (CPT) "The oak is quite apparent with sweet blueberry fruit and leafy tannins. This is a medium weighted wine but everything is in balance and control. It's probably a medium term wine." (JW) "It's distinctly less dense with some savoury edges to the fruit. There's a touch of mint, but the wine has much more weight and mouth-feel than I expected. Considering the vintage, this is a very good wine. The 2001 is a rich, round wine with fantastic balance. It has potent aromas of blackberries and fresh oak and excellent integration of fruit and oak tannins. This is a sensational young wine." (JH) "It has superb richness and fleshiness. It's thickly textured – like the 1999 – with plenty of blackberry/blueberry fruits and abundant soft tannins." (HH)

"The 2000 is incredibly convincing considering the vintage." (JW) "All the vintages are outstanding. The wines are very consistent, with lovely succulent fruit and concentration. The 1998 stands out, but the 2001 could well equal it." (JS)

(CPT) – CH'NG POH TIONG
(JH)   – JAMES HALLIDAY
(HH) – HUON HOOKE
(JS)   – JOANNA SIMON
(JW) – JOSEPH WARD

Penfolds

BIN 707

OVERVIEW: When Max Schubert returned from Bordeaux and began his quest to make a great Australian wine, his mind was on Cabernet rather than Shiraz. Even in 1948, Penfolds made Cabernet-based wines from Block 42, a small patch of vines planted in the Kalimna Vineyard.

Some years ago a bottle of 1948 Penfolds Kalimna Cabernet Sauvignon was opened at a Sydney Wine Show dinner. The wine was memorable not only because of its remarkable concentration, balance and quality, but also because of its extreme rarity. The wine (two bottles with duck-egg coloured capsules) surfaced from a derelict but cool Sydney cellar in the late 1980s. The wine has never been seen since!

Clearly, however, Max Schubert would have considered the mature old Kalimna vines, planted in the mid 1880's, to be an important source for his new experimental wine. Indeed, during the very early days, Schubert experimented with Cabernet Sauvignon as the possible contender for his Grange project. In the end, however, pragmatism won the day. He recognised that Block 42 could not always deliver the consistency of quality he needed, because of variable vintage conditions. Nor could it supply the volume required for a commercially viable fine wine.

The plantings of Cabernet Sauvignon around Australia were extremely limited. Although the variety showed enormous promise, Coonawarra was in the process of rediscovery and Margaret River was a viticultural backlot (the first commercial vineyard had yet to be planted). When Bin 707 Cabernet Sauvignon was first released in the mid 1960s, Grange had been around for 15 years. However, it did reflect something of a coming of age. Cabernet Sauvignon was seen as an important premium grape variety with a future and Penfolds was keen for some of the action!

The significance of Bin numbers can always yield surprises. Curiously, Bin 707 was named by an ex Qantas marketing man after the Boeing 707! It should be pointed out, however, that brand marketing was in its infancy and that few would have predicted that Penfolds Bin numbers would carry so much cachet in the future. The original Bin 707s (first vintage 1964) were based on warmer climate fruit largely from the Barossa Valley and Adelaide environs. The wine was discontinued after the 1969

**PENFOLDS
BIN 707
CABERNET
SAUVIGNON**

First Vintage: 1964

Variety: Cabernet Sauvignon

Origin: A multi-district blend from South Australia's Barossa Valley, Coonawarra, Padthaway, Robe, Bordertown.

Fermentation: 10 tonne stainless steel tanks with wax lined, wooden header boards. All components complete fermentation in barrel.

Maturation: 18 months in 100% new American oak hogsheads (300 litres).

Comments: Bin 707 was not made from 1970-1975 – nor in 1981, 1995, 2000 or 2003. Packaged in laser-etched bottles since the 1997 vintage.

PENFOLDS BIN 707
CABERNET SAUVIGNON

vintage because of the inconsistency of quality fruit supply and a niggling but practical concern about house style and the spectrum of cool climate Cabernet fruit aromas, flavours and structure. By the release of the 1976 vintage, the first to use Coonawarra fruit, such concerns had been largely sorted out. Within a few years of this relaunch, Penfolds Bin 707 was already considered a benchmark Australian Cabernet.

If you can wait the distance, Bin 707 builds up into a wonderfully complex and engaging wine.

The Penfolds philosophy of winemaking is unique because of Penfolds' commercial evolution from major fortified wine to table wine producer. The concepts of multi-district blending and house style are central to fortified wine production. This orientation and culture, based on achieving consistency in quality and reliability in the market place, remains intact. The success of the Penfolds brand is largely based on a highly identifiable thumbprint. When it comes to Bin 707, winemakers are looking for ripe Cabernet characters, concentration and chocolaty tannin structures.

Penfolds Bin 707 draws fruit mainly from Coonawarra, Padthaway, Barossa Valley and select parcels from Penfolds' Bordertown Vineyard. In cooler, sometimes well-regarded vintages, Penfolds is unable to use perfect, high quality fruit for this style. For example, the 2000 Limestone Coast vintage is widely considered a good year. The fruit profile, however, was considered by the winemakers to not be 'true-to-style'. Consequently, a 2000 Bin 707 was not made. This example clearly illustrates the strength of the Penfolds winemakers' commitment to consistency of style and quality.

Huon Hooke comments, "The Bin 707s come of age around 1984. Many of the best vintages – usually the even years – are sensational." Asked whether he prefers the Bin 389 to Bin 707, Joseph Ward responds, "It really depends whether you like the softer tannins of Bin 389, or the muscular structure of the Bin 707. Certainly the 1990 Bin 707 Cabernet opened a lot of eyes in the US and has since become recognised as an important Australian and international Cabernet".

Bin 707 is the Penfolds Cabernet Sauvignon equivalent of Grange Shiraz. Together, the two wines represent the Penfolds red wine style at its most rich and powerful. Everything about Bin 707 is large scale. Winemakers seek physiologically ripe fruit with equally strong flavours derived from partial barrel fermentation

BIN 707

and maturation in new American oak hogsheads for 18 months. These wines are not shrinking violets. Bin 707 is an immensely concentrated style with dark berry/dark chocolate fruit balanced by well-seasoned new oak, plenty of fruit sweetness and powerful, but not overwhelming tannins. This is a medium to long-term cellaring style of wine. If you can wait the distance, Bin 707 builds up into a wonderfully complex and engaging wine.

PENFOLDS BIN 707
CABERNET SAUVIGNON

1964 `Now – Past` ★

Brick red. Complex sweet mocha/black fruit/leathery/cedar aromas with some minty nuances. The palate is fully mature with plenty of tobacco/cedar/mocha-berry characters and fruit sweetness. The tannins are soft and fine. A long savoury finish. Entirely sourced from the Kalimna Vineyard's Block 42 established in 1888. Expect bottle variation.

1965 `Now – Past`

Brick red. A fragile wine but still fresh with savoury/mocha/earthy/sandalwood aromas and a soft mellow/mature palate. Drink now.

1966 `Now`

Brick red. A rich deep meaty wine with black fruit/dark chocolate/spice aromas. The palate is velvety-textured and sweet with plenty of concentration and flavour length.

1967 `Now`

Brick red. A smooth fleshy wine with earthy/olive/berry aromas and some mint. A mellow sweet balanced palate with gamy/spicy flavours and fine lacy tannins.

1968 `Past`

Brick red/brown. Overdeveloped wine with toffee/caramel/old leather aromas. The palate is drying and very tannic. Tasted from a half bottle but the wine, on previous record, is clearly past its best.

1969 `Past`

Brick red. Complex leathery/mocha aromas with some leafy notes. The palate is quite leathery and drying with fine slightly bitter tannins.

1970–1975

Not made.

1976 `Now` `2010`

Brick red. Intense dark chocolate/meaty/liquorice aromas. A deeply concentrated palate with dark chocolate/blackcurrant fruit, malty oak and fine sweet grainy tannins.

1977 `Now` `2007`

Medium brick red. Well developed wine with spicy/olive/berry aromas and some earthy notes. The palate is well-balanced with plenty of sweet fruit, fine savoury tannins and vanilla oak. On the downhill stretch.

1978 `Now` `2008`

Brick red. Sweet, solid wine with autumnal/dried fig/warm earth aromas. Blackcurrant/cedar, classic Cabernet flavours on the palate with fine-grained tannins which build up firm and dry at the finish. A lovely mature wine at its peak. Better than at the previous *Rewards of Patience* tasting!

1979 `Past – Now`

Brick red. Chocolaty/earthy/baked aromas and flavours. The palate is quite tarry and austere with some leafy tannins, but dries off at the finish.

1980 `Past – Now`

Brick red. Vellum/leather/olive aromas with some barnyard notes. A dry unyielding palate with fine bitter/green tannins and firm grippy finish.

1981

Not made.

1982 `Past – Now`

Red brick. Controversial wine! Distinctive cherry/tomato leaf, almost porty aromas and flavours. The palate is smooth, rich and fleshy, but the fruit lacks focus.

1983 `Now` `2010`

Red brick. Intense complex leather/cigar box/brassy aromas. A supple, concentrated palate with leather/cigar box/smoky flavours and fine but pronounced tannins. An elegant style of Bin 707 still holding well. Bushfire/drought year. ★

Outstanding vintages ★

1984 Now · 2010
Medium red brick. A stylish wine with earthy/meaty/
cigar box aromas. The palate is rich and solid with
earthy/meaty/cedar flavours and supple lingering
tannins. Not regarded as a strong vintage but has
developed impressively.

1985 Now · 2007
Red brick. Leather/vellum/ripe berry fruity aromas.
A sinewy, almost tough palate, with some sweet
leathery fruit. Finishes grippy and dry. Drink soon.

1986 Now · 2015 ★
Medium red brick. Very complex beautifully
developed wine with blackcurrant/sous bois/cedar
aromas and some leafy Cabernet notes. A powerful,
rich and concentrated palate with deep set sweet
blackcurrant/chocolate/minty fruit and ripe tannins.
A persistent dry finish. Classic year.

1987 Now · 2007
Red brick. A scented wine with dusty/leafy/cassis
fruit. The palate is savoury with some cassis/spicy
notes and fine tannins. Finishes quite hard and dry.

1988 Now · 2018
Red brick. Powerful earthy/blackcurrant/damson
aromas with some mocha/nutty oak. A structured,
almost muscular palate with concentrated earthy/
blackcurrant/damson flavours and finely grained
tannins. Finishes firm and tight.

1989 Now · 2007
Medium crimson. Cassis/leafy aromas with some
minty notes. The palate is solid and chewy with sweet
cassis/minty flavours and leafy tannins.

1990 Now · 2020 ★
Deep crimson. Intense, sweet, rich and ripe wine with
plenty of blackcurrant/plum/mulberry/dark chocolate
aromas. A dense concentrated palate with cassis/
chocolate flavours, underlying mocha oak and fine
ripe tannins. A great vintage.

1991 Now · 2016 ★
Medium deep crimson. Complex developing sweet
fruit aromas of black fruits/chocolate/vanilla. The
palate is beautifully concentrated with plenty of
blackcurrant Cabernet characters and long fine
grainy tannins.

1992 Now · 2012
Medium deep crimson. A fragrant scented wine with
mulberry/blackcurrant pastille/leafy aromas and
some new oak. The palate is well-concentrated and
solid with cassis/leafy flavours and strong slightly
grippy tannins.

1993 Now · 2012
Crimson-purple. A cool vintage year. Leafy/minty/
dark fruit aromas with some beefy nuances. The
palate is strongly concentrated and chunky with
beefstock/meaty flavours and green edged tannins.
Muscular style.

1994 2006 · 2025
Crimson-purple. Saturated black fruits and mocha
aromas. A very concentrated powerful palate with
blackcurrant fruit, mocha/malt oak and masses of ripe
tannins. Still very young.

1995
Not made.

1996 2008 · 2025 ★
Crimson-purple. Beautifully balanced wine with sweet
intense mulberry/cassis/dark chocolate fruit. Dense
concentrated palate with layers of flavours, plenty of
sweet fruit and ripe tannins. A very great wine.

1997 2008 · 2020
Deep crimson-purple. Intense mulberry/cassis/
coffee/leafy aromas. The palate is savoury with bitter
chocolate/cassis flavours, a core of fruit sweetness and
firm tannins. An early maturing wine.

Outstanding vintages ★

PENFOLDS BIN 707
CABERNET SAUVIGNON

1998 `2010` `2025`

Deep red-purple. Very intense blackcurrant/coffee aromas with some spicy notes and integrated oak. A very powerful concentrated palate with plenty of cassis/mocha flavours and ripe velvety tannins. A substantial wine with excellent cellaring potential.

1999 `2010` `2020`

Deep red-purple. Raspberry/mulberry aromas with some mocha/smoky oak. Well concentrated wine with plenty of sweet cassis/mulberry fruit and chocolaty tannins. Finishes quite grippy. Slightly in the shadow of the 1998 but needs more time to reveal itself.

2000

Not made.

2001 `2008` `2020`

Deep red-purple. Fragrant blackcurrant/violet aromas with some new spicy vanilla oak characters. The palate is still very youthful with blackcurrant/blackberry fruit, plenty of mid-palate richness and mouth coating tannins. A very promising vintage.

Outstanding vintages ★

BIN 707

COMMENTARY: "The 1964 vintage is a beautifully mature Cabernet with smoky/tobacco/ripe sweet fruit. I hope I age this well." (JW) "It has terrific fruit sweetness on the palate with concentration and creamy, slightly honeyed oak. It's very complex and long with a touch of peppermint." (JS)

"The 1965 is more fragile than the 1964, but is still fresh and enjoyable. It has plenty of sandalwood/tobacco notes and sweet fruit." (CPT) "The American oak is poking through here. While it contributes a wonderful sweetness to the Bin 389 style, I am puzzled by the influence of American oak with some of these older Bin 707s." (JH)

"The 1966 is a rich deep meaty wine with a gutsy high-ripeness and lots of liquorice and tar. This is a solid rather than an elegant wine." (HH) "But it's a remarkably fresh wine with plenty of sweet mocha/black fruit aromas and flavours." (CPT) "The wine is still very much alive with substantial body and tannins. The 1967 shows earthy/olive/berry/mint aromas. The wine is still holding on, courtesy of the tannins, which are not overly aggressive." (JH) "There's a touch of fennel/aniseed on the nose and palate, but it's still got some bright blackcurrant fruit and a slightly gamy/spicy middle. The wine's not huge, but mellow, sweet and well-balanced. The 1968 is maderised – completely past it." (JS) "It smells of old leather. It's very grippy and drying, definitely over the hill." (HH)

Bin 707 was not made between 1970 and 1975.

"The 1977 is a well-balanced wine with spicy/leafy/olive/berry aromas and some sweet vanilla oak." (JH) "The wine is a good drink, but is beginning to slide down the hill. It has some cedar/dried fruit/toffee aromas with a fresh loose-knit palate." (JW)

"The 1978 has a spicy/dried fig Cabernet nose with some sweet autumnal/brick notes. The wine is a bigger, chunkier version of Bordeaux with blackcurrant/cedary notes." (JS) "It's a solid, tannic wine with deep/dense fruit and plenty of dusty/leafy Cabernet characters. The 1979 is a very chocolaty wine. It's not particularly varietal or well defined, but the palate is big, soft and fleshy with some baked fruit flavours." (HH) "I thought it was fractionally musty with some earthy/leafy/chocolate/mint notes, but I sense the wine is weakening off now. It needs to be drunk soon. The 1980 is a very firm wine with green bitter tannins." (JH) "I was keener on the wine. It has beautiful ripe cassis fruit and spicy/cedar flavours. The tannins are substantial, but they integrate nicely into the wine." (JW) "I'm more negative about the wine. The palate is very dried out and austere." (HH)

"The 1981 was not made. The 1982 has stewy/tomato paste aromas and a rather clumsy coarse palate. The characters in the wine give a contrived cherry/vegetal fruit profile. There are some porty notes, but the wine is sweet, rich, smooth and fleshy." (HH)

"The 1983 has a deep smoky nose with plenty of sweet fruit. The palate is supple, concentrated and elegant despite the tannins." (JS) "I really like this wine a lot. It's complex and solid with a serious aged red wine nose of leather/earth/cigar box and old pennies! The palate is rich and smooth, with lovely flavours and plenty of tannins." (HH)

"The 1984 is a very stylish wine with very pure/perfectly ripened black fruit/olive aromas. The palate has excellent structure and weight." (JH) "It has plenty of dried black fruits/leather/spice aromas. It's a big wine in terms of fruit and

195

PENFOLDS BIN 707
CABERNET SAUVIGNON

tannins, though not as precise as it should be. But who cares – it's got so much power and intense fruit." (JW)

"The 1985 has leather/sweet spices on the nose with a palate dominated by oak." (CPT) "This is a very leafy wine which is a touch off-putting. The tannins have really taken charge." (JW) "It's still a decent drink, but it has become a very dry, earthy leathery old red." (HH) "The 1986 is a lovely wine with a cassis/flinty/herbaceous nose and wallops of cassis fruit in the mouth. The palate is fresh and crisp with supporting tannins." (CPT) "It's a very powerful wine with some solid mid-range berry/olive/earth aromas, but those tannins are starting to poke through. Indeed there seems to be an Indian arm wrestle happening with some of these older wines – the tannins seem to be winning the struggle." (JH) "It has savoury, leafy/sous-bois/foresty aromas and a very rich concentrated palate. This is a serious Cabernet." (HH)

"The 1987 is attractively mature with a spicy Cabernet nose, but it is just a little dominated by wood on the palate. The 1986 rather overshadows this wine!" (JS) "I like the 1987 too. It has light cassis/spicy aromas but plenty of cassis/mocha fruit and firm tannins on the palate." (CPT)

"The 1988 is a powerful earthy wine with typical mature Coonawarra type fruit. The palate is intense but there is an austere Medoc-like structure." (JH) "The wine is very chocolaty and rich. It has a very serious weight and structure." (HH) "There are plenty of sweet plums and blackcurrants on the nose. The palate is darker and more brooding with some liquorice and black olive notes and more damson-like flavours. The style is quite muscular with strong tannins." (JS)

"The 1989 had lovely dark chocolate/cassis aromas with good supporting tannins." (CPT) "This is an easy drinking wine with noticeably sweet berry fruit and a ripe soft, slightly stewy palate. The 1990, on the other hand, instantly proclaims the vintage with its ripe blackcurrant/plum/mulberry aromas. The palate is perfectly poised and balanced, intense and long yet elegant." (JH) "The 1991 shows plenty of blackcurrant Cabernet character with some chocolaty/honeycomb notes. The palate is massive, with loads of flavours and slabs of tannins, but it's ripe, smooth and in harmony too." (HH) "It's ripe and complex with black fruits/chocolate and vanilla. The palate is supple and seductive with long fine 'fluttering eyelash' tannins." (JH)

"The 1992 has a ripe sweet blackberry cordial nose. There's plenty of sweet pastille fruit and concentration on the palate. The oak is fairly prominent." (JS) "There is a strong tannin attack on the palate. The fruit is there, but damned if I can get to it." (JW) "I particularly like this style. It's very scented, supple, round and gently sensuous on the palate." (JH)

"The 1993 is very minty/leafy, a cool year Cabernet. The palate is a touch lean with very firm tight tannins." (HH) "Those tannins are pretty tough but there is a fair amount of fruit." (JW) "It's a very muscular style of wine with some beefstock/meaty notes." (JS)

"The 1994 is a rich ripe style with plenty of plum fruit and ripe tannins." (CPT) "The wine also has some mocha/spice/sweet cassis aromas. The palate is deep and plummy and mixes well with the tannins. The fruit keeps building to a long finish." (JW) "It's not a blockbuster, but it has some serious depth of flavour. It finishes gripping and tannic, but the wine is still too young.

BIN 707

The 1995 was not made. The 1996 has a core of fruit sweetness which shines through, but the tannins are very big. The wine is in evolution with sweet mulberry/cassis aromas and flavours. It's a delicious wine with plenty of long term cellaring potential." (HH)

"The 1997 is a distinctively savoury wine and far less herbaceous than I expected. It has some earthy/bitter chocolate flavours and the tannins tremble on the brink." (JH) "The 1998 is a rich, ripe, deeply concentrated wine with cassis/dark chocolate fruit and rich tannins." (CPT) "The colour of the wine is almost black! It has some creamy cassis/coffee/spice on the nose and intense piercing blackcurrant fruit and silky tannins on the palate, a very impressive wine." (JS) "This is a major wine, a blockbuster with densely concentrated fruit, massive tannins and plenty of new oak. The wine needs ages to develop, but it is remarkably smooth and balanced." (HH)

"The 1999 has voluminous blackcurrant, blackberry fruit, lashings of oak (welded into the profile of the wine) and substantial tannins." (JH) "The wine has sweet cassis/plum aromas and very apparent oak. It has chewy ripe fruit and chocolaty notes on the palate. This is a good wine. In any other line up this wine would be a heavyweight." (JW)

"The 2000 was not made. The 2001 has a lovely nose with elements of violets/anise and jam. This is a big solid wine with plenty of fruit and tannins and balance." (HH) "It's difficult to know where this wine will go, but it has plenty of floral/black cherry/plum fruit and rich/tough tannins." (CPT) "This is a very promising wine with a vivid, young blackcurrant fruit underpinned by spicy/vanilla oak. This wine has excellent depth and breadth." (JS)

"The 1990 Bin 707 Cabernet opened a lot of eyes in the United States and has since become recognised as an important Australian and international Cabernet." (JW) "From 1984 Penfolds Bin 707 has come of age. There are so many sensational wines. As well as the 1991, it is generally the even years that seem to shine – 1984, 1986, 1988, 1990, 1994, 1996 and 1998." (HH)

(CPT) – CH'NG POH TIONG
(JH)   – JAMES HALLIDAY
(HH)   – HUON HOOKE
(JS)   – JOANNA SIMON
(JW)   – JOSEPH WARD

Penfolds

KALIMNA
CABERNET SAUVIGNON

OVERVIEW: First planted in the mid 1880s, Block 42 comprises the oldest Cabernet Sauvignon vines in Australia and, for that matter, the world. Max Schubert was aware of this remarkable resource and he isolated and experimented with the crop at each vintage. In the early days he considered Block 42 a source of his Grange project – hence the release of the 1953 Grange Cabernet. However, the low yielding Block 42 (a section of the Kalimna Vineyard) provided neither enough fruit, nor the required consistency every vintage.

Max Schubert had a very clear idea of what constituted ideal Cabernet fruit – it had to have deep colour, concentration, power, pure fruit definition and chocolaty ripe tannins. Block 42 has always provided high quality fruit, but has rarely fulfilled the texture and weight required to be given the full Penfolds treatment, particularly the critical element of barrel fermentation. The impossibly rare 1948 Penfold Kalimna Cabernet Sauvignon from Block 42 is the earliest example of a modern Penfolds dry red table wine style.

The experimental 1961 and 1963 vintages were both precursors to the release of Bin 707. The 1963 Bin 64 Kalimna Cabernet, another Block 42 wine, won the Jimmy Watson trophy at the Melbourne Wine Show, providing further impetus. Max Schubert struggled with this grape variety at first. However, improved viticulture and the acquired wisdom of succeeding vintages resulted in the release of Bin 707, with the inaugural vintage, 1964, being produced entirely from Block 42 fruit.

Block 42 is a remarkable piece of viticultural dirt which has contributed very useful, if not essential, blending material for both Grange and Bin 707. During the 1970s and 1980s no Block 42 Kalimna Cabernet was made. The 1996 South Australian vintage, however, was generally exceptional, giving John Duval the option of making a single Block 42 wine once again. The sheer quality and balance of the Cabernet fruit harvested across all contributing regions in that vintage, allowed both a Bin 707 and a separate Block 42 to be vinified in 1996.

The 1996 Block 42 completed its fermentation in barrel and was then matured in new American oak hogsheads for approximately 18 months. The wine is largely a homage to the original 1953 Grange Cabernet, one of the most important wines ever released in Penfolds' winemaking history.

PENFOLDS
BLOCK 42
CABERNET
SAUVIGNON

First Vintage: 1948

Variety: Cabernet Sauvignon

Origin: Block 42 – Kalimna Vineyard, South Australia.

Fermentation: 10 tonne stainless steel static fermenter with wax lined, wooden header boards. Fermentation completed in barrel.

Maturation: 18 months in new American oak hogsheads (300 litres).

Comments: Block 42 played a critical role in the development of Grange and particularly Bin 707.

PENFOLDS BLOCK 42
CABERNET SAUVIGNON

1953 `Now`   ★
GRANGE CABERNET
Medium deep, brick red. Sweet developed and superbly complex gamy/cassis/cedar/tobacco aromas. The palate is well-concentrated and beautifully balanced with sweet gamy/cassis/spicy/tobacco flavours interwoven with fine grained tannins. Finishes long and sweet. A very great wine.

1961 `Now`
BIN 58 KALIMNA CABERNET
Medium deep, brick red. Perfumed tobacco/earth/cedar aromas with grilled nut nuances. A firm but fruit-sweet palate with cedar/dried fig/chocolate flavours and fine sinewy tannins. VA (volatile acidity) noted on the finish.

1963 `Now`   ★
BIN 64 KALIMNA CABERNET
Medium deep, brick red. Lifted but rich, dried earth/toasted nut/mocha/spice aromas. A substantial wine with ripe date/prune/mocha flavours, dense fine-grained tannins, great concentration, richness and length. An exceptional bottle. Jimmy Watson Trophy winner.

1964 `Now`   ★
BIN 707 CABERNET SAUVIGNON
Brick red. Complex sweet mocha/blackfruit/leathery/cedar aromas with some minty nuances. The palate is fully mature with plenty of tobacco/cedar/mocha-berry characters and fruit sweetness. The tannins are soft and fine. A long savoury finish.

1996 `Now`   2020 ★
BLOCK 42 CABERNET SAUVIGNON
Deep red-purple. Intense blackcurrant/dark plum/dark chocolate aromas with some malt/nutty oak. A richly concentrated wine with deep-set cassis/dark plum/chocolate/vanilla fruit, ripe cedary tannins and plenty of flavour length.

Outstanding vintages ★

COMMENTARY: "This was a very great bracket. The 1953 Grange Cabernet is a fabulous wine – still alive and kicking – with solid gamy/spicy/autumnal fruit. It is an elegant, perfectly balanced wine with both power and sleekness. Perfect!" (JS) It's a beautiful wine reminiscent of an old Chateau Latour with its cedary tones and warm, mouth-filling palate." (JW) "You wouldn't think this wine is 50 years old. The wine is just sheer perfection. It has a long lingering finish like peacock tail feathers. Perhaps it belongs to a universal brotherhood of great wines – it has the length and feel of a mature Grand Cru Burgundy." (JH)

"The 1961 Bin 58 Cabernet is a pretty tough wine with multi-spices/dried fruits and gripping tannins. It's a lovely drink now, but it will start to deteriorate." (JW) "The wine is almost faultless and pristine, but it has a very strongly built palate with dried figs/dates/dark chocolate flavours and persuasive tannins that build up to the finish like an iron tonic on the palate." (HH)

"The 1963 Bin 64 Cabernet is a very voluptuous wine with penetratingly sweet fruit on the palate." (CPT) "This was a Jimmy Watson Trophy winner at the Melbourne Wine Show. I am almost running out of superlatives, but this is a wonderfully structured wine with clean dried earth/toasty aromas and a chunky palate structure. It's not as refined as the 1953 Grange, but it's a beautiful wine all the same." (HH) "The extra richness and weight carries the VA very well. This is an Alice in Wonderland wine with its wondrously rich, powerful structure." (JH)

"The 1964 Bin 707 Cabernet has classical cedar blackcurrant aromas with some chocolaty nuances and a creamy vanilla quality. It's round, full, ripe and chocolaty with blackfruit/spicy fruit supported by spicy/vanilla-tinged oak." (JS) "This is a sensational bottle with perfect structure and harmony. It's still got life ahead of it." (JW)

"The 1996 Block 42 Cabernet smells rich and ripe on the nose, but is very tight and closed and deeply concentrated on the palate." (CPT) "Coming 32 years after the previous wine, it is hard to bring this wine into a context. If we approached this tasting in reverse order we might not have made comments about tightness. This wine is destined to be a very great classic. It is in perfect balance with remarkable texture. It is one of the longest prospective wines in the Penfolds portfolio. It is likely to outlast us all." (JH)

(CPT) – CH'NG POH TIONG
(JH) – JAMES HALLIDAY
(HH) – HUON HOOKE
(JS) – JOANNA SIMON
(JW) – JOSEPH WARD

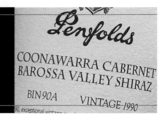

OVERVIEW: The Special Bin Red releases reflect a culture of research, experimentation and innovation at Penfolds. This goes beyond winemaking to consideration of vineyard site, vineyard management and fruit selection. When Max Schubert began his Grange project he used a 'control wine' to compare the results of his work with barrel fermentation and maturation in American oak. Although the control wine (several hundred dozen were bottled) showed "all the characteristics of a good, well-made wine in the orthodox mould", the wine did not reach the standard of the first experimental Grange. "It did, however, set the guidelines for production and marketing of a whole range of special one-off red wines which have been sought after, vintage by vintage, to this day." (Max Schubert).

Some of the Special Bin releases represent work in progress. Others highlight outstanding parcels of fruit. The 1962 Bin 60A is considered by many to be the greatest Australian wine ever made. Indeed, Max Schubert's direct contemporary André Tchelistcheff (1901-1994), the founding father of the modern Californian wine industry, once demanded of a room of startled Napa Valley vignerons, "Gentlemen, you will all stand in the presence of this wine!".

> The 1962 Bin 60A is considered by many to be the greatest Australian wine ever made.

The 1962 Bin 60A is now over 40 years old and continues to impress tasters. James Halliday remarks, "This is a glorious, absolutely wonderful wine with potent cedar/blackcurrant/espresso aromas. The palate has magnificent texture, structure and length – a finely woven tapestry of innumerable flavours". Bin 60A is eagerly sought after on the secondary wine market. While not reaching the giddy heights of old vintages of Grange, it attracts an impressive volume of bidding, usually from a swag of Australian winemakers eager to try the wine. Bin 60A is Penfolds' most successful show wine ever, having won 19 trophies and 33 gold medals in a relatively brief period.

Bin 7 (also a two-thirds Coonawarra Cabernet Sauvignon/one-third Kalimna Shiraz blend) was a famous show wine of its day, but it never reached the legendary status of Bin 60A. The 1962 Bin 60 was the reverse of Bin 60A, a blend of one-third Coonawarra Cabernet/two-thirds Barossa Shiraz. Max Schubert once said, "It was never up to the Bin 60A, but it was still a bloody good wine". The 1966 Bin 620, a 100% Coonawarra Cabernet Sauvignon Shiraz blend, was almost as legendary as Bin 60A in its time. Certainly, it was a convincing example of Coonawarra's potential as a fine Cabernet Sauvignon producing region.

PENFOLDS SPECIAL BIN RED WINES

The 1973 Bin 169 Coonawarra Claret and Bin 170 Kalimna Shiraz, released as single region wines, were originally earmarked to be blended together, perhaps becoming a 1970s version of Bin 60A. The panel noted that if the two had been released as a single blended bottling, it could well have been a much better wine.

When Penfolds purchased Bill Redman's Sharam's Block Vineyard in Coonawarra, Max Schubert was initially quite concerned about the reliability and vintage consistency of this cool-climate, maritime-influenced region. Cabernet Sauvignon, with its thick skins and small berries, can be quite grippy in texture, particularly after a cool growing season. Indeed, up to this period Coonawarra was more famous for its Shiraz-based wines. The success of many of these early experimental Bins – particularly Bin 60A and Bin 7 – highlighted the advantages of multi-district blending and the sheer potential quality of Coonawarra Cabernet Sauvignon. Indeed these early Special Bin Reds and unreleased experimental wines paved the way for the re-commencement of production of Bin 707 in 1976.

These early Special Bin Reds and unreleased experimental wines paved the way for the re-commencement of production of Bin 707 in 1976.

The release of Bin 80A, Bin 820, Bin 90A and Bin 920 (as their names suggest) are a homage to Max Schubert and his two most famous experimental wines. Using special parcels of fruit, these wines were largely vinified, matured and blended to Max Schubert's original specifications. At the time, the 1982 vintage was considered an extraordinary vintage. Bin 820, like most other wines from Coonawarra, has not evolved as predicted, although it was enjoyed by some members of the panel.

Ch'ng Poh Tiong says, "I really liked this wine with its perfumed cassis fruit, mature palate full of fresh acidity and ripe tannins". Bin 80A, Bin 90A and Bin 920, however, are all cellaring well. Indeed Huon Hooke declares the Bin 90A to be "A great wine with plenty of sweet plum Barossa Shiraz characters. It's very youthful and pristine with masses of beautifully ripe blackberry/cassis fruit framed by persistent, ample, fine-grained tannins. A future classic".

The Special Bins to date derive from Penfolds' own Coonawarra, Koonunga Hill and Kalimna Vineyards. Future releases may embrace new viticultural regions. Over the past decade Penfolds has planted vineyards in new and established wine regions. Winemakers will have a larger spectrum of regional provenance to choose from in the future.

PENFOLDS SPECIAL BIN RED WINES

1956 `Now` ★
BIN 136 MAGILL
BURGUNDY
Brick red. Scented and developed cedar/cigar box/
meaty aromas. A soft, mellow, silky wine with coffee/
cedar/mocha flavours and fine-grained tannins.
Beautiful wine.

1962 `Now`
BIN 60 KALIMNA SHIRAZ COONAWARRA
CABERNET SAUVIGNON
Brick red. Intense sweet plum/prune/dried fig aromas
with some raisin/bitumen notes. A mouth-filling
palate with plenty of developed sweet mocha/berry/
leather flavours, leafy, Cabernet-like tannins and
lingering finish.

1962 `Now` ★
BIN 60A COONAWARRA
CABERNET SAUVIGNON KALIMNA SHIRAZ
Deep brick red. Intensely complex. Beautifully
perfumed blackcurrant/coffee/dark chocolate/leather
aromas. The palate is smooth and supple with mocha/
black fruit flavours, lovely concentration and fine lacy
tannins. A magnificent wine. A great Australian classic.

1966 `Now`
BIN 620 COONAWARRA
CABERNET SAUVIGNON SHIRAZ
Brick red. Rich blackcurrant/mocha/leafy/aniseed
aromas. A substantial palate with deep set chocolate/
truffle/leather characters and chewy firm dry tannins.
Still has plenty of sweet fruit.

1967 `Now`
BIN 7 COONAWARRA
CABERNET SAUVIGNON – KALIMNA SHIRAZ
Brick red. Aromatic and developed blackberry/
mocha/sandalwood/polished leather/marmalade aromas.
The palate is rich and mature with opulent mocha/
blackberry flavours and mouth-filling soft tannins.
Finishes surprisingly firm and leathery.

1973 `Now`
BIN 169 COONAWARRA CLARET
Brick red. Developed cassis/mocha/dusty/leafy
aromas. A lean wine with cassis/coffee/dusty/walnut
flavours and sinewy tannins. Finishes dry, grippy and
hard. Believed to be 100% Cabernet Sauvignon. Also
labelled as Bin CC. Drink up.

1973 `Now`
BIN 170 KALIMNA SHIRAZ
Brick red. Elegant prune/raspberry-comfit/spice/
cedar aromas. The palate still has plenty of sweet
raspberry/cedar/mocha fruit, mid-palate richness and
fine-grained tannins. A lovely wine.

1980 `Now` ──────── `2020` ★
BIN 80A COONAWARRA
CABERNET SAUVIGNON KALIMNA SHIRAZ
Brick red. Attractive aromatic sweet cassis/
sandalwood/meaty/malt aromas with a hint of mint.
A soft well-balanced wine with blackcurrant/malt/
cedar flavours and supple fine chocolaty tannins.
A classic Penfolds vintage.

1982 `Now`
BIN 820 COONAWARRA
CABERNET SAUVIGNON SHIRAZ
Brick red. Developed red cherry/blackcurrant/
tomato leaf – slightly stewed fruit aromas. The wine is
well-concentrated with cassis/blackberry jam flavours
and fine grained, slightly leafy tannins.

1990 `2010` ──────── `2035` ★
BIN 90A COONAWARRA
CABERNET SAUVIGNON KALIMNA SHIRAZ
Deep crimson. Intense fresh dark chocolate/malty
aromas with a touch of cigar box. The palate is
beautifully concentrated and balanced with lovely
chocolate malt characters, mocha/grilled nut/sous-
bois complexity, plenty of sweet fruit and lacy fine
tannins. A superb wine.

Outstanding vintages ★

1990 `2010` `2030` ★

BIN 920 COONAWARRA
CABERNET SAUVIGNON SHIRAZ

Deep crimson. Intense blackcurrant/plum/blackberry
aromas with some dark chocolate/smoky/cedar notes.
A superbly balanced, deeply concentrated wine with
deep-set blackcurrant/chocolate/spicy fruit and rich
ripe chocolaty tannins. Sumptuous!

Outstanding vintages ★

PENFOLDS SPECIAL BIN RED WINES

COMMENTARY:

1956 PENFOLDS BIN 136
MAGILL BURGUNDY

"This is a simply delicious old wine with scented cedar/cigar box/leather aromas and a soft luscious sweet palate." (JH) "It's decidedly mature with leather/game/cedar/prune characters and slight rancio/burnt notes." (JS) "The wine has lifted creamy mushroom/Chinese joss stick aromas and a fresh well-balanced palate." (CPT) "It has lovely coffee/mocha/nut aromas and some caramel tones. It's still a nice bottle, but I think it's past its best." (JW) "The Bin 136 Burgundy is a seamless, beautiful old wine with a silky, very fine-grained, texture. It's probably been better, but in no way is it over the hill." (HH)

1962 BIN 60 KALIMNA
SHIRAZ COONAWARRA
CABERNET SAUVIGNON

"This is still very alive and sound, with a deep coffee/mocha/raisiny fruit and firm tannin spine. There's a real VA kick to the finish." (HH) "It's a mouth-filling, sweet-fruited wine with blackberry/chocolate/spice fruit and soft tannins." (JS) "I think the tannins are quite intrusive, but it has plenty of good aged characters. It needs drinking soon." (JW)

1962 BIN 60A COONAWARRA
CABERNET SAUVIGNON
KALIMNA SHIRAZ

"This is a glorious, absolutely wonderful wine with potent cedar/blackcurrant/espresso aromas. The palate has magnificent texture, structure and length. A finely woven tapestry of innumerable flavours." (JH) "It's sublime, with a long list of adjectives to describe it. The palate is supple and beautifully harmonious. It caresses the palate with its sweet flavours and succulence." (HH) "It's a really beautiful wine with well developed sweet fruit and ripe, well-balanced tannins. A very great Australian wine." (JW)

1966 BIN 620 COONAWARRA
CABERNET SAUVIGNON SHIRAZ

"I found this wine very enjoyable with its sweet 'root beer' aromas and fresh flavours." (CPT) "It's a very sweet concentrated wine with slightly porty flavours and a burnt Madeira tang." (JS) "This is a very powerful robust wine with blackcurrant/leather/chocolate aromas and substantial chewy tannins – those tannins take the citadel by storm." (JH)

1967 BIN 7 COONAWARRA
CABERNET SAUVIGNON
KALIMNA SHIRAZ

"This is still an agreeable old red with a polished leather, old woodwork/timber nose and a hint of VA. The palate is drying and leanish with a fair kick of tannin to finish. It lacks the suppleness and succulence of the 60A and Magill Burgundy." (HH) "I found it rich and opulent with mouth-filling tannins!" (JH) "It has really evolved sandalwood aromas and fresh crisp acidity. It still has a lively palate." (CPT) "It's a pretty special wine, but should be enjoyed before the tannins take over." (JW)

1973 BIN 169 COONAWARRA
CLARET

"The wine has a very dusty nose but there are leafy/smoky/blackcurrant Cabernet-characters on the palate. After initial smoothness the wine becomes lean and dry." (JS) "It has pristine Cabernet fruit aromas and firm robust tannins – reminiscent of Bin 620." (JH)

1973 BIN 170
KALIMNA SHIRAZ

"This has a marvellous nose – sweet raisin/ prune/blackberry, almost super-ripe fruit. It has slightly grainy tannins that become quite grippy. A lovely old red wine." (HH) "This has meaty/dried fruit/cedar spice aromas and warm ripe fruit on the palate. The tannins get in the way a bit, but the fruit is there at the end. It has plenty of fruit sweetness and excellent purity." (JW) "It has smouldering chocolate mocha aromas. The tannins are dry, but there's enough fruit to overcome this." (CPT)

1980 BIN 80A COONAWARRA
CABERNET SAUVIGNON
KALIMNA SHIRAZ

"This is a gentle, well-balanced wine with soft chocolate/blackcurrant fruit." (JS) "It's an elegant aromatic wine with cedar/spice/ sandalwood/blackberry and currant aromas with piercing flavours – a long glistening wine." (JH) "The Cabernet is quite evident. It has a fine, elegantly balanced palate with suppleness and fine-grained texture. It's on its way to being a Penfolds classic." (HH)

1982 BIN 820 COONAWARRA
CABERNET SAUVIGNON

"This is very herbaceous with some currant/ spice nuances. It's riper and sweeter on the palate but that stemminess persists." (JW) "I think it's going downhill." (JH) "I really like this wine with its perfumed cassis fruit, mature palate full of fresh acidity, and ripe tannins." (CPT)

1990 BIN 90A COONAWARRA
CABERNET SAUVIGNON
KALIMNA SHIRAZ

"This is a great wine with plenty of sweet plum Barossa Shiraz character. It's very youthful and pristine with masses of beautifully ripe blackberry/cassis fruit framed by persistent, ample, fine-grained tannins. A future classic." (HH) "Those ripe blackberry spicy Barossa Shiraz characters dominate the wine. It has a big rich tannic palate with masses of black fruits, ripeness and spice. It will last for a very long time." (JS) "This is an open and lacy wine, a generous weaving of fruit, oak and tannins. It's a touch finer and slightly more elegant than the Bin 920." (JH)

1990 BIN 920 COONAWARRA
CABERNET SAUVIGNON SHIRAZ

"This is a very fine wine with its cassis/ blackberry (slightly leafy) vanilla aromas. The palate is sweet and ripe with plenty of plummy/ blackcurrant fruit and significant but ripe tannins. It has tremendous persistence on the palate." (JW) "This has a fresh coconut/cedar/ crème de cassis Cabernet nose and is much more attractive than the Bin 80A. The palate seems slightly unbalanced with light-weight fruit followed by a rush of grippy tannins. I'm not sure that this really works." (HH) "It's a pure joyful expression of cassis, plum and blackberry. It has tremendous structure and texture – perfect tannin balance and flavour!" (JH)

(CPT) – CH'NG POH TIONG
(JH) – JAMES HALLIDAY
(HH) – HUON HOOKE
(JS) – JOANNA SIMON
(JW) – JOSEPH WARD

OVERVIEW: Penfolds has a long tradition of fortified wine production going back to its origins in the mid 1800s. Then, fortified wines were extremely fashionable throughout the world with Sherry, Madeira and Oporto (Port) enjoying considerable fame in the 19th and early 20th centuries.

Wines are 'fortified' when grape spirit is added. This addition contributes significantly to wine stability. Yeasts and bacteria cannot live in solutions of more than around 18% alcohol. The practice of fortification was a practical method of wine stabilisation in many wine producing countries. Sherry and Port style wines were particularly suited to the climate and frontier culture of Australia in the 1800s. Indeed, by 1881 Penfolds was responsible for one-third of South Australia's wine production and almost all of it was fortified wine.

Classification, batch vinifying and barrel maturation play an important part in Penfolds Tawny production.

Penfolds continues to have a remarkable share of the Australian fortified (specifically tawny-style) wine market. Penfolds Club Tawny began life in the 1940s as Penfolds Five Star Club Tawny Port. The term 'Port' is no longer used by Penfolds, in keeping with international standards and trade agreements. The Penfolds tawny range comprises: Penfolds Club, Penfolds Club Reserve, Penfolds Bluestone 10 Year Old Tawny, Penfolds Grandfather Liqueur Tawny and Penfolds Great Grandfather Liqueur Tawny.

These wines are all aged in small old oak casks at Penfolds' Kalimna Cellars in the Barossa Valley. All are multi-regional blends, a key feature of the Penfolds house style. Max Schubert's idea of being able to make an 'all-round' table wine is partially a reflection of Penfolds winemaking culture during the 1940s and 1950s. Winemakers were able to source fruit of specific quality and character from several different vineyards and growers.

Classification, batch vinifying and barrel maturation play an important part in Penfolds Tawny production. Fruit richness, grape tannin balance, the 'maturation effect' (from aging in old oak hogshead casks) and grape spirit/brandy character are essential elements of the Penfolds style. Indeed, selection for style is the crucial factor.

The Riverland and the Barossa Valley are the principle sources of Penfolds' fruit for these wines. Club, Club Reserve and, to a lesser extent, Bluestone 10 Year Old Club Tawnies, have a significant

Riverland component. Grandfather and Great Grandfather Liqueur Tawnies are largely Barossa Valley wines. They are all based on Shiraz, Mataro (Mourvèdre) and smaller percentages of Cabernet Sauvignon and Grenache – grape varieties introduced to Australia during the very early 19th century. While the tawny wines differ in concentration, richness and complexity, there is a continuity of house style based on rich, full-bodied fruit. Selection of fruit begins in the vineyard. Winemakers are looking for optimum ripeness, a combination of flavour composition, vitality and potential alcohol levels of around 14-15 Baumé. The various Penfolds Tawnies are differentiated by overall structure and weight. The style of fruit used for the Grandfather and Great Grandfather Liqueur Tawnies is similar to the requirement for St. Henri and Bin 389 with their pristine fruit dimension.

Vinification takes place in small, stainless steel fermenters and each style component is batched. During fermentation the wine is regularly pumped over to extract colour and flavour. Fortification takes place towards the middle stages of fermentation. Fruit and sugar sweetness is a key element of the Penfolds tawny style. The choice of fortification spirit is an important one. Apart from adding the style and quality of spirit, complexity and mouth-weight can also be affected.

Penfolds uses two different spirit types which have a similar character – rich, full and oily, varying only in the level of intensity. The primary function of both spirits is to accentuate primary fruit qualities and add initial complexity. A richer, more intense spirit is used to complement the richer, more intensely concentrated Grandfather and Great Grandfather Liqueur Tawny styles. The styles are further differentiated after fortification. Pressings of varying percentages are added to the early drinking Club styles to add structure and balance. The Grandfather and Great Grandfather Tawnies are made from 100% free run wine and rely on the fuller spirit and extended small old oak maturation to gain overall complexity and optimum balance.

The Penfolds Tawnies are all aged in Solera Systems at Penfolds' Kalimna Cellars maturation shed. The wines are all aged in 280 litre hogsheads, averaging between 20 and 60 years old! The maturation process deliberately takes place under corrugated iron roofing. At the height of summer the temperatures on the top

> Penfolds uses two different spirit types which have a similar character – rich, full and oily, varying only in the level of intensity.

stack can be as high as 55°C. In winter the temperatures can fall below 8°C. These cyclic swings in temperature are vital to the maturation process – evaporation, concentration and controlled oxidation all play their part in the complexing of aromas and flavours.

The Solera is a fractional blending system which develops a continuity and consistency of style. The Penfolds Club wines use a modified Solera System for early release with an average age of around three years. The Reserve and Bluestone spend a longer time achieving more complexity and richness.

Penfolds Grandfather Liqueur Tawny is batch aged in old oak hogsheads for an average period of eight years before it enters the six-stack known as 'Grandfather Solera'. During this initial period these batches comprise the components of a single vintage, grape variety and vineyard. At the end of this initial maturation period the components are classified and blended to achieve the style required to maintain consistency of the Solera. This is a complex selection process because each of the components ages slightly differently. Shiraz, for example, with its overall opulence and fruit density, ages more slowly. Mourvèdre matures more rapidly and provides enhanced complexity. Cabernet (used to a lesser extent) contributes mouth-feel and yet another layer of fruit intensity.

Each year winemakers draw one twelfth of the Solera's volume from the sixth stage, the lowest and oldest level of the Solera. This sixth stage is then topped from the fifth, the fifth from the fourth, and so on. The process is completed when the first stage has topped up the second. The first stage is then itself topped up with the blended eight year old Grandfather Liqueur Tawny.

Theoretically, the wine drawn from the oldest level (sixth stage) of the Solera is 20 years of age, having been in the fractional blending system for 12 years. During the entire maturation process the wines become more concentrated and complex. Opulence, weight and sweetness are intertwined and balanced by the alcohol, acidity, oak nuances and volatility. The highly evocative term, 'rancio' is used by tasters to describe this character. The wine has a dense tawny colour with a green patina, seductive rich spicy/nutty/paneforte aromas and extraordinary intensity and viscosity on the palate.

Penfolds Grandfather Liqueur Tawny is batch aged in old oak hogsheads for an average period of eight years before it enters the six-stack known as 'Grandfather Solera'.

PENFOLDS FORTIFIED WINES

Joanna Simon comments that the Penfolds Grandfather Liqueur Tawny, "Has classic sweet dried-fig, rancio fruit and a sweet, full, lush, ripe palate finishing with a VA spirit lift". Huon Hooke describes the wine as, "Superb, an incredibly complex, rich wine with walnutty, dried peel aromas and layers and layers of flavour".

The Great Grandfather Liqueur Tawny (first release 1994) was introduced to celebrate Penfolds' 150th anniversary. Blended from exceptionally aged Solera material and "other great stuff lying around the cellar", the wine has an average age of 30+ years. It is immensely complex and powerful. Huon Hooke describes the Series I release as, "An extraordinary wine, wonderfully nuanced and full of twists and turns". James Halliday notes the Series IV release is "An intensely spicy wine with great life and length – a classic tawny style". Great Grandfather Liqueur Tawny is Penfolds' rarest wine. While only 1,994 bottles were released in 1994, 2,500 are now produced with each release. The latest release was Series IV in 2003.

215

PENFOLDS GRANGE

"Grange Hermitage has
always been a controversial
and an individual wine.
It is my belief that if these
two characteristics can be
combined, then at least half
the ingredients necessary for
success have been achieved."

– MAX SCHUBERT

EST 1844

> Grange is a beautifully seductive, richly concentrated wine which evokes the spirit of the Australian landscape.

OVERVIEW: Penfolds Grange is an Australian icon, a National Trust of South Australia Heritage-listed wine which captures both a 'sense of country' and the essence of Australian agricultural ingenuity and innovation. The story of Grange is steeped in the Australian ethos. Max Schubert, the creator of Grange, is an Australian folk hero – a man who battled against the odds and then succeeded in creating one of the very great wines of the world.

Penfolds Grange is unique. It is a beautifully seductive, richly concentrated wine which evokes the spirit of the Australian landscape. Its natural affinity is with Shiraz. Penfolds' remarkable winemaking philosophy ensures each vintage of Penfolds Grange, has its own vintage character, which continually evolves and surprises. The best vintages can last for 50 years (and perhaps beyond) as *The Rewards of Patience* tasting proves.

When Grange reached its 50th anniversary milestone in 2001, it was considered appropriate to review all vintages of Grange with the exception of the 1951, but including the exceedingly rare 1953 Grange Cabernet (see pp198). The 1951 was not tasted because it has the unusual distinction of being an historical curio and Australia's most expensive wine. It may well be past its best, but has fetched over AUD$52,000 at auction!

Ch'ng Poh Tiong comments, "It is a great honour to be invited to a 50 year review of Grange. I don't know quite what I have done in my past life to deserve this." James Halliday describes the occasion as "like a great First Growths tasting all rolled into one."

The Grange tasting was held in the Balcony Room, the Government Caucus room at the South Australian Parliament House, looking out towards the Adelaide Oval. In 2000 the South Australian Parliament created a new political electorate called 'Schubert' in honour of Max Schubert and his extraordinary contribution to the prestige of South Australia and its wine industry. This historical tasting was recorded and acknowledged in Hansard, the official transcript of the Parliament.

Originally called Penfolds Grange Hermitage, Penfolds Grange is a distinctive style. A very perfumed, concentrated wine, it combines the intensely rich fruit and ripe tannins of Shiraz with the fragrance and complementary nuances of new, fine-grained

PENFOLDS GRANGE BIN 95 SHIRAZ

First Vintage:
1951 Experimental
1952 Commercial

Variety: Shiraz and small percentages of Cabernet Sauvignon.

Origin: A multi-district blend from South Australia. Predominately Barossa Valley.

Fermentation: 10 tonne stainless steel fermenters with wax lined, wooden header boards at Nuriootpa. Open, wax lined concrete (3-6 tonne) with wooden header boards at Magill. All components complete fermentation in barrel.

Maturation: 18-20 months in new American oak hogsheads (300 litres).

Comments: Named after the Grange cottage built in 1845 on the Magill Estate and itself named after Mary Penfold's family home in England. Labelled 'Grange Hermitage' until the 1989 vintage; and 'Grange' since the 1990 vintage. Made at Magill until 1973 then Nuriootpa, Barossa Valley until 2000 and back at Magill since 2001. Packaged in laser etched bottles with identification numbers since the 1994 vintage. Limited availability in all Penfolds markets.

PENFOLDS GRANGE
BIN 95 SHIRAZ

American oak. Partial barrel fermentation takes place at the tail-end of primary fermentation (at 2-3 degrees Baumé). It weaves the two elements together, producing a 'meaty' complexity and roundness of flavours on the palate. As Joseph Ward observes, "Barrel fermentation gets the oak into the wine and the wine into the oak".

A portion of Cabernet is used in some years to further enhance aromatics and palate structure. The 1999, 2000 and 2001 vintages, however, are all 100% Shiraz. Penfolds Grange is released as a five-year old wine. This maturation period is a legacy of Max Schubert's trials through the 1950s. Through these he came to understand the minimum age at which this remarkable wine could begin to be appreciated.

> He knew intuitively that fruit power, concentration and ripe tannins were key components of optimum quality.

Penfolds Grange is usually a multi-regional, multi-vineyard blend. Indeed, the 2001 vintage is the exception to the rule, being a 100% Barossa Valley wine. One of the great strengths of the Penfolds Grange style is that it does not rely on the performance of a single vineyard. Max Schubert recognised that Grange should be based on a riper spectrum of fruit. He knew intuitively that fruit power, concentration and ripe tannins were key components of optimum quality. He was well ahead of his time. His experimental work in the 1950s confirmed his view that South Australian Cabernet of that era was unreliable. Schubert observed, "The imbalance of the fruit invariably manifested itself on the palate with a noticeable break in the middle and a thin, astringent finish".

When Max Schubert embarked on his winemaking voyage of discovery and innovation during the late 1940s, the Australian table wine market was only just emerging. By the standards of today, the fledgling wine industry was relatively amateurish and fragmented. The criticism fired at Max Schubert's early Granges reflected the conservatism prevalent throughout winemaking circles. Australian red wines at that time were relatively elegant wines with medium concentration and matured in old oak.

Max Schubert remembered the jibes, "A concoction of wild fruits and sundry berries with crushed ants predominating" or perhaps more famously "Schubert, I congratulate you. A very good dry port, which no-one in their right mind will buy – let alone drink".

Grange was a radical departure from the norm.
Everything about the wine was substantial.
The fruit was ripe and concentrated and the
new American oak featured strongly.

MAX SCHUBERT
1915-1994

Penfolds
Grange

VINTAGE 1998   BIN 95

With the benefit of hindsight, it is perhaps unsurprising that Grange attracted so much criticism. The wine was a radical departure from the norm. Everything about the wine was substantial. The fruit was ripe and concentrated and the new American oak featured strongly. The barrel ferment characters and level of VA (volatile acidity), both features of the style, were also greatly misunderstood. To add insult to injury, the Grange project was utilising a substantial amount of working capital in the form of unreleased and maturing wine. The infamous tasting of Grange by Penfolds board members, Sydney wine identities, friends and top management which resulted in the 1957 decision to cease Grange production was a fait accompli and a disaster for Schubert.

Yet, after 50 years these earlier vintages of Grange are in remarkable condition. James Halliday observes, "The 1952 is still very complex and rich, with no hint of drying out. When I came back to the glass three hours later it still smelled and tasted sweet". Huon Hooke describes the 1952 as "A ripsnorter – the best bottle in recent memory".

The 1953 also turned a few heads. Joanna Simon describes it as, "Terrifically balanced with rich texture and impressive depth". James Halliday is even more enthusiastic, "The 1953 is lusciously ravishing and should still present well at the next *Rewards of Patience* tasting". Alas, these wines are astonishingly rare – and expensive.

The famous 1955 was released twice, first as a commercial release and then as a show wine, and is more readily available on the secondary market – albeit at relatively high prices. Joseph Ward describes the wine as, "Very appealing with soft tannins and plenty of palate richness". These old vintages of Grange were bottled under various Bin numbers. 1951 was released as Bin 1 and 1952 as Bin 4. The Bin numbers, which relate to the Bins the bottles were stored in, became notoriously complicated. By 1964 the Bin number was standardised to Bin 95.

Disregarding a Penfolds management directive, Max Schubert continued to make Grange with the full support of Jeffrey Penfold-Hyland, who was Assistant General Manager of his family's South Australian operation. Without a budget, Max Schubert had to make do with used American oak hogsheads,

After 50 years these earlier vintages of Grange are in remarkable condition.

221

PENFOLDS GRANGE
BIN 95 SHIRAZ

although the winemaking technique comprising partial barrel fermentation was continued. However, the maturation time in oak was halved to just nine months.

The 1957 and 1958 Granges are extremely rare these days. Although they don't have the complexity of earlier vintages, they are still holding – just. The 1959 was also a hidden Grange, but was released commercially after Penfolds' management rescinded its earlier decision to stop making the wine. Don Ditter, who succeeded Max Schubert as Chief Winemaker observes, "The 1957, 1958 and 1959 (vintages) reflect a time when we were unable to purchase and mature the wine in new American oak. In the end, we employed and completed fermentation and maturation in used oak hogsheads. We never quite picked up the same characters. All the same, these are interesting wines and after almost 50 years they are still holding together".

> The experimental work carried out by Max Schubert and his team during the 1950s left lasting impressions.

By the early 1960s Penfolds Grange had secured its future. The experimental work carried out by Max Schubert and his team during the 1950s left lasting impressions. Penfolds' work in research and development is legendary. Elements of the fortified winemaking culture were maintained, particularly submerged cap fermentation. As well, new ideas (within the constraints of the knowledge of the time) were employed, resulting in an emerging Penfolds house style. This is typified by the use of American oak and partial barrel fermentation.

Ray Beckwith's contribution as Penfolds' scientist should also be acknowledged in this context. His remarkable research in wine stability and analysis of winemaking procedures provided Max Schubert with a competitive edge. The 1960 to 1977 Penfolds Grange vintages were regularly entered into Australian Wine Shows with considerable success. Both the 1965 and 1967 vintages won the prestigious Jimmy Watson Trophy at the Melbourne Wine Show. Grange earned a considerable swag of Gold, Silver and Bronze medals in all Australian capital city wine shows. The 1962 won over 50 gold medals in its show career!

Huon Hooke notes that these wines still show, "Great finesse and texture". Regarding the 1962-1971 bracket, Joanna Simon comments, "There are some really magnificent wines in this flight", whilst James Halliday notes, "The oak is perfectly integrated in all of these Granges – a remarkable bracket of wines".

By the early 1980s Penfolds stopped entering Grange into wine shows, largely because it is such a distinctive style that most wine judges could spot it easily in a blind tasting. There was nothing further to be gained. This was perhaps illustrated by the poor wine show results of the 1976 Grange, a wine which Max Schubert regarded as a classic Grange vintage. Notwithstanding, Penfolds has periodically entered Grange into various international wine competitions with considerable success – the 1971, for instance, created a sensation when it beat the best Rhône Valley wines at the Gault-Millau Wine Olympiad in Paris in 1979.

James Halliday singles out the 1976, "It's a silky, smooth, aromatic display of dark plum/blackberry and vanilla. The wine has fantastic generosity with majestic blackberry flavours and masculine structure – an outstanding wine". Interestingly, in 2001, Robert Parker Jr, the influential US wine critic, awarded the 1976 vintage 100/100 points.

The 1955 Grange was named by *Wine Spectator* magazine as one of the top 12 wines of the 20th century.

Since the early 1970s Penfolds Grange has created a strong international image for Australian wine. Every time a person opens a bottle of fine, mature Grange, it strengthens the wine's reputation. Positive critical reviews also help. Hugh Johnson, the notable UK wine critic, once called it "The one true First-Growth of the Southern hemisphere". Robert Parker Jr claimed Grange is, "A leading candidate for the richest, most concentrated dry red table wine on Planet Earth". *Wine Spectator* magazine has conferred two important honours. The 1990 Penfolds Grange was awarded Wine of the Year in 1995, and the 1955 Grange was named as one of the top 12 wines of the 20th century.

Australian critics and publications have also acknowledged the achievements of Grange. In 1995 Huon Hooke, wine writer for *The Sydney Morning Herald*, said, "Grange is now priced on a par with First Growth Bordeaux – such as Lafite and Margaux (sic). There is no longer any doubt that it is one of the greatest wines in the world". Both *Winestate* magazine and *Gourmet Wine Traveller* have championed successive vintages. In 1991 Langton's Fine Wine Auctions created Langton's Classification of Australian Wine. Classified 'Exceptional', Penfolds Grange heads up this internationally recognised list of benchmark Australian wines.

The rise of an Australian secondary wine market and Penfolds Grange are intrinsically linked – Grange still represents a significant proportion of the trade on this market in Australia. Indeed, it has had a strong profile for several decades with a remarkable, documented track record of performance in all vintages. Until recently, Access Economics, Australia's leading economic 'think tank', used 1971 Grange as a benchmark indicator of overall wine investment performance. Although Grange prices ebb and flow with economic conditions and the reputation of vintage, its sustained strong track record over time illustrates Grange's solid reputation for longevity amongst collectors and wine enthusiasts. Indeed, Grange has weathered several economic cycles and trends within the ultra-fine wine secondary market.

> Its sustained strong track record over time illustrates Grange's solid reputation for longevity amongst collectors and wine enthusiasts.

Max Schubert retired as Chief Winemaker at Penfolds in 1973, but remained involved as a mentor and 'Winemaker Emeritus' for another 20 vintages. He was recognised in his lifetime with membership of the Order of Australia (AM) in 1984 and the inaugural McWilliam's sponsored Maurice O'Shea Award in 1990. *Decanter* magazine (UK) conferred on him its 'Man of the Year' award in 1988.

Max Schubert, who died in 1994, was a self-taught, practical winemaker with a natural inquisitiveness for winemaking theory. He had a whimsical and romantic view of winemaking too. He once said, "I'd like to think that the wines with which I have been associated are descended from one ancestral vineyard established many years ago, marrying with another, and another, and even another if you like, thus creating and establishing a dynasty of wines. These may differ in character year by year, but all bear an unmistakable resemblance and relationship to each other. This approach and concept has been of great assistance to me, not only in the technical sphere, but as a means of stimulating my imaginative powers as far as winemaking is concerned. All winemakers should possess a good fertile imagination if they are to be successful in their craft".

Don Ditter, an early graduate of Roseworthy Agricultural College who joined Penfolds as a laboratory assistant in 1946, was appointed by Max Schubert as his successor in 1973. This was a time of considerable technical advances in winemaking. The 1976, and the very great 1986 Grange, Don Ditter's last vintage before retirement, epitomise this remarkable period.

The winemaking talents of John Duval were spotted early by Don Ditter and Max Schubert. Duval's family, Morphett Vale grape growers, were early suppliers to Penfolds. Many of the Shiraz vines at Magill Estate are derived from cuttings from John Duval's family vineyard. John Duval, however, represented a new generation of winemaker with a very strong, pure science and applied winemaking background.

For ten years he played an understudy role to John Davoren (the creator of St. Henri), Kevin Schroeter, Don Ditter and Max Schubert. He assumed the mantle of Penfolds Chief Winemaker at a remarkably young age. Even so, he had a fully immersed knowledge of Penfolds' winemaking philosophy and house style. Duval's contribution to the evolution of Grange has been critical. His stewardship has probably seen the greatest developments and innovation in viticulture and winemaking. The 1990, 1991 and 1996 Granges are regarded by many as extraordinary wines with incredible power and finesse.

James Halliday calls the 1990 Grange, "Flawlessly supple". Huon Hooke describes the 1991 as "Fascinating; slowly, slowly unfolding. It's hard to imagine a better wine". Ch'ng Poh Tiong finds the vintages in the 1990s had, "The greatest consistency; a straight line of impressive wines". Joseph Ward observes of the 1996, "It's still very elemental, but the fruit builds tremendously. This is destined to be a great wine".

Peter Gago assumed the role of Penfolds Chief Winemaker in 2002, being only the fourth in 55 years. A graduate in mathematics and science, Peter also completed a degree in oenology from Roseworthy College, now part of the University of Adelaide. His inherent winemaking and communication skills – he was a teacher for eight years – were quickly recognised by Penfolds. Soon after joining the team, he became Penfolds Red Wine Oenologist, a hands-on role maintaining the existing Penfolds wine portfolio and helping to develop new wines for an increasingly global market.

While working with John Duval and Steve Lienert (Penfolds' Red Winemaker, now with Penfolds for over a quarter of a century), Peter Gago's contribution to Grange is evident in the 1998 vintage. James Halliday describes it as, "Oozing plum/blackberry/ blackcurrant from every pore. It's sumptuously smooth, like a

The 1990, 1991 and 1996 Granges are regarded by many as extraordinary wines with incredible power and finesse.

PENFOLDS GRANGE
BIN 95 SHIRAZ

velvet cushion – a gorgeous wine". *The Rewards of Patience* tasting panel also recognised the potential of the 2001. James Halliday comments, "Classic Grange with immaculate balance and flavour length".

Penfolds Grange is considered by many to be the ultimate Australian wine experience.

In the context of the international market, Peter Gago's stewardship of Penfolds Grange comes at an important time for Australian wine. One commentator recently remarked that the job of Penfolds' Chief Winemaker is an honour surpassed only by being captain of the Australian cricket team or Prime Minister of Australia!

Penfolds Grange is considered by many to be the ultimate Australian wine experience. At the Penfolds Red Wine Re-corking Clinics – now held throughout the world – collectors, wine enthusiasts and Grange owners bring their bottles (or even a single bottle) to be assessed by Penfolds winemakers. It has become something of an annual ceremony, where stories and anecdotes are swapped while bottles are checked, topped up, re-corked and recapsuled. The eclectic crowd ranges from millionaire wine collectors to doctors and labourers, taxi drivers and priests. Australians from all walks of life are immensely proud of the worldwide success of Grange.

In the late 1940s, post-war Australia was embarking on a journey to modern nationhood. Max Schubert, himself a returned soldier, dreamed of making something different and unique in the world of wine. The development of Penfolds Grange reflects a national mood, a sense of purpose, and an enthusiasm for progress. Australia is a young country and does not have the highly evolved traditions of the old world. The future is its reference point. The stature of Penfolds Grange has been achieved, not through centuries of heritage and accumulated wealth, but through the trial, error and persistence of a new nation.

Max Schubert described Penfolds Grange as "buoyant, almost ethereal" – evocative of companionship, happiness and wonder, it is the essence of the fine wine experience.

PENFOLDS GRANGE
BIN 95 SHIRAZ

1951 `Past – Now`

Not tasted at The Rewards of Patience tasting, but several bottles were opened during the 2002/2003 Penfolds Red Wine Re-corking Clinics. The first experimental Grange, it is extremely rare. A valuable collector's item because of its historic significance. Rare, hand blown bottles. The wine itself is past its peak, although some bottles still have fruit sweetness and flavour length. The wine has largely a dull, tawny colour and skeletal palate structure with little flesh and fading tannins.

100% Shiraz. Released as Bin 1. 50% Magill Estate 50% Morphett Vale (Adelaide environs). A hot, very dry growing season. 160 cases/5 hogsheads made.

1952 `Now` ★

Medium deep brick red. Very lifted complex wine with sweet earth/dark chocolate/mocha/jam aromas with some liquorice/leather notes. A rich and sweet palate with soft jam/mocha/earthy flavours, supple grainy tannins. A lovely bottle. First commercial vintage. Very rare.

100% Shiraz. Magill Estate/Morphett Vale. Average growing season with normal rainfall conditions. Around 100/150 cases released for less than AUD$1 a bottle at release. Some half bottles were also released as Bin 4.

1953 `Now` `2010` ★

Medium deep brick red. Intensely aromatic wine with plenty of mocha/dark chocolate/meaty fruit. A very concentrated, beautifully balanced wine with mocha/dark chocolate/meaty flavours, plenty of fruit sweetness and fine cedary/grainy tannins. Still holding up brilliantly well. Very rare.

87% Shiraz 13%, Cabernet Sauvignon. Bin 2. Magill Estate, Morphett Vale (Adelaide) and Kalimna Vineyard (Barossa). 260 cases made. Some half bottles (375ml) were released. First vintage and then uninterrupted use of Kalimna fruit, hence the term 'mother vineyard'. Released as Bin 2. (Also Bins 10 & 86C.)

1954 `Now`

Medium brick red. Sandalwood/cinnamon/smoky/chocolate aromas with some maderised characters. The palate is beginning to dry out, but is well concentrated with some roasted/smoky/chocolate flavours and leafy/savoury tannins. Very rare.

98% Shiraz, 2% Cabernet Sauvignon. Magill Estate (Adelaide) and Kalimna Vineyard (Barossa Valley). Internal criticism of Grange led Max Schubert to lighten the style slightly. Only nine months in oak. Cool to mild growing season followed by a mild to warm vintage. Released as Bin 11 and Bin 12.

1955 `Now` ★

Deep brick red. Bright red currant/dried fig/dark chocolate/prune aromas. The palate is elegant but well concentrated with red currant/dark chocolate/prune flavours and fine loose-knit tannins. A great Grange vintage. Increasingly rare.

90% Shiraz, 10% Cabernet Sauvignon. Magill Estate (Adelaide), Morphett Vale (Adelaide), Kalimna Vineyard (Barossa Valley) and McLaren Vale blend. The most decorated Grange – winner of 12 trophies and 52 gold medals on the Australian wine show circuit. Only 9 months in oak. A favourite of Max Schubert, partly because it won a gold medal in the Open Claret Class at the 1962 Sydney Wine Show (some members of the judging panel had previously been vocal critics of the style). Mild to warm growing conditions interrupted by above average rainfall. A warm dry vintage followed. Chosen by the US publication, Wine Spectator, as a 'Wine of the Millenium'. Released as Bin 95. (Also Bins 13, 14, 53, 54 & 148A.)

1956 `Now`

Medium brick red. Aromatic leathery/old parchment/mocha nose. The palate is medium concentrated with leather/mocha/dark chocolate flavours and sweet lacy tannins. Finishes quite firm and acidic. Very rare.

96% Shiraz, 4% Cabernet Sauvignon. Magill Estate (Adelaide), Morphett Vale (Adelaide) and Kalimna Vineyard (Barossa Valley). Only nine months in oak. A cool, mild growing season. Released as Bin 14.

Outstanding vintages ★

1957 `Now`

Deep brick red. A leaner wine with savoury earthy/leafy/dark chocolate characters, some bitumen nuances and fine slightly bitter tannins. Finishes dry and firm. Fading. Very rare.

88% Shiraz, 12% Cabernet Sauvignon. Magill Estate (Adelaide), Morphett Vale (Adelaide) and McLaren Vale. A so-called 'hidden Grange' because the wine was made without the knowledge of Penfolds management who had ordered Max Schubert to cease production. Matured in previous year's Grange barrels. A mild dry growing season. Released as Bin 50 and Bin 113.

1958 `Now`

Deep brick red. Complex and developed, slightly maderised wine with earthy/mushroom/truffle aromas. The palate is dry and savoury with some meaty/mushroom flavours but it finishes skeletal and dusty dry. Very rare.

94% Shiraz, 6% Cabernet Sauvignon. Magill Estate (Adelaide), Morphett Vale (Adelaide), Kalimna Vineyard (Barossa Valley), Barossa Valley and McLaren Vale. A 'hidden Grange'. Mild to warm growing season. Released as Bin 46. (Also Bins 47 & 49.)

1959 `Now`

Deep brick red. A savoury wine with earthy/dried meat/barnyardy aromas. Elegantly structured palate with some earthy/dark chocolate/blackberry flavours and strong chalky tannins. Increasingly rare.

90% Shiraz, 10% Cabernet Sauvignon. Magill Estate (Adelaide), Morphett Vale (Adelaide) and Kalimna Vineyard (Barossa Valley). Cool to mild growing season followed by a warm dry vintage. Released as Bin 95. (Also Bins 46 & 49.)

1960 `Now`   2010   ★

Medium brick red. Complex smoky/meaty/fig-jam aromas with hints of leather/spice. A lovely fruit sweet concentrated wine with plenty of mocha/dried fig/black berry flavours and fine drying tannins. Increasingly rare.

92% Shiraz, 8% Cabernet Sauvignon. Magill Estate (Adelaide), Morphett Vale (Adelaide) and Kalimna Vineyard (Barossa Valley). A hot dry growing season.

1961 `Now`

Medium brick red. Very aged plum/prune/leathery/earthy aromas. Palate is substantial with thick, coarse tannins and plenty of plum/prune/spicy/woody flavours. Increasingly rare.

88% Shiraz, 12% Cabernet Sauvignon. Magill Estate (Adelaide), Morphett Vale (Adelaide), Modbury Vineyard (Adelaide), Kalimna Vineyard (Barossa Valley) and Coonawarra. A hot, dry growing season with hot vintage conditions.

1962 `Now`   2012   ★

Deep brick red. A lovely aged wine with complex black berry/cedar/mocha/smoky/vanilla aromas. An elegantly proportioned palate with prune/mocha/dark chocolate fruit and supple/slinky tannins. Superb flavour length and balance. A classic Grange vintage. Increasingly rare.

87% Shiraz, 13% Cabernet Sauvignon. Magill Estate (Adelaide), Kalimna Vineyard (Barossa Valley) and Adelaide Hills. Barossa Valley fruit becomes ascendant component. An ideal, warm (fairly dry) growing season followed by a warm, dry vintage.

1963 `Now`   2013   ★

Deep brick red. Immensely complex and powerful wine with intense chocolate/coffee/plum/liquorice/sandalwood aromas. Very seductive, richly concentrated palate with mocha/plum/cedar flavours, plenty of sweet fruit and ripe velvety tannins. A wonderful vintage. Increasingly rare.

100% Shiraz. Kalimna Vineyard (Barossa Valley), Barossa Valley, Magill Estate (Adelaide), Morphett Vale (Adelaide) and Modbury Vineyard (Adelaide). A warm, dry growing season.

1964 `Now`

Medium brick red. A savoury wine with herb garden/prune/meaty aromas with hints of mint/spice. The palate is restrained with herb/chocolate flavours and fine, leafy, loose-knit tannins. An elegant style with a clean dry finish. Increasingly rare.

90% Shiraz, 10% Cabernet Sauvignon. Magill Estate (Adelaide), Kalimna Vineyard (Barossa Valley) and Barossa Valley. A wet growing season followed by a fine, cool vintage.

Outstanding vintages ★

PENFOLDS GRANGE
BIN 95 SHIRAZ

1965 `Now` `2011`

Medium deep brick red. Developed bitter dark chocolate/menthol/spicy aromas. Plenty of chocolaty/mocha/blackberry/prune flavours combine with firm tannins. A well concentrated wine which finishes chalky and tight. Increasingly rare.

95% Shiraz, 5% Cabernet Sauvignon. Kalimna Vineyard (Barossa Valley), Barossa Valley, Magill Estate (Adelaide), Morphett Vale (Adelaide) and McLaren Vale. Jimmy Watson Trophy Winner (a prestigious Melbourne Wine Show award). A warm, dry growing season.

1966 `Now` `2016` ★

Medium deep brick red. A very powerful compact wine with meaty/black cherry/sandalwood aromas. A very mellow, beautifully balanced and concentrated palate with sweet meaty/black cherry/mocha/sandalwood flavours, underlying malt/vanilla characters and smooth velvet tannins. A classic Grange year. Increasingly rare.

88% Shiraz, 12% Cabernet Sauvignon. Kalimna Vineyard (Barossa Valley), Barossa Valley, Magill Estate (Adelaide) and Morphett Vale (Adelaide) blend. A dry growing season was followed by an ideal warm vintage.

1967 `Now` `2015`

Deep brick red. Cedar/chocolate box/blackberry/leafy aromas with hints of liquorice. A rich, ripe wine with blackberry/spicy/mocha fruit and fine leafy loose-knit tannins. Finishes chalky and firm but with excellent flavour length.

94% Shiraz 6%, Cabernet Sauvignon. Kalimna Vineyard (Barossa Valley), Barossa Valley, Clare Valley and Magill Estate (Adelaide). A warm, dry growing season. Won the Jimmy Watson Trophy at the Melbourne Wine Show. A generally dry growing season followed by a warm vintage.

1968 `Now`

Medium brick red. Complex herb garden/baked earth/meaty aromas. The wine still has some fruit-sweetness with baked earth/meaty/herb/minty flavours and fine slightly leafy tannins. Beginning to dry out.

94% Shiraz, 6% Cabernet Sauvignon. Kalimna Vineyard (Barossa Valley), Barossa Valley, Magill Estate (Adelaide), Clare Valley, Adelaide Hills and Coonawarra. A hot dry vintage with only intermittent rains during the growing season.

1969 `Now`

Medium brick red. Intense dark chocolate/briary/leafy aromas. A dry, austere palate with some briary/chocolate/leafy flavours and sinewy tannins. Just a hint of fruit sweetness.

95% Shiraz, 5% Cabernet Sauvignon. Kalimna Vineyard (Barossa Valley), Barossa Valley, Magill Estate (Adelaide), Clare Valley, Morphett Valle (Adelaide) and Coonawarra. Mild, wet conditions prevailed during the growing season and vintage.

1970 `Now` `2008`

Medium brick red. Complex mushroom/cedar/cigar box aromas. The palate is quite structured with mushroom/cedar flavours and some raisin/leathery notes. The tannins are quite leafy and muscular, but balanced by a core of fruit sweetness. Finishes very firm. Beginning to lose fruit.

90% Shiraz, 10% Cabernet Sauvignon. Kalimna Vineyard (Barossa Valley), Barossa Valley and Magill Estate (Adelaide). A dry, mild growing season and vintage.

Outstanding vintages ★

1971 `Now` 2016 ★

Medium deep brick red. Intensely complex smoky/meaty/mushroom/mocha cedar aromas. A rich, beautifully balanced wine with deep set meaty/mocha/cedar/vanilla fruit, and fine ripe velvety tannins. Finishes long and sweet. A great Grange – reminiscent of the 1953.

87% Shiraz, 13% Cabernet Sauvignon. Kalimna Vineyard (Barossa Valley), Barossa Valley, Magill Estate (Adelaide), Clare Valley and Coonawarra. "If you had to point to a wine which fulfiled the ambitions of Grange, it would have to be the 1971." – Max Schubert, 1993. Topped the Gault-Millau Wine Olympiad in Paris in 1979, beating some of the best Rhône wines and creating a sensation. A great South Australian vintage. Ideal, generally warm conditions throughout the growing season and vintage.

1972 `Now` 2012

Medium deep brick red. Intense liquorice/dark chocolate/blackberry/violet aromas with hints of vanilla/spice. A loose-knit palate with herb/camomile/meaty/mocha flavours and fine cedary tannins. A lovely, elegant wine.

90% Shiraz, 10% Cabernet Sauvignon. Kalimna Vineyard (Barossa Valley), Barossa Valley, Magill Estate (Adelaide), Modbury Vineyard (Adelaide) and Coonawarra. A very good Grange vintage. However, a single batch was unintentionally oxidised before bottling, resulting in significant bottle variation. A mild, dry growing season and vintage.

1973 `Now`

Medium deep brick red. Mushroom/orange marmalade aromas. Some meaty/demi-glace flavours but sappy/bitter tannins dominate the palate. Fruit is fading.

98% Shiraz, 2% Cabernet Sauvignon. Kalimna Vineyard (Barossa Valley), Barossa Valley, Magill Estate (Adelaide) and Modbury Vineyard (Adelaide). A dry growing season followed by a cool vintage. Last vintage made completely in open, wax-lined concrete fermenters (completed in barrel) at Magill Estate.

1974 `Now`

Medium deep brick red. Redcurrant/smoky/dried-fig/leafy aromas. A well concentrated wine with mocha/gamy/dried fig flavours and fine chalky tannins. A slightly underpowered finish.

93% Shiraz, 7% Cabernet Sauvignon. Kalimna Vineyard (Barossa Valley), Barossa Valley and Magill Estate (Adelaide). Winemaking transferred to Nuriootpa. Vinification in stainless steel tanks, completed in barrel. A very wet growing season made more difficult by the outbreak of downy mildew just prior to harvest.

1975 `Now` 2010

Deep brick red. Savoury, wet bitumen/blackberry/mocha aromas. A thickly textured, muscular wine with farmyardy/bitumen flavours, plenty of concentration and grippy tannins. A dark horse.

90% Shiraz, 10% Cabernet Sauvignon. Kalimna Vineyard (Barossa Valley), Barossa Valley and Coonawarra. A cool summer was followed by a mild, dry vintage.

1976 `Now` 2030 ★

Deep brick red. Immensely powerful blackberry/dark chocolate/paneforte/liquorice aromas. A very complex, concentrated palate with deep blackberry fruits and dark chocolate/cedar flavours. The tannins are supple and fine but build up firmly towards the finish. A beautifully proportioned wine with power and finesse. A great Grange vintage.

89% Shiraz, 11% Cabernet Sauvignon. Kalimna Vineyard (Barossa Valley), Barossa Valley, Magill Estate (Adelaide) and Modbury Vineyard (Adelaide). The 25th anniversary of Grange. Max Schubert considered it, "More in the old style: a good vintage". These days it is regarded as a great vintage. First Australian wine to cross the AUD$20 barrier at release. An ideal warm, dry growing season.

Outstanding vintages ★

PENFOLDS GRANGE
BIN 95 SHIRAZ

1977 `Now` `2012`

Deep brick red. Intense blackberry/smoked oyster/meaty aromas. The palate is quite forward and developed with meaty/leather/spice/bitumen flavours and fine, grainy, slightly sappy tannins. Finishes dry and tight.

91% Shiraz, 9% Cabernet Sauvignon. Kalimna Vineyard (Barossa Valley), Barossa Valley, Magill Estate (Adelaide) and Clare Valley. Cool, mild conditions prevailed during the growing season.

1978 `Now` `2018` ★

Deep brick red. Mature gamy/earthy/apricot/chocolate aromas with some minty nuances. A richly concentrated wine with plenty of sweet dark chocolate/prune/dark fruit flavours and savoury, cedary tannins. A very good Grange year.

90% Shiraz, 10% Cabernet Sauvignon. Kalimna Vineyard (Barossa Valley), Barossa Valley, Magill Estate (Adelaide), McLaren Vale, Clare Valley and Coonawarra. A warm, dry growing season followed by mild vintage conditions.

1979 `Now` `2018`

Deep brick red. A complex, aromatic wine with dark chocolate aromas and lifted rum and raisin fruit characters. The palate is big and solid with plenty of fruit sweetness, earthy/chocolate complexity and ample (but drying) tannins.

87% Shiraz, 13% Cabernet Sauvignon. Kalimna Vineyard (Barossa Valley), Barossa Valley, Clare Valley, Magill Estate (Adelaide) and McLaren Vale. An unusually wet (but hot) growing season. Magnums first released.

1980 `Now` `2025` ★

Deep crimson brick red. Intense plum/blackberry/menthol/mocha/liquorice aromas. The tannins are pronounced but offset by stylish, rich, concentrated dark berry/chocolaty fruit. A powerful and generously proportioned wine.

96% Shiraz, 4% Cabernet Sauvignon. Kalimna Vineyard (Barossa Valley), Barossa Valley, Clare Valley, Magill Estate (Adelaide), McLaren Vale and Coonawarra. A fine, warm growing season followed by a cool but late vintage. First vintage adopting consistent use of signature red Penfolds capsules.

1981 `Now` `2025`

Deep crimson brick red. Liquorice/dried fig/baked red fruit aromas. A powerfully concentrated and muscular wine with chocolate/raisin fruit, earthy nuances and a touch of American oak. The tannins are soupy and dense and build up very chalky and dry at the finish. Will it ever soften out?

89% Shiraz, 11% Cabernet Sauvignon. Kalimna Vineyard (Barossa Valley), Barossa Valley, Magill Estate (Adelaide), Modbury Vineyard (Adelaide), Clare Valley and Coonawarra. A warm, hot, drought-affected summer followed by a warm, dry vintage.

1982 `Now` `2010`

Deep crimson. Aromatic sweet cassis/blackberry/herb garden aromas. A supple, refined wine with sweet, cassis/cedary flavours, spicy oak and fine chocolaty tannins. A good vintage.

94% Shiraz, 6% Cabernet Sauvignon. Kalimna Vineyard (Barossa Valley), Barossa Valley, Magill Estate (Adelaide), Modbury Vineyard (Adelaide) and Clare Valley. A mild growing season followed by a hot vintage. Most 1982 Penfolds wines have a particular vintage character, often described as "exaggerated ripe fruit".

Outstanding vintages ★

1983 `Now` ————————— 2030 ★

Deep crimson. Ripe powerful prune/plum/black cherry/mocha/smoky aromas. A luscious, richly textured palate with prune/plum/dark chocolate/liquorice flavours and dense ripe tannins. A superbly concentrated wine. A great Grange vintage.

94% Shiraz, 6% Cabernet Sauvignon. Kalimna Vineyard (Barossa Valley), Barossa Valley, Magill Estate (Adelaide) and Modbury Vineyard. A bizarre growing season marked by drought, the Ash Wednesday bushfires and March flooding. A very low-yielding vintage resulting in wine of immense concentration.

1984 `Now` ————————— 2015

Deep crimson. Perfumed, red berry/cassis/toasty/mocha/herb aromas and some malt oak characters. The palate is seductively smooth with redcurrant/leafy blackcurrant fruit and soft, slinky tannins. A really well-balanced, delicious wine.

95% Shiraz, 5% Cabernet Sauvignon. Kalimna Vineyard (Barossa Valley), Barossa Valley, Magill Estate (Adelaide), McLaren Vale, Clare Valley and Coonawarra. A cool growing season followed by a cool, dry late vintage.

1985 `Now` ————————— 2015

Deep crimson. Intense plum/camomile/violet/earthy aromas. An elegantly structured wine with blackberry/black olive/plum flavours, good fruit sweetness and firm savoury tannins.

99% Shiraz, 1% Cabernet Sauvignon. Kalimna Vineyard (Barossa Valley), Barossa Valley, Clare Valley and Modbury Vineyard (Adelaide). Cool to mild growing season and vintage punctuated by intermittent rains. Late rains delayed picking.

1986 `Now` ————————— 2030+ ★

Deep crimson. Immensely rich and powerful dark chocolate/mocha/cedar/cigar box aromas. The palate is sumptuously concentrated with dark chocolate/blackberry/dried fig fruit, plenty of malty oak, massive sweet, dense, ripe tannins and superb flavour length. A very great Grange vintage.

87% Shiraz, 13% Cabernet Sauvignon. Kalimna Vineyard (Barossa Valley), Barossa Valley, Clare Valley, McLaren Vale and Modbury Vineyard (Adelaide). A mild, relatively dry growing season and vintage. An important and very successful vintage.

1987 `Now` ————————— 2025

Medium crimson. Appealing red berry/mint-chocolate aromas and subtle oak nuances. A well concentrated wine with redcurrant/blackberry/chocolate/mint flavours and fine, leafy, chewy tannins. Very firm, dry finish. An elegant Grange.

90% Shiraz, 10% Cabernet Sauvignon. Kalimna Vineyard (Barossa Valley), Barossa Valley and McLaren Vale. A cool vintage marked by October hailstorms and variable yields.

1988 `Now` ————————— 2020

Medium crimson. Developed ethereal meaty/gamy/smoky aromas. A muscular palate with meaty/chocolate/mocha flavours, some malt oak characters and savoury, spicy tannins. An elegant style.

94% Shiraz, 6% Cabernet Sauvignon. Kalimna Vineyard (Barossa Valley), Barossa Valley, Padthaway and McLaren Vale. Ideal growing season followed by a warm dry vintage.

1989 `Now` ————————— 2020

Medium crimson-purple. Intense rum/raisin/chocolate (a touch herbal) aromas and flavours. Plenty of fruit sweetness and cassis/chocolate notes, but tannins build up quite firm and tight at the finish.

91% Shiraz, 9% Cabernet Sauvignon. Kalimna Vineyard (Barossa Valley), Barossa Valley and McLaren Vale. Extreme heat and heavy March rains followed an ideal, warm growing season.

Outstanding vintages ★

233

PENFOLDS GRANGE
BIN 95 SHIRAZ

1990 `Now`   2040 ★

Deep crimson. Immensely concentrated, beautifully perfumed wine with deep, dark, chocolate/spicy/mocha/malty aromas. A very rich, ripe, supple palate with deep blackberry/chocolate/liquorice fruit, malt/vanilla oak nuances and satin smooth tannins. A superbly-balanced wine. A very great Grange vintage with tremendous finesse and understated power.

95% Shiraz, 5% Cabernet Sauvignon. Kalimna Vineyard (Barossa Valley), Barossa Valley, Clare Valley and Coonawarra. Voted 'Red Wine of the Year' by Wine Spectator magazine in December 1995. A very great Australian vintage with a perfect warm, dry, growing season and harvest.

1991 `Now`   2035 ★

Deep crimson. Gloriously ripe, dark berry/chocolate/smoked meaty aromas interwoven with mocha/malty oak. A multi-layered, textured, loose-knit wine with penetrating, rich, dark berry/chocolate/spicy fruit, underlying savoury oak and fine grainy tannins. A substantial wine with superb balance and flavour length. Another great Grange vintage.

95% Shiraz, 5% Cabernet Sauvignon. Kalimna Vineyard (Barossa Valley), Barossa Valley and McLaren Vale. A warm, dry year with even ripening conditions. Vintage started early.

1992 `Now`   2022

Deep crimson. Smoky/dark chocolate/blueberry/plum aromas. Well rounded, balanced palate with ripe blueberry/plum/dark chocolate flavours and fine grained slightly leafy tannins. Finishes very firm and tight.

90% Shiraz, 10% Cabernet Sauvignon. Kalimna Vineyard (Barossa Valley), Barossa Valley, Coonawarra and McLaren Vale. A cool to mild growing season marked by intermittent rains.

1993 `Now`   2018

Deep crimson. Very scented apricot/camomile/dark berry/smoky aromas with faint hints of mint. The palate is rich and concentrated with apricot/prune/chocolate flavours and supple grainy tannins. Finishes quite firm. An earlier maturing wine from the latest Grange vintage on record.

86% Shiraz, 14% Cabernet Sauvignon. Kalimna Vineyard (Barossa Valley), Barossa Valley and Coonawarra. A very wet growing season was followed by warm, drier conditions, resulting in a very late but sound quality vintage fruit. An Indian Summer in Coonawarra delivered fully ripened fruit.

1994   2008   2030 ★

Deep crimson. Intense plum/dark cherry/blackberry/dark chocolate aromas with some menthol notes. Very powerful and concentrated with blackberry/dark chocolate/mocha flavours and rich granular tannins. A great and often overlooked vintage.

89% Shiraz 11%, Cabernet Sauvignon. Kalimna Vineyard (Barossa Valley), Barossa Valley, Mclaren Vale and Coonawarra. A dry, mild even-ripening vintage in the Barossa. Intermittent rains but mild conditions in McLaren Vale and a warm, dry autumn in Coonawarra delivered a very high quality vintage.

1995   2006   2020

Deep crimson. Scented, herb garden/blackberry/spicy nose. Elegantly structured but well-concentrated wine with blackberry/cedar/spice flavours and ample, fine, but leafy tannins. An earlier drinking Grange.

94% Shiraz, 6% Cabernet Sauvignon. Kalimna Vineyard (Barossa Valley), Barossa Valley and Magill Estate (Adelaide). A period of drought and September frosts reduced potential yields. Warm, dry conditions prevailed until late March/early April when a cooler weather pattern marked by drizzle set in.

Outstanding vintages ★

1996 `2006` `2040` ★

Deep crimson-purple. Decadently rich, gloriously exuberant wine with rich ripe blueberry/dark chocolate/musky plum/meaty aromas. A very rich, sweet concentrated palate crammed with musky plum/mocha fruit and balanced with savoury, cedar oak and abundant ripe chocolaty tannins. Classic Grange.

94% Shiraz, 6% Cabernet Sauvignon. Kalimna Vineyard (Barossa Valley), Barossa Valley, McLaren Vale and Magill Estate (Adelaide). Superb winter rainfall replenished soil moisture levels. This was followed by mild and dry weather conditions resulting in a vintage of exceptional quality.

1997 `2007` `2030`

Deep opaque crimson. Sumptuous, fragrant, rum/dark chocolate/blackberry/blueberry aromas with some herbal/violet notes. The palate is deeply concentrated with cranberry/blueberry/dark chocolate flavours, lovely oak integration and smooth fine tannins. Finishes chalky and firm. A remarkable wine considering vintage conditions and its place between the great 1996 and 1998 Granges.

96% Shiraz, 4% Cabernet Sauvignon. Kalimna Vineyard (Barossa Valley), Barossa Valley, McLaren Vale and Bordertown. Late spring rains followed a generally wet winter. Generally dry, cool conditions prevailed during October and November. A hot burst of weather arrived during summer but cooler temperatures and a week of rain during February slowed down ripening. A warm dry period followed over vintage.

1998 `2010` `2040` ★

Deep crimson-purple. Beautifully perfumed and exotic musky plum/blackberry/blackcurrant aromas with plenty of malty/meaty/apricot complexity. Opulently rich and seductive plum/apricot/blackfruit/meaty flavours with toasty/malty/savoury oak and fine velvety sweet tannins. A superbly-balanced, sumptuous wine with all the hallmarks of a great, long-living Grange.

97% Shiraz, 3% Cabernet Sauvignon. Kalimna Vineyard (Barossa Valley), Barossa Valley, Magill Estate (Adelaide) and Padthaway. A mild early growing season was followed by very hot, dry weather with virtually all dam water reserves exhausted. An exceptional vintage.

1999 `2010` `2035` ★

Deep crimson-purple. Concentrated, elemental wine with ripe blackberry/liquorice/scented plum aromas and perfectly seasoned malty/savoury oak. The palate is powerfully rich with deep-set blackberry/plum/dark chocolate/malty flavours balanced by fine grained tannins. Finishes firm with plenty of flavour length. A classic Grange reflecting the sheer class of the 1999 Barossa vintage.

100% Shiraz. Kalimna Vineyard (Barossa Valley), Barossa Valley, Magill Estate (Adelaide), McLaren Vale and Padthaway. Dry winter conditions were followed by intermittent rains. Rain fell during November and December, but just enough to maintain healthy vines. The Barossa Valley and McLaren Vale experienced heavy rains in March and ripening slowed. Despite this, vineyards with good drainage produced fruit of exceptional quality. Padthaway escaped the burden of March rain and experienced a great vintage.

Outstanding vintages ★

PENFOLDS GRANGE
BIN 95 SHIRAZ

2000 `2010` `2025`

Deep crimson-purple. Cedar wood/cassis/raspberry/ menthol aromas with some leafy complexity. An elegant (rather than blockbuster) style with fleshy, redcurrant/raspberry/cassis fruit, savoury oak and leafy, fine tannins.

100% Shiraz. Kalimna Vineyard (Barossa Valley) and Barossa Valley. After a dry, cool spring and a warm, sometimes hot summer, rains fell in late February/ March resulting in a difficult year. A stop-start vintage.

2001 `2010` `2040` ★

Deep purple. Very elemental blackberry/raspberry/ eau-de-vie aromas and sweet malt/savoury oak. A strikingly rich, concentrated wine with deep-set musky blackberry/dark chocolate fruit flavours, underlying savoury oak and ripe smooth tannins. Finishes long and sweet. Immaculately balanced wine. Almost certainly a great Grange.

50% Kalimna Vineyard (Barossa Valley) and 50% Barossa Valley. Winter rains replenished soil moistures which sustained vineyards during a very hot, dry summer marked sometimes by extreme heat. By late February/March cool, dry temperatures prevailed, stabilising Baumé levels. A superb vintage.

Outstanding vintages ★

PENFOLDS GRANGE
BIN 95 SHIRAZ

COMMENTARY: "The 1952 is a big, brawny tannic wine with sweet rich molasses/treacle/jam/blackstrap liquorice aromas. It still has plenty of richness and density, but there's not a lot of fruit sweetness. I am amazed it's still hanging on. This is the best bottle of this vintage I can recall tasting." (HH) "This is a quirky but lovely wine with leafy/cedar/smoky fruit and a crisp attack. There's not a huge amount of fruit sweetness but there's still life." (JW) "It's a very complex wine. It's still quite rich and sweet with earthy/compost fruit. The sweetness promised by the bouquet floods the mouth. It has plenty of liquorice, jam flavours and soft tannins. When I came back to the glass three hours later, it still smelled and tasted sweet." (JH)

"The 1953 has a rich nose with fresher gamy/sandalwood notes and concentrated autumnal/spicy fruits on the palate. The wine has impressive depth and a rich texture." (JS) "The wine is more masculine than the 1952, with leather/chocolate/mocha/spicy fruit and a long persistent finish. I think it will continue to evolve." (CPT) "The wine is crammed with dark chocolate/berry fruit and tannins. This is the most lusciously ravishing of the older Granges – and it still has a future." (JH) "This is a very great wine. It's very complex and rich with a smoked-meaty/gamy nose. The VA (volatile acidity) shows, but it's not interfering with the wine. The palate has lots of fruit sweetness still remaining and a very deep, thick chewy texture. This is a dense, gutsy multi-layered wine which also has elegance and style. This will keep for at least another six years." (HH)

"The 1954 is a bit bonier than the 1953, with a creamy, toffee, slightly maderised nose. The wine has seen better days, but it still has signs of fruit sweetness, some rancio/maderised notes and a ping of acidity." (JS) "The 1954 is firm and complex with sandalwood/coffee aromas and a precise long palate. There are faint touches of mint, but it has good balance and savoury, long tannins." (JH) "The fruit has been overcome by tannins and acid. There are some evolved mushroom/leather, slightly varnishy notes and mouth-puckering tannins." (JW)

"The 1955 is still a beautiful drink, but it is beginning to fade and dry. It smells of prune juice and dried figs, but the palate is lean with dry, papery tannins at the finish. It still retains finesse, but the wine is certainly on the down hill slide." (HH) "I thought the wine had a wonderful nose, complex and vibrant red fruits/prunes/dried figs and hints of orange pomader. There's not quite as much on the palate and the flavours fade a bit, but it's a mouth-filling wine." (JS) "It has much in common with the 1953. Though elegant, the wine is clearly defined and focused. While the fruit is perhaps fading, the wine lasts well in the glass." (JH)

"The 1956 was slightly corked but it has always been a decent mid-ranked Grange." (HH) "You can see the fruit is still there, but the tannins and acid build up at the finish." (JW)

"The 1957 to 1961 was a significantly lesser bracket in quality and style." (JH) "Yes. It was a less impressive bracket, but I still feel like a millionaire drinking these wines! The 1957 is quite tight with a smoky nose with hints of port and blue/black fruits. It is very vivacious indeed with lovely intensity and concentration." (CPT) "It has a chocolaty/wood smoke/VA nose and medium complexity. The palate is lean, slightly hollow and lacks fruit sweetness, richness and nuance on palate. It's still drinkable, but not very interesting." (HH)

"The 1958 has mushroom/earthy aromas and some hints of saturated/wet cork characters.

It has some richness on the palate with chunky – not too dry – tannins." (JH) "It has some truffly/mushroom/orange marmalade notes, but there's a mustiness that develops on the palate. I think the finish is very dry." (JS)

"The 1959 is very reductive on the nose and needs major airing." (CPT) "It smells quite bilgy. It's lean, plain, tannic, angular and lacks fruit sweetness and charm." (HH) "It's a very tough bird. It smells of leather/dried fruits and cedar. There's a big tannin kick which dominates the palate. The fruit comes out only at the finish." (JW) "It has more richness and breadth on the palate. It's rounder and sweeter without being porty. The finish is very dry." (JS) "I have seen better bottles of the 1959, but it has secondary earthy/savoury/dried meat aromas and some dark chocolate notes on the palate. It's quite elegant with surprisingly fine tannins." (JH)

"The 1960 is complex and attractive and comes up in the glass. It smells quite raisiny with molasses/fig-jam/chocolate/old-leathery notes. It has quite a rich, fruit-sweet palate with a lovely old-wine taste, an array of appealing flavours and plenty of drying tannins. Delicious!" (HH) "It has lively elegant cassis/spicy fruit. The palate is very fresh with delicious acidity, finishing with very grippy tannins." (CPT) "It has plenty of smoked meat/cedar/leather aromas with a soft fruit attack on the palate." (JW) "I find it a fresh, elegant, harmonious wine with a touch of vanilla and gentle berry fruit." (JH)

"The 1961 has pruny/plum/eau-de-vie aromas and a slight mustiness that seems to clear off in the glass. The palate is quite fleshy with plummy/pruny/spicy flavours – some woody/oaky notes – and good texture and length." (JS) "There is an element of VA in all the above wines, but it is part of the style. Unless it intrudes, there's no point talking about it. The 1961 hasn't aged with the grace of the others." (JH)

"The 1962 is very complex and pretty for Grange, with dried fruit/tobacco leaf/cedar/smoke aromas. The palate has a great dried fruit/mocha entry. The fruit is encased in chewy tannins. It's a medium weight wine with plenty of ripeness but a drying finish." (JW) "This is really quite a beautiful wine, with lovely old singed barbecued meats, burnished old wooden furniture, and old-leather aromas. There are some honey/cigar box/smoky nuances too. The palate is lean and elegant. It lacks the usual Grange concentration, but it has a lovely refined texture." (HH) "It has a lightly aromatic mix of red berries/blackberry/cedar/mint and vanilla. The wine caresses the mouth with its gloriously rich myriad flavours. A lovely bottle." (JH)

"The 1963 is a powerhouse of plum/blackberry and liquorice. The palate is seductively rich, velvety and soft. It doesn't quite have the finesse of the 1962, but it has delicious flavours." (JH) "It has beautifully rich fruit on the palate with plums/prunes and cassis, some spice/cedar/sandalwood notes, beautifully integrated oak and fine grained tannins." (JS) "It's a lovely supple sweet wine." (CPT)

"The 1964 is a lighter Grange with chocolaty/meaty/animal/funky aromas and flavours. The palate is elegant with a clean dry, claret-like finish. Yum!" (HH) "The aromas are quite baked with prune/black fruits and some spicy characters. The ripe fruit becomes quite attenuated on the mid-palate and finishes quite dry." (JW) "It's a drier style of Grange with complex, savoury dried herb/spice mint aromas. There are plenty of dark chocolate/blackberry flavours and soft tannins." (JH)

PENFOLDS GRANGE
BIN 95 SHIRAZ

"The 1965 has a raisiny/mushroom nose with a touch of maderisation. The palate is big and ripe – a touch porty – with dark chocolate flavours and assertive tannins." (JS) "It has lovely chocolate/minty flavours and a taut, firmly spined palate. It lingers well too. There is no danger of its falling over." (HH)

"The contribution of Cabernet in the 1966 is unmistakable. Indeed, on the nose, this is like cassis masquerading as a red wine. This is a very aristocratic wine with a supple velvety palate and wonderful structure." (CPT) "It's a vigorous, sweet-fruited wine with dried fig/plum/spicy/cedary fruit and penetrating, persistently long flavours." (JW) "It is a powerful, compact, interesting wine with touches of blackcurrant/sandalwood and vanilla. The palate is still cruising along with layers of fruit and perfect tannins." (JH)

"The 1967 has plenty of sweet, black fruits and hints of mushrooms on the nose. It's not a big Grange, but it has a classic ripe black fruit spicy profile. It finishes too dry on the palate." (JS) "It has a very hard tannic palate. There are some slightly singed meaty/Madeira aromas, but generally it lacks balance and complexity." (HH) "I find it more impressive on the palate than the nose. It's balanced, but not very characterful." (CPT)

"The 1968 has piquant smoky aromas with some mint berry fruit. The tannins tend to poke out." (JH) "I find smoky/toffee aromas and some green herbal/mushroom notes. It's alive but doesn't have much fruit complexity or richness." (JS)

"The 1969 has some dried red fruit/mint/cedar fruit but there are some stewed/oxidised fruit flavours. The palate is a little tired." (JW)

"It lacks greater intensity, but it has some pleasant mushroom/truffle aromas and fresh soft plum/prune flavours." (CPT) "It's decidedly briary, with woody/leafy aromas and spicy/minty flavours. It's not as lush as most Granges." (JH)

"The 1970 is an Aladdin's lamp of spicy/raisin/cedar cigar box aromas. It's almost decadently sweet and raisiny – but not porty. It's not as good as the 1966 or 1967." (JH) "There are plenty of leather/raisin aromas. The palate is fairly lean and drying. It lacks real richness and fruit sweetness." (HH)

"The 1971 bears a tremendous family resemblance to the 1963. It is an aromatic wine with an exotic black cherry/sandalwood/spicy nose, a terrifically sweet ripe palate and beautifully integrated oak. A great Grange." (JS) "Instantaneously it shows incredible complexity, multi-spice/mocha/cedar aromas and a panoply of flavours – all within an explosion of sweet fruit/mocha and vanilla. This is a direct and immediate descendant of the 1952 and 1953." (JH) "It has a superior nose with lots of crushed-ant/barbecued meats and charcuterie complexity. It's intense and layered, but slightly maderised. The palate is smooth and fine with lovely sweet fruit. The tannins still make their presence felt, but it's not tongue-crunching these days! Still a beaut drink. Probably will last another 20 years." (HH)

"The 1972 is ready to drink now with dried fruit and some minty/leafy notes. The palate is soft, warm and cedary and has developed nicely – but it won't get any better." (JW) "It smells of chocolate and plums on the nose. It's rich and ripe, but not particularly multi-dimensional. There's a nice lingering sweetness on the finish." (CPT) "This was a good bottle with strong black fruits/dark chocolate and hints of vanilla.

The palate has great balance. The wines in this 1972-1981 bracket rely on brute force rather than elegance and finesse." (JH)

"The 1973 is an earthy, slightly musty wine. It has strength and muscle on the palate." (HH) "You can see the sweet fruit and tannins." (JH)

"The 1974 has an attractive tobacco/spice/roasted meat nose with some biscuity oak. The palate is very sweet and creamy and textured with roasted gamy notes and a touch of tar. It's not a huge wine, but well-balanced with a leathery/chocolaty finish." (JS) "While it's fairly tannic and lacks a certain vinosity, this is a good outcome for a very difficult vintage." (JH) "It has very aged meaty/porty/smoky/molasses/tawny port-like fruit. The palate is smooth and mellow with fine grained tannins. A soft, dry wine which finishes a touch short." (HH)

"The 1975 has unusual herbal/camphor notes and farmyard/coffee characters. The wine has a distinctly barnyardy palate with strapping tannins. It finished very dry." (JS) "It is certainly quite smelly! It is reminiscent of oyster shells. I think it's slightly sulphidic. It's a very tannic, thickly textured, coarse wine." (HH) "The tannins are firm and mean, but the fruit does persist through to the finish." (JW) "It's a very potent, savoury wine with dense dark fruits and strong tannins. It may not come into balance, but it may be worth trying some patience." (JH)

"The 1976 is a silky smooth aromatic display of dark plum/blackberry and vanilla. The wine has fantastic generosity with majestic blackberry flavours and masculine structure – an outstanding wine." (JH) "This is a considerable step up in quality (in this bracket). 1976 is, after all, the year of the Dragon! It has cassis, alcohol and hints of port on the nose. There's plenty of ripe, rich fruit balanced by fresh tannins and

acidity." (CPT) "It has a big aromatic, sweet ripe nose with plenty of fig jam/blackberry/blackcurrant/Chinese spice fruit. The palate is massive and mouth-filling with ripe blackberry/blackcurrant fruit and layers of chocolate/spice flavours. The oak is beautifully integrated and the tannins are big and ripe. An amazing wine." (JS)

"The 1977 is beginning to fade. It has some baked fruit/redcurrant on entry but some worrisome hard tannins." (JW) "It's got lots of grip and grunt with dominating oak tannins. It's a very firm, dense, thick wine and not particularly nuanced. But it has loads of flavour and body." (HH)

"The 1978 smells of animal/mushroom and truffles on the nose. The palate has plenty of rich, dark fruits and rich tannins but they need further integration." (CPT) "I think the wine comes together quite well with leafy/earthy/cassis aromas, a savoury earthy/dark chocolate spectrum of flavours and firm tannins." (JH)

"The 1979 has gentle plummy fruit and some camphor nuances. The palate is soft and plummy with some spice/dark chocolate notes and substantial dry tannins – considering the relatively light fruit." (JS) "It has some plum/liquoice/spice/curranty aromas. The tannins are certainly more evident, but the fruit is still doing nicely." (JW)

"There's nothing subtle about the 1980. It has plenty of earthy/mocha/chocolate/molasses aromas and flavours. The palate is very generous and sweet fruited with pronounced but grainy tannins." (HH) "It is a rich, ample wine with plenty of dark plum/blackberry fruit and nice oak. The palate lives up to the bouquet. The tannins are quite pronounced but this is off-set by the stylish concentrated dark blackberry/blackcurrant flavours." (JH)

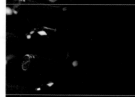

PENFOLDS GRANGE
BIN 95 SHIRAZ

"The 1981 is oaky and super-tannic!" (CPT) "It's not nearly ready, but it's showing lots of plum/mocha/vanilla fruit and a very concentrated tannic palate." (JS) "It has lifted dark chocolate/raisin aromas and a huge tannin grip. It's a whopper, but a rough, unsubtle wine." (HH) "Those tannins growl ferociously!" (JH)

"The 1982 shows strong cassis/berry aromas with a touch of mint. There is no trace of DMS (dimethyl-sulphide). There are some slight confectionery/crème brûlée characters on the palate, with tannins coming through on the finish." (JH) "This is a voluptuous, persistent wine. The alcohol dominates on the nose, but the palate is big, ripe and fleshy with plenty of concentration and intensity." (CPT) "I find slightly stewed/herbal nuances in the wine, but the fruit's pretty sweet." (JW)

"The 1983 has big sweet black fruit/plum aromas and hints of spice. The palate is rich, ripe and richly textured with concentrated blackberry/ prune/liquorice fruit and big ripe tannins." (JS) "It has fabulous toasty/smoky/old leather upholstery aromas. The palate is wonderfully concentrated, fleshy and rich with great flavour and style. It has beautiful balance despite lots of tannin. A very big wine with a great future. I can see echoes of the 1971 and 1953 in this." (HH)

"The 1984 is an aromatic wine with an array of mint/herb/berry aromas and seductively soft palate." (JH) "It has lovely smoky/chocolaty/ toasted-nut/slightly cassis-like aromas. The palate is deliciously fleshy, with loads of primary fruit still showing. An impeccably balanced wine." (HH) "This is a really nice wine with plum/spice/vanilla sweet fruit and substantial but rounded tannins and fresh flavours." (JW)

"The 1985 is very tight, taut and tannic with cassis notes." (CPT) "It's a firm, savoury style,

but it's looking OK with olive/blackberry fruit and soft tannins." (JH) "It has prunes and blackcurrants on the nose with plenty of plum/ liquorice flavours. The palate seems quite ripe and supple until you're hit by a wall of hard, firm tannins." (JS)

"The 1986 is a sumptuous wine with a delicious array of flavours and fine structure. It has lovely toasted nuts/sweet-earth/cedar/cigar-box aromas and amazing intensity." (HH) "It's a fantastically rich wine with rich blackcurrant fruit and layer-upon-layer of melded blackcurrants and tannins." (JH) "I find the nose quite closed, but the palate is massively proportioned and richly textured with blackcurrant/blackberry essence, spicy/grilled meat/chocolate flavours and ripe tannins." (JS) "The wine is very powerful with blackberry/ plum/cocoa fruit and strong muscular tannins. There's a little disagreement between the fruit and tannins, but the fruit wins the day!" (JW)

"The 1987 shows plenty of black/blue fruits and alcohol. Although there's fruit on the palate, the tannins are quite assertive." (CPT). "It has a chocolaty/roasted meat/slightly burnt nose. The palate is big and raunchy with grippy – somewhat rustic – tannins. The flavours are all up-front and fall away towards the back palate. Probably needs a bit more time." (HH)

"The 1988 is a very elegant Grange with floral/raspberry/summer pudding aromas. The palate is soft and creamy with raspberry essence/ milk chocolate/coffee fruit and firm tannins. It's not a huge wine but it has immediate appeal." (JS) "I see a cooler spectrum of redcurrant/ leafy/spicy fruit and touches of oak. The wine tastes a touch green with grippy tannins." (JW)

"The 1989 has a sweet rum-and-raisin/milk chocolate aroma and flavours. The tannins are slightly drying." (JH) "I find this wine very

242

seductive with alcohol/violets/cassis and other rich, ripe fruits. The tannins are deliciously ripe with balancing acidity. This is the most elegant, feminine Grange since 1972." (CPT) "It's a sweet, aged, open-knit wine with a rather jammy, over-ripe nose. The palate is slightly hot with chocolate/golden syrup flavours and grippy tannins." (HH)

"The 1990 has almost immediately assumed perfection and ultimate elegance. It's flawlessly supple, smooth, fine and long – with the finest imaginable tannins!" (JH) "It's a great Grange with rich/spicy/deep black fruit aromas and biscuity oak. The palate is beautifully textured with very rich, ripe, black fruit/chocolate/coffee fruit and satin smooth tannins." (JS) "It does not appear quite as oaked as other vintages (like the 1981 and 1983), but it is quite a masculine style." (CPT) "The wine is still very primary with clear plum/blackberry anise fruit and some vanilla oak. But the ingredients are all there. It has great concentration and depth of fruit." (JW)

"The 1991 is a very complex wine. As with the 1990, some oak shows, but it's still youthful with vanilla/chocolate/smoked meat/leather aromas and nuances of sweet chocolate/fruitcake and roasted nuts. The palate is superbly balanced with penetrating fruit and tremendous power. It is hard to imagine a better wine – from now to eternity!" (HH) "It's oozing with gloriously ripe, sweet dark fruits and the oak makes a positive contribution. The palate is immensely voluptuous, multi-layered and textured with substantial fruit and tannins." (JH) "It's quite a difficult wine, largely because of the tannins, but it is a very promising well-balanced Grange." (JS)

"The 1992 smells of plum/blackberry/ chocolate/vanilla fruit. The palate is developing nicely, moving from sweet to dry with ripe

tannins and fine mid-palate sweetness. It's a lovely harmonious Grange with excellent persistency." (JW) "It has smoky/dark chocolate/ ripe blue fruit aromas and flavours with ripe supple tannins." (CPT) "The wine is getting better and better. It has a clean, seductively open array of red and black fruits, vanilla and spice with very good balance and texture." (JH)

"The 1993 shows plenty of ripe blue fruits balanced by fresh acidity and elegant tannins." (CPT) "It has sweet black fruits and smoky notes on the nose. The palate is ripe, full and concentrated with plenty of sweet blackberry/ dark chocolate fruit and ripe tannins." (JS) "The wine has dark berry aromas and minty/ compost/vegetal overtones. It's a lighter framed, soft and earlier maturing wine." (HH)

"The 1994 has great blackberry/plum fruit driven aromas. It has great power, depth and complexity. The tannins are melded to blackberry/chocolate fruit." (JH) "It has plum/roasted aromas and a blast of spicy oak. The palate is ripe with a rich fruit attack and plenty of tannins. The fruit builds right through to the finish." (JW) "This a very fresh, youthful wine with rich, ripe fruits backed up by complementary rich, ripe tannins." (CPT)

"The 1995 has sweet, intense blackberry fruit and vanilla, toasty oak. It rather lacks the elegance and harmony of top vintages – the ample tannins take over the palate and build firmer towards the finish." (HH) "It's quite scented with spicy/berry fruit. It follows – logically – into a dryish style with good texture but slightly rough tannins." (JH)

"The 1996 is a big, big wine with very ripe blackberry cordial/briary/fresh fig aromas. The palate is huge, ripe and rich with plenty of figs and blackberries, dark chocolate and coffee.

It's mouth-filling with ripe tannins." (JS) "It has a very impressive ripeness with smoky/blue/red fruits and violet aromas. The palate is layered with nuanced flavours, silky rich tannins. In dimension – if not in texture – this reminds me of a young vintage port." (CPT) "This is an amazingly fresh wine with bright blackberry/blueberry aromas and hints of jam. It has a big, soft, sweet-berry, mouth-filling palate with fine tannins running the full length." (HH)

"The 1997 is not meant to be as good as this! It has sumptuous blackberry/blueberry fruit with wonderful fruit and oak integration." (JH) "This is not a huge wine, but it has lovely plum/berry/liquorice aromas and spicy oak characters. It has great ripeness, sweetness and tannins on the palate." (JW) "I agree. It has very good flavour and fruit, not quite as deep and long as the 1996 or as concentrated as 1998, but it's a very good Grange – surprising in fact." (HH)

"The 1998 oozes plum/blackberry/blackcurrant from every pore. It's sumptuously smooth like a velvet cushion – a gorgeous wine." (JH) "It has massively sweet fruit with raspberries and plums on the nose and palate. It has even sweeter fruit than the 1996 with smooth, satin tannins and rich, very concentrated flavours." (JS) "This is one of the greatest Granges of all. It has sumptuous, exotic blackberry/plum/cranberry fruits and toasty charred oak nuances. The wine is massive and opulent with an amazing array of fragrances and flavours." (HH)

"The 1999 is back to sweet, black fruit/prune/liquorice fruits. The palate is rich, ripe and full of plenty of dark chocolate fruit flavours and plenty of new oak. It's still a very good Grange." (JS) "It is very reminiscent of Côte Rotie with perfumed violets and rich, red and fragrant blue fruits. The palate has the texture of a piece of new velvet." (CPT) "It's a touch more austere than the 1998, with concentrated blackberry/liquorice fruit and already perfectly integrated oak. It's a powerful, masculine style." (JH) "The 1990s shows the greatest consistency. These Granges reflect a superb level of understanding and sensitivity towards fruit quality, vintage character and winemaking philosophy." (CPT)

"The 2000 has perfumed plum/blackberry aromas and touches of mint. The tannins are already in the ascendancy." (JW) "It has a very spicy/peppercorn/vegetal nose – very typical of 2000." (HH) "It's a highly scented wine with minty/leafy nuances and new oak. It is similarly quirky on the palate with exotic red fruits and raspberry cordial flavours. The soft tannins are a plus." (JH)

"The tasting ends with the 2001, a classic Grange with dark, blackberry/plum fruits and very good oak integration. The palate is strikingly rich and concentrated with immaculate balance and flavour length." (JH) "It has a huge, sweet fruit attack with wonderful power and balance. It's huge now and will go on and on." (JW) "It's incredibly sweet and ripe with musky/spice/chocolate flavours, huge concentration and ripe tannins and great length. Great Grange!" (JS) "It has sweet, very ripe blackberry and eau-de-vie aromas – a classic Barossa vintage character. The palate is sumptuously rich with heaps of super-ripe concentrated fruit and lashings of smooth tannins. This is a big, bumptious, riot of a wine." (HH)

(CPT) – CH'NG POH TIONG
(JH)   – JAMES HALLIDAY
(HH)   – HUON HOOKE
(JS)   – JOANNA SIMON
(JW)   – JOSEPH WARD

"Schubert had not only created
Australia's greatest red wine,
but laid the ground for the
revolution in Australian red
winemaking..."

– JAMES HALLIDAY

CH'NG POH TIONG – SINGAPORE

Ch'ng Poh Tiong is the publisher of *The Wine Review, A Guide to Champagne*, and the world's first *Guide to Bordeaux* in Chinese. Poh Tiong's articles have also appeared in magazines, including Harper's, Decanter and Silver Kris, Singapore Airlines' inflight magazine.

As well as speaking at wine events around the world, Poh Tiong works as a consultant. His clients include FairPrice and Liberty Supermarkets and Conrad International Singapore. Poh Tiong lectures on wine extensively across Asia including: Malaysia, Thailand, Indonesia, Hong Kong, China and Taiwan. He also speaks on wine to private clients, including international law firms, multinational banks and corporations, France's Sopexa, and the Wine Institute of California.

Ch'ng Poh Tiong is the founder of the Lianhe Zaobao Wine Review Annual Wine Challenge, Singapore's first independent wine competition. He was a judge of the 1999 Robert Mondavi *Decanter* magazine 'Wine by the Glass' Competition. He has also judged wines in England, South Africa and Japan. His most recent publication is *Tables Singapore 2003*, an annual, independent dining guide to the 'Great & Greatest Tables' of Singapore.

COMMENTARY: I was struck by how well Penfolds wines age, particularly Grange, St. Henri, Bin 707 and RWT. Actually, what I really meant to say is that I was very impressed with the way the wines have evolved. After all, most wines have short to medium-term aging potential, but only great wines are capable of evolving into something more complex than the exuberance of their youth.

I also discovered when wines are tasted in the cold of the morning, they are less expressive than when the outside temperature is higher. Indeed, this is the very same discovery I've made when tasting Bordeaux primeurs or futures over the course of a week in spring in Bordeaux. When it's cold, as spring days can be, the wines are numbed and closed. And if a wine is young, acid and tannic, the acidity and tannins are even more tight and taut.

By way of corollary, I've found that when I open wines in the tropics, given our higher temperatures and humidity, the wines are also more giving of their aromas and fruit. This is a great

> Ch'ng Poh Tiong is the founder of the Lianhe Zaobao Wine Review Annual Wine Challenge, Singapore's first independent wine competition.

Only great wines are capable of evolving into something more complex than the exuberance of their youth.

bonus of course. However, we must also be careful that the higher temperatures and humidity do not, at the same time, rob the wine of its vivacity.

Finally, a word about what I think is Australia's next great wine. Based on what I have tasted in the past, and during *The Rewards of Patience* tasting, it's confirmed for me that Australia's next Great Wine is Grenache. The palate profile of this varietal in the southern Rhône, Spain and Australia is so very different. Sure, you get the generosity of fruit in all three major Grenache regions. But down under in Australia, the tannins are effortlessly velvety without sacrificing important structure and backbone. I am stunned by Grenache's adaptation and transformation in the hands of the growers who believe in this varietal in Australia.

Ch'ng Poh Tiong

JAMES HALLIDAY – AUSTRALIA

James Halliday needs no introduction in Australia – he's an acclaimed wine writer, Australian and international wine show judge and founder of two of the country's leading wineries: Brokenwood and Coldstream Hills.

He has written or co-authored over 45 books on wine since 1979, and has been a contributor to others notably, the *Oxford Companion to Wine* and *Larousse Encyclopaedia of Wine*. He won the Charles Heidsieck Award for Excellence in Wine Journalism in 1983. In 1993 he was joint winner (with Hugh Johnson) of the James Beard Award and Clicquot Award, as well as runner up for the Glenfiddich Award. He won the James Beard Award in 1994 and most recently, the Wine Literary Award (San Francisco) in 2002.

A wine show judge since 1977, James Halliday is currently the chairman of six regional wine shows, and judges at many others including shows in the United Kingdom, Europe, the United States, South Africa and New Zealand.

James Halliday's contribution to the Australian wine industry was recognised when in 1995 he was presented with the country's most prestigious wine award, the Maurice O'Shea Award, for his outstanding contribution to the Australian Wine Industry.

COMMENTARY: How or why a country with such a keenly developed tall poppy syndrome could ever be regarded as complacent, I do not understand. Or is it that the very accusation of complacency stems from the syndrome? I don't profess to know the answer, but *The Rewards of Patience* V was not only the best tasting yet, but it underlined the incredible riches of Australia's 150 years of vinous history.

True, the wine lands of Burgundy and Germany stretch back 2000 years or more, and wine has been an integral part of civilisation for two or three times longer than that. But Bordeaux was a creature of the late 18th century (courtesy of the soil draining technology of the Dutch) and the classification of Bordeaux wines did not take place until 1855.

It was only 30 years later that what is known today as Kalimna Block 42 was planted to Cabernet Sauvignon. And no matter how long the periscope of history is, this is the oldest planting of

> James Halliday's contribution to the Australian wine industry was recognised when he was presented with the country's most prestigious wine award.

REFLECTIONS
ON THE REWARDS OF PATIENCE

Cabernet Sauvignon in the world. What is more, it was planted on its own roots and can (with total legitimacy) be described as pre-phylloxera. (Some sleight-of-hand here, for phylloxera has never wrought its havoc on South Australia's vineyards, regardless of their age.)

Penfolds acquired the Kalimna Vineyard from D and J Fowler in 1945. One of the most memorable tastings of *The Rewards of Patience V* took place at the original homestead (1896) on the property. Rain, drove us from the planned tasting between the rows, so we moved to the open verandah of the house.

> What other wine company in the world could stage a tasting of such breadth and depth? The answer is – absolutely none!

The tastings included all but one of the 100% Cabernet Sauvignons known to have been made by Penfolds from the block. The missing link was a 1948 Cabernet Sauvignon which had been given to John Duval, and which he shared with the judges at Len Evans' Chairman's dinner at the Royal Sydney Wine Show some years ago. I was one of four *Rewards of Patience V* participants present at that dinner and shared in what was a magnificently rich wine – to my mind a more direct forefather of the 1996 Block 42 than any of the four intervening wines, except perhaps the mighty 1953 Grange Cabernet Sauvignon.

Why didn't Max Schubert persist with the Block 42 sourced Grange and why has only one Block 42 been made since 1996? Schubert's answer was the shortage of Cabernet Sauvignon (other than the limited resource of Block 42); Duval's answer is that the Barossa Valley is not the perfect climate for Cabernet, with an implicit acknowledgment that Block 42 provides a cornerstone for Bin 707.

Be that as it may, this tasting was the highlight of four transfixing days. (Yes, even more than the 50 consecutive vintages of Grange, however unlikely it is that this latter tasting will ever be repeated.) It underlined the value of the inheritance we have from the second half of the 19th century, the sheer quality of the wines in question, and the uniqueness of the resource.

The last was the major take home message from *The Rewards of Patience* tasting. What other wine company in the world could stage a tasting of such breadth and depth? The answer is – absolutely none!

James Halliday

HUON HOOKE – AUSTRALIA

A leading independent wine writer, Huon Hooke makes his living entirely by writing, judging, lecturing and educating about wine. A journalist first, and a wine professional second, he has tertiary qualifications in both fields and has been writing about wine since 1983. His current quota includes two weekly columns in *The Sydney Morning Herald's Good Living* section and *Good Weekend* magazine, and regular articles in *Australian Gourmet Traveller Wine* magazine, for which he is a contributing editor.

He co-authors the best-selling annual Penguin *Good Australian Wine Guide*, writes for the British wine magazine, *Decanter* and the various wine-related publications of Italy's Slow Food organisation, judges at least ten wine competitions a year in Australia and overseas, runs wine courses in his home town, Sydney (notably at the Sydney University Continuing Education Centre), and chairs the judging panel of the annual Tucker Seabrook Restaurant Wine List of the Year Awards. He's been a wine show judge for 16 years.

A journalist first and wine professional second, he has tertiary qualifications in both fields and has been writing about wine since 1983.

COMMENTARY: For a wine lover, being invited to *The Rewards of Patience* tastings is the ultimate kid-in-a-lolly-shop experience. I was reminded, not for the first time, what a wealth of superb wine Penfolds produces. Not only is there high quality over many vintages at the top end, with Grange, Bin 707, Bin 389 et al, but quality is also there at the lower end, where Koonunga Hill and Rawson's Retreat provide amazing value and can age remarkably well. Most of the Koonunga Hill reds, dating back to 1976, are still drinking well. This is a rare thing for such an inexpensive red wine.

It seems to me that the greatness of Penfolds is almost taken for granted these days. We are spoilt rotten with good wine and there is a certain ho-hum factor in a company that puts out such consistently superb, age-worthy wine, year after year. Jaded members of the trade and media, not to mention the public, need to be reminded periodically of what an outstanding company it is. These days we are so inundated with new wines, many of them made in flashy, opulent styles, arrestingly packaged and designed for immediate gratification, that we are like the dog with the bone looking at its own reflection in the water. We are drawn to the other, seemingly more attractive bone and in the lunge for it, we drop the one we already had. The easy availability of most of the

REFLECTIONS
ON THE REWARDS OF PATIENCE

Penfolds wines seems to make them less exciting than the tiny output of some fashionable new boutique. Widely advertised discount prices add to the perception that Penfolds wines aren't quite as special as they were.

> Penfolds' consistency of style creates an impression of a wine company with a definite philosophy of winemaking and an unwavering integrity in the way it goes about its business.

Well, I'm happy to say the wines are still where they've been for the 20-odd years I've been writing about wine - at the top of the tree. The consistency of quality is quite amazing, notwithstanding the style variations produced by seasonal conditions. And that is another of the fascinations of these tastings – vintage characteristics are clear throughout the portfolio. The great quality years tended to be great throughout, from Koonunga Hill up to Grange, and there are distinct vintage patterns in structure and flavour. There could scarcely be a better example of how different a trio of consecutive vintages can be than 2000, 2001 and 2002.

Penfolds' consistency of style creates an impression of a wine company with a definite philosophy of winemaking and an unwavering integrity in the way it goes about its business. No doubt this has a lot to do with the 'firm hand on the tiller'. There have been only four Chief Winemakers at Penfolds since Max Schubert set the direction in the 1940s: Max Schubert, Don Ditter, John Duval and now Peter Gago. Hence, Penfolds has been more immune to fads and fashions than other wineries.

We live in the age of sound bites and short attention spans. It's heartening to see Penfolds swimming against the tide and sending out messages (this book and the re-corking clinics are unique) that encourage us all to cellar wine and give it time so that it can build complexity and realise its full potential. Even if we drink young, current-release wine most days of our lives, let's not forget the joys of drinking a well matured bottle on a special occasion.

Huon Hooke

JOANNA SIMON – UNITED KINGDOM

Award-winning wine writer for London's *The Sunday Times*, Joanna Simon writes a column in its *Style* magazine, neatly sandwiched between Tom Conran and AA Gill. She also contributes to the Travel, Books and Doors sections and has edited three large-scale part works, the last one in 2001.

Since her 1987 appointment to *The Sunday Times*, she has written a weekly article as well as contributing to many other publications worldwide including: *Decanter, Australian Gourmet Traveller Wine, Harpers, Condé Nast Traveler, Tatler, Whisky Magazine, BBC Good Food*, and *Country Living*. Before joining *The Sunday Times*, she was editor of *Wine* magazine and before that editor of *Wine & Spirit International*.

Her books include: *The Sunday Times Book of Wine*, first published in 2001 and now in ten languages; *Discovering Wine*, which has sold nearly 300,000 copies in 12 languages, and which was published in a completely revised edition in May 2003; and *Wine with Food*, the research for which involved several years of strenuous eating and drinking. *Wine with Food* has been published in many languages, including Japanese, German, Portuguese and Dutch.

Also a broadcaster, Joanna Simon presented *The Bottle Uncorked* in 1999 – BBC Radio 4's first series devoted entirely to wine. Her television appearances have included advice on matching food and wine, buying fine and rare wines at auction, and vodka. When not writing, tasting, talking about wine or visiting the world's vineyards, she spends as much time as possible in a remote part of France.

COMMENTARY: When I tell people what I do, they invariably say, "What a wonderful job!". I try to make it sound tough, with tales of tasting raspingly tannic young reds and searingly acid whites in freezing European cellars at 8.30 in the morning. But they still look envious, rather than sympathetic.

So when I told friends and colleagues that I was going from London to Adelaide and back via Dubai, Perth and Singapore in slightly less than six days, with the sole purpose of spending three days on the ground tasting a few hundred wines, their reaction was oddly gratifying. "You're completely mad," said one and all, although some put it less politely.

> Since her 1987 appointment to *The Sunday Times*, she has written a weekly article as well as contributing to many other publications worldwide.

In truth, I had my own doubts, especially on that first morning. Taking my seat in Mount Lofty House an hour after getting off the plane, I reached down to get a pen from my bag on the floor. The floor came up to meet me halfway and then spun around, taking James, Joseph, Ch'ng Poh Tiong, Peter, Huon, Andrew and John with it. Not a drop had passed my lips, but I was deeply jet-lagged.

Once a few drops had passed my lips in both directions (yes, it grieves me, too, to think of the fabulous, historic wines I spat out), I felt much better. Who would not have been revitalised by tasting a flight of Bin 407s starting with a 1990 that was full and supple, well-developed and yet still fresh?

Inspiring wines showed the resourcefulness and talent of Penfolds' very short succession of Chief Winemakers.

And that was only 407. Over three days, there were, among others, 20 vintages of Magill Estate, 33 of Bin 389, 28 of Bin 707, 44 of St. Henri Shiraz and 50 of Grange. While the flight (a complete liquid history) of St. Henri demonstrated, that this is Penfolds' unsung hero, the quality and longevity of Grange over half a century shows beyond doubt why it has achieved its legendary status, not just in Australia, but in the world at large. Tantalisingly, it also showed that some of the greatest Granges are comparatively low in alcohol. The 1955 is 12.6% and the 1971 is 12.3%. Now, there's something for winemakers everywhere to ponder.

There were also 11 Special Bin reds spanning three-and-a-half decades – inspiring wines that showed the resourcefulness and talent of Penfolds' very short succession of Chief Winemakers (whom we were privileged to have tasting with us, the late Max Schubert excepted of course). And then there was the Block 42 flight: five wines from four hectares planted in the 1880s and said to be the oldest Cabernet Sauvignon vineyard in the world. As I tasted the 1953 Grange Cabernet (a Block 42 wine and the only Grange Cabernet ever made), I signed off my tasting note with the word "perfect" – and knew I'd made a terrible mistake. I had spat it out. With that, I drained my glass and swallowed. I like to think I learn by my mistakes.

Joanna Simon

JOSEPH WARD – UNITED STATES OF AMERICA

For the past twelve years, as Wine Editor and Wine Columnist for *Condé Nast Traveler*, Joseph Ward has been visiting the world's wine regions and interviewing winemakers. His articles conjure a vivid sense of place, which he considers essential to understanding fine wines.

He has reported on the familiar: Napa, Bordeaux, and Tuscany, and the less well known: Chile, Casablanca, South Africa's Walker Bay and New Zealand's Central Otago, always looking for exciting, distinctive wines. Joseph Ward has a special interest in the wines of Australia and New Zealand. *Condé Nast Traveler* has been a leader among American magazines in reporting on these two countries.

An experienced journalist, Ward began writing about wine for *The Wall Street Journal* Europe in 1983. He lived in Europe for fifteen years and understands the markets on both sides of the Atlantic. His articles have appeared in various publications including *Smart Money* magazine, *The Washington Post*, and *The International Herald Tribune*. For seven years Ward was the wine columnist for Canada's *The Financial Post*. His book, *How To Buy Fine Wines: The Christies Guide*, written with Steven Spurrier, was one of the first books to deal with wine auctions and wine as an investment.

COMMENTARY: As great, and as much fun, as *The Rewards of Patience* tasting was, it would have been better as a five day event. As we rushed to finish sessions on the first two days, and even the third day, one or more wines were short changed in the discussion.

The wine that most deserved further discussion was the Bin 707. From 1986, maybe even 1984, there are some stunning 707s, and very few duds. When there is a problem, it is with tannins and acidity, and this is less of a problem of late. There is an amazing amount of fruit in the top vintages of 707. While the cassis and plum are textbook Cabernet, the texture is something else entirely. The wines are concentrated and rich with a sweet fruit character seldom found in Cabernet, certainly not in Bordeaux, nor in Napa where concentration is often accompanied by an over-extracted (definitely not sweet) character.

An experienced journalist, Ward began writing about wine for *The Wall Street Journal* Europe in 1983. He lived in Europe for fifteen years and understands the markets on both sides of the Atlantic.

The best 707s are singular, exotic (to a non-Australian palate) yet recognisably Cabernet Sauvignon. Although I am reasonably familiar with recent vintages of Bin 707, I have had limited experience with older wines. I found the evolution of a style over nearly 40 years to be one of the most fascinating experiences of the week. The 1964, of course, is brilliant, but atypical. It is not until the mid 80s that the winemakers let the fruit rip and the wine becomes both great, and unmistakably Australian.

The Grange tasting was overwhelming. The young wines are so rich, so concentrated, and so powerful that they nearly trigger sensory overload. Fruit, oak, tannin all just wash over the palate like a giant wave. I can't imagine drinking a young Grange. With the older vintages one has to be constantly aware, because there is something interesting in every crevice and corner.

The fruit remains intense for a long time, delaying the onset of a mature phase. The persistence of the fruit, not just through the wine, but through the decades, is what sets Grange apart. Structure is important, of course, but structure, as we've seen, is seldom a problem with Penfolds reds. Fruit justifies structure.

> The Grange tasting was overwhelming. The young wines are so rich, so concentrated, and so powerful that they nearly trigger sensory overload.

I hope to be around long enough to taste the 1990, 1996 and 1998 Granges as they approach maturity, because they are as great and as complete as any young wines I have tasted. I suspect the 1996 will develop a bit like the 1986, the 1990 will be the most balanced and assured at every stage of development, and the 1998 will be the most talked about, and maybe the most controversial of the young Granges.

I regret that I never had an opportunity to taste older vintages of St. Henri when they were in their prime. It was frustrating to taste the first dozen or so vintages and to get so little out of them. The 1976 was superb, as was the 1986, but since 1990 the wine has become consistently excellent. Were the older vintages this fresh and supple when young? Or is St. Henri stylistically different? Whatever, the 1990, 1994, 1996, 1998, 1999, and 2001 are outstanding – big without being overpowering; very ripe, yet still fresh. Balance and elegance set St. Henri apart from the other top Penfolds reds.

Joseph Ward

THE STORY OF GRANGE
BY MAX SCHUBERT

So much has been spoken and so much written about Grange Hermitage over the years that, as its originator, I welcome the opportunity of adding my own measure to the volume that has gone before, particularly as the spoken and written word has not always been laudatory but often quite distinctly the reverse.

Grange Hermitage has always been a controversial and an individual wine. It is my belief that if these two characteristics can be combined, then at least half the ingredients necessary for success have been achieved.

Grange Hermitage has been argued and debated around countless dinner tables. In its early years it was insulted and classified among the lowest of the low – yet, through all this it has stood out as an individual wine with its own particular personality and has been consumed in copious quantity whether it be with praise and pleasure, or with dislike and condemnation.

It has been almost unbeatable in wine shows, whether it be in the young vintage classes or the old open classes, having accumulated since 1962 some 126 gold, 76 silver and 42 bronze medals, plus 28 trophies and seven championship awards. It has even won two Jimmy Watson trophies, which is surprising as it is not the type of wine that usually wins Jimmy Watson awards – not because of its quality, but because of its style.

It is a truly controversial wine, never without interest and always open to debate one way or another. How, then, did an individual wine of this nature come into being?

It was during my initial visit to the major wine-growing areas of Europe in 1950 that the idea of producing an Australian red wine capable of staying alive for a minimum of 20 years and comparable with those produced in Bordeaux, first entered my mind. I was fortunate to be taken under the wing of Monsieur Christian Cruse, one of the most respected and highly qualified wine men of the old school of France at that time, and he afforded me, among other things, the rare opportunity of tasting and evaluating Bordeaux wines between 40 and 50 years old which were still sound and possessed magnificent bouquet and flavour. They were of tremendous value from an educational point of view and imbued in me a desire to attempt to do something to lift the rather mediocre standard of Australian red wine in general at that time.

> It is a truly controversial wine, never without interest and always open to debate one way or another. How, then, did an individual wine of this nature come into being?

THE STORY OF GRANGE
BY MAX SCHUBERT

The method of production seemed fairly straightforward, but with several unorthodox features, and I felt that it would only be a matter of undertaking a complete survey of vineyards to find the correct varietal grape material. Then, with a modified approach to take account of differing conditions, such as climate, soil, raw material and techniques generally, it would not be impossible to produce a wine which could stand on its own feet throughout the world and would be capable of improvement year by year for a minimum of 20 years. In other words, something different and lasting.

The grape material used in Bordeaux consisted of our basic varieties, namely Cabernet Sauvignon, Cabernet Franc, Merlot and Malbec, and these were used in varying percentages to make the Bordeaux wines. Only Cabernet Sauvignon and Malbec were available in South Australia at the time, but a survey showed that they were in such short supply as to make them impracticable commercially – after all, the development of a new commercial wine, particularly of the high grade range, depends on the quality and availability of the raw material, the maintenance of standard, and continuity of supply.

I elected to use Hermitage or Shiraz only (which was in plentiful supply) knowing full well that if I was careful enough in the choice of area and vineyard and coupled that with the correct production procedure, I would be able to make the type and style of wine I wanted. If necessary, I could always use a small percentage of Cabernet or Malbec from our own Kalimna Vineyard in the Barossa Valley as a balancing factor to lift flavour and character. As it happened, this was not necessary – at least, not in the early Granges.

It was finally decided that the raw material for the first experimental Grange Hermitage would be a mixture of Shiraz grapes from two separate vineyards and areas consisting of Penfolds Grange Vineyards at Magill in the foothills overlooking Adelaide and a private vineyard some distance south of Adelaide. I had already observed that both vineyards produced wines of distinctive varietal flavour and character with a great depth of colour and body weight, and felt that by producing them together, the outstanding characteristics of both vineyards would result in an improved all-round wine eminently suitable for my purpose.

> The outstanding characteristics of both vineyards would result in an improved all-round wine eminently suitable for my purpose.

Accordingly, during the 1951 vintage, the first Grange experimental wine was made, incorporating five new untreated oak hogsheads which I had observed were used to such good effect in France and other European countries. The objective was to produce a big, full-bodied wine containing maximum extraction of all the components in the grape material used.

The procedure to be employed was first to ensure that the grape material was sound and that the acid and sugar content was in balance consistent with the style of wine as specified. Using the Baumé scale, this was to be not less than 11.5 degrees and not more than 12 degrees with a total acidity of not less than 6.5 and not more than 7 grams per litre. With strict attention to detail and close surveillance, this was achieved.

The grapes were gathered and crushed and the must – consisting of skins, seeds and other solids comprising the fleshy part of the grape – and juice were pumped into a 12-tonne open concrete fermentation tank. During this operation, the must received a dose of sulphur dioxide, to neutralise the wild yeasts, and also an injection of pure yeast culture previously acclimatised to the level of sulphur dioxide used. The tank was filled to the exact level required. Boards, known as heading-down boards, were placed across the surface of the must in the open tank, with a narrow gap between each board. These were secured by two strong pieces of timber placed across the boards and locked in position underneath four lugs built into the upper tank walls. Fermentation began almost immediately and as carbon dioxide gas pressure developed, the juice was forced through the narrow gaps between the boards, keeping the skins and other solids completely immersed underneath the surface.

> The objective was to produce a big, full-bodied wine containing maximum extraction of all the components in the grape material used.

Although this was all fairly basic, it was important in achieving complete extraction during fermentation particularly, if viewed in conjunction with other procedures which followed. For instance, it was thought that in order to obtain full extraction, a much longer period of fermentation and skin contact would be required, necessitating strict fermentation control. This was to be achieved by controlling the temperature generated by the fermentation, on the basis that the lower the temperature, the slower the rate of fermentation, since there would be a considerable reduction in the heat generated by the yeast in its

THE STORY OF GRANGE
BY MAX SCHUBERT

frantic efforts to multiply and convert the grape sugars into alcohol. Of course, vice versa, by allowing the temperature to rise, an increase in the fermentation rate would result. Temperature control was to be achieved by incorporating a heat exchanger in the process.

The actual fermentation rate in this case was governed by the predetermined length of fermentation, which was set at 12 days. This required a fermentation sugar conversion rate of approximately one Baumé degree per day. A further measure of control was achieved by using a graph system which showed the ideal fermentation line over a 12-day period compared with the actual fermentation line, which was governed by daily temperature and Baumé readings of the fermenting juice. A glance at the graph immediately showed the degree of cooling or heating required to maintain an even daily rate of fermentation over the period stipulated.

> The fermenting wine was a beautiful rich, dark, ruby red already showing above-average body, bouquet and fruit flavour.

I had previously determined that to assist in obtaining full extraction it would be necessary to separate the fermenting juice from the skins by completely draining the tank. This would cause all the solids, including the heading-down boards and cross pieces, to settle on the bottom of the tank. Then we would pump the juice back over the top so that it would percolate through the skins and other solids, thus extracting further essentials in colour, flavour and character. As the tank filled, the head-boards would rise on the surface until they were again locked into position by the cross pieces. It was a comparatively simple matter to incorporate a heat exchanger in this process, using salt brine as the coolant to achieve temperature control as indicated by the graph.

Fermentation proceeded slowly but evenly and the development of colour, body and character was extremely interesting. As the process approached its end, I decided that extraction from the solids was sufficient and that no useful purpose would be served by prolonging skin contact.

The fermenting wine was a beautiful rich, dark, ruby red already showing above average body, bouquet and fruit flavour. In addition, a general slowing down of fermentation, which is normal during the latter stages, meant that temperature was no longer a problem, and cooling could be dispensed with. In fact, a slight increase in temperature was desirable at this stage as an

encouragement for the flagging yeast to complete the conversion of the remaining sugar into alcohol.

The wine was then separated from the solids for the last time, a portion was transferred to the five new untreated oak hogsheads, and the remainder to a 1000 gallon (4550 litre) well-seasoned dry red cask. This was to be the control wine used to measure the success or failure of the new experimental hogshead wine.

The solids which were left in the fermenting tank were removed and pressed and the pressings stored in small seasoned casks holding 30 gallons, or about 140 litres. This would be used later on as a topping-up wine, to keep the containers filled to the brim at all times. Topping-up is a preventative measure against bacterial infection, and also makes good the removal of lees or deposits which accumulate on the bottom of containers during the self-clarification process following completion of fermentation. It was also intended to use the pressings as a balancing medium for the experimental wine before bottling, if required.

The experimental hogsheads were stored in underground cellars where the temperature was constant at 15°C and fermentation was completed in 12 days as previously determined. Within a month, vast differences became apparent between the experimental hogsheads and the control cask. Whereas the control wine showed all the characteristics of a good, well made wine cast in the orthodox mould, the experimental wine was strikingly different. The volume of bouquet, comprising raw oak mixed with natural varietal fruit, was tremendous. These characteristics were also very apparent on the palate. The overall flavour was much more intense than the control, and for a big young wine, the balance was superb. To my mind, even at this early stage, there was no doubt that this wine would be different, with almost unlimited potential if handled correctly.

During the months that followed, treatment was confined to the removal of lees from all containers, including the control cask, and the addition of small amounts of tannic acid. After 12 months, both wines were crystal clear, with superb dark, full, rich colour and body – but there the similarity ended. The experimental wine was bigger in all respects. It was a big wine in bouquet, flavour and balance. The raw wood was not so apparent, but the fruit characteristics had become pronounced and defined, with more

The overall flavour was much more intense than the control, and for a big young wine, the balance was superb.

than a faint suggestion of cranberry. It was almost as if the new wood had acted as a catalyst to release previously unsuspected flavours and aromas from the Hermitage grape.

I was delighted with the result of the experiment so far. To my mind, the marriage of all components had taken place and it required only the sealing of all these wonderful characteristics into bottles for the marriage to be consummated.

After a total wood storage of 18 months, and without any further treatment, the wine was bottled and binned away in underground bins where the temperature was more or less constant at 15°C.

Several hundred dozen of the control wine were also bottled and, while it developed into an exceptionally good wine in the orthodox manner, it never reached the heights of the first experimental Grange Hermitage. It did, however, set the guidelines for the production and marketing of a whole range of special red wines which have been sought after, vintage by vintage, to this day.

In the meantime, the 1952 vintage had come and gone with an increase in quantity production of Grange Hermitage, using the same raw material and method of production with similar results. It was a superb wine to my mind.

> As vintage followed vintage, the accumulation of bottled stock grew and the improvement shown in the earlier vintages was all that I had hoped for.

A variation occurred in 1953 in that, in addition to Hermitage, a straight Cabernet Sauvignon from our Kalimna Vineyard in the Barossa Valley was made experimentally, employing the same method of production as for Grange. The quantity made was five hogsheads as in 1951. The decision to make an experimental Cabernet at all, despite the shortage of this variety, was influenced by the fact that in 1953 the analytical balance of the grapes was similar to that laid down for Grange.

To obtain balanced Cabernet, at least in my sphere of operations at that time, was rare, and while the volume of flavour and character of the finished wine was usually magnificent, the imbalance of the fruit invariably manifested itself on the palate with a noticeable break in the middle and a thinnish, hard, astringent finish. However, this was not so with the 1953 vintage and I still rank this wine as one of the best Grange-style wines made.

As vintage followed vintage, the accumulation of bottled stock grew and the improvement shown in the earlier vintages was all that I had hoped for. Gone was any suggestion of raw wood, and a complete wine was emerging with a full, buoyant, almost ethereal nose of great intensity and a palate which was full of rich flavour and character. The balance in every vintage, I thought, was near perfect. The time appeared to be ripe to remove the wraps and allow other people to see and evaluate this wondrous thing.

Besides, my superiors at head office in Sydney were becoming increasingly aware of the large amount of money lying idle in their underground cellars at Magill.

Representative bottles from each vintage from 1951 to 1956 were called for, and a wine tasting arranged by the then managing director. Those invited included well-known wine identities in Sydney, personal friends of the board, and top management. The result was absolutely disastrous. Simply, no one liked Grange Hermitage.

It was unbelievable, and I must confess that for the first time, I had misgivings about my own assessment of Grange. However, I was determined to prove the Sydney people wrong and, with the help and support of Jeffrey Penfold-Hyland, who was then Assistant General Manager of our South Australian operations, numerous tastings were arranged in and around Adelaide and at Magill. We availed ourselves of every opportunity, donating various vintages to wine and food societies, Beefsteak and Burgundy Clubs, and wherever wine drinkers congregated. However, the general reaction was little better than the earlier disaster in Sydney.

It may be illuminating at this time to record some of the assessments made by experts and critics alike in public and in my presence during the darkest hours of Grange Hermitage. Some of the remarks were downright rude and pained me no end:

"A concoction of wildfruits and sundry berries with crushed ants predominating."

This, by a well-known, respected wine man.

"Schubert, I congratulate you. A very good, dry port, which no one in their right mind will buy – let alone drink."

> The balance in every vintage I thought was near perfect. The time appeared to be ripe to remove the wraps and allow other people to see and evaluate this wondrous thing.

THE STORY OF GRANGE
BY MAX SCHUBERT

Then there was the smart person who wanted me to give him a couple of dozen. He was not going to pay for it because he did not think it was worth anything. Another very smart one wanted to buy it and use it as an aphrodisiac. His theory was that the wine was like bull's blood in all respects and would raise his blood count to twice the norm when the occasion demanded. A young doctor friend even thought he could use it as an anaesthetic on his girlfriend. I could go on, but I think that will give you an idea of Grange's initial reception by most people at that time.

> The final blow came just before the 1957 vintage when I received written instructions from head office to stop production of Grange Hermitage.

There were, of course, some notable exceptions, whose faith in Grange never wavered. They were people such as Jeffrey Penfold-Hyland, without whose support Grange would have died a natural, but not peaceful death, George Fairbrother, that doyen of wine judges, Tony Nelson, at that time managing director of Woodley Wines, Douglas Lamb, who needs no introduction from me, and Dr Max Lake who, I recall, either purchased for a song or consumed most of the 1953 experimental Cabernet himself.

There were others who would not commit themselves, but preferred to wait and see. At least they did not condemn and were prepared to give the wine a chance. To all these I offer my gratitude.

The final blow came just before the 1957 vintage when I received written instructions from head office to stop production of Grange Hermitage. The main reasons given were that I was accumulating large stocks of wine which to all intents and purposes were unsaleable and that the adverse criticism directed at the wine was harmful to the company image as a whole. It appeared to be the end.

However, with Jeffrey Penfold-Hyland's support, I disregarded the written instructions in part, and continued to make Grange in reduced quantities. Finance was not available to purchase new hogsheads, but some benefit was gained by using hogsheads from previous vintages. This undercover production continued through to 1959 and the wines made, although good, lacked that one element which made the difference between a good wine and a great wine.

In all, it was 10 years from the time the first experimental Grange was made before the wine gained general acceptance and the prejudices were overcome. As the earlier vintages matured in bottle and progressively became less aggressive and more refined, people generally began to take notice, and whereas previously it had been all condemnation, I was now at least receiving some praise for the wine. A little of this filtered through to my board of directors, with the result that just before the 1960 vintage, I was instructed to start making Grange Hermitage officially again, with ample funds available for this purpose. Since that time, Grange Hermitage has never looked back.

In 1962, after many years' absence from Australian wine shows, the company decided again to take part in these competitions, and Grange was first submitted as an entry in the Open Claret class in the Sydney Show of that year. It was awarded a gold medal. This was the 1955 vintage which, in my humble opinion, was one of the best Granges ever produced. This wine won more than 50 gold medals, until its retirement from the show arena in the late 1970s, not because it was defective in any way – in fact, in 1977 it was awarded the trophy for the best dry red in the Melbourne Show – but because my board wished to give later vintages the opportunity of winning or adding to the number of gold medals already won.

> I wish to pay tribute to the many winemakers, technicians, cellar managers, senior cellar hands and vineyard supervisors who, over the years, so ably assisted me in the making of Grange.

In retrospect, the 1950s were exciting years of discovery, faith, doubt, humiliation and triumph. The 1960s were rewarding years of contentment in the knowledge that the continued making of Grange was in good hands.

I wish to pay tribute to the many winemakers, technicians, cellar managers, senior cellar hands and vineyard supervisors who, over the years, so ably assisted me in the making of Grange. Each one had a part to play in every vintage made, and even though I always retained absolute control of all stages of Grange production and, indeed, company production generally, without their help, support, interest and co-operation, it would have been almost impossible for me to cope, particularly in the later years before my retirement in 1975.

THE STORY OF GRANGE
BY MAX SCHUBERT

I would also like to express the hope that the production and the acceptance of Grange Hermitage as a great Australian wine has proved that we in Australia are capable of producing wines equal to the best in the world. But we must not be afraid to put into effect the strength of our own convictions, continue to use our imagination in wine-making generally, and be prepared to experiment in order to gain something extra, different and unique in the world of wine.

The acceptance of Grange Hermitage as a great Australian wine has proved that we in Australia are capable of producing wines equal to the best in the world.

Taken from a paper delivered at the first Australian National University Wine Symposium in Canberra in September 1979.

"You must go forward, because if you can't, you must go backwards. If you believe what you're doing can't be improved on, you're mistaken."

– MAX SCHUBERT

Introduced in 1991, Penfolds Red Wine Re-corking Clinics provide Penfolds wine collectors and enthusiasts with an opportunity to have their wines assessed and, if necessary, topped up and re-corked. Over 45,000 bottles belonging to more than 9,000 wine consumers have been given a 'health check' since this programme began. The clinics take place each year, on a two-year rotational basis, in major Australian cities and recently in New Zealand, the United Kingdom and the United States.

Penfolds Red Wine Re-corking Clinics were inspired by the practice of re-corking old bottles by United Kingdom wine merchants and Bordeaux chateaux. In fact, Max Schubert would re-cork old vintages of Grange for his friends. A number of these bottles have turned up at Australian wine auctions over the years. Penfolds has reinvented this largely ad hoc practice into a serious after-sales service for Penfolds wine collectors and enthusiasts. After many years in the cellar, corks can deteriorate and the level of the wine in bottle may ullage. If not checked, it is possible the wine may overdevelop or oxidise, rendering it undrinkable.

Penfolds' experience with re-corking is unmatched by any other wine company in the world. It has developed an awareness of diverse cellaring conditions, giving winemakers an insightful understanding of the maturation process. There is no question that ideal cellaring conditions are not only a matter of a cool temperature and optimum relative humidity, but also overall constancy of temperature and environment. Bottles lying in warmer cellars may develop more quickly, but not necessarily to the detriment of the overall quality of the wine. Conversely, storing wines in very cold cellars can retard the maturation process. The issue of cellar provenance is becoming more and more important, especially as wine markets become increasingly global. Ideal cellaring conditions (as outlined here) are the preferred option.

The problem with corks (other than the infuriating occurrence of cork taint) is that they deteriorate with time. Typically wine will soak through the cork or find a way between the cork and the wall of the bottle neck and start leaking out. The level of the wine in the bottle will consequently fall below the base of the neck and increase the risk of oxidation. Cellaring conditions can therefore influence the life of the cork. Air conditioning without

Bottles lying in warmer cellars may develop more quickly, but not necessarily to the detriment of the overall quality of the wine.

humidifiers, can dry out corks and shorten their life. Usually, however, corks do not present a problem until after an extensive period of cellaring.

Clinics offer owners of Penfolds red wines which are 15 years and older the opportunity to have their wines assessed by a Penfolds winemaker and, if necessary, opened, tasted, topped up, re-corked and recapsuled (with branded corks and capsules) on the spot. Special equipment has been developed to optimise this process, including the use of inert gas to prevent oxidation and portable reverse pressure (vacuum) re-corking machines. All the features of a modern bottling line are replicated at the clinic.

Bottles in acceptable condition receive a special numbered clinic back label certifying the soundness of the wine. It's signed by a Penfolds winemaker and endorsed by specialist wine auctioneers, Langton's Fine Wine Auctions and Christies. All re-corked bottle numbers are recorded in a data bank. Bottles found in unacceptable condition are sealed with a plain, unbranded cork, but neither topped up, nor certified, nor recapsuled – effectively weeding poorly cellared wines out of the system.

Penfolds has been experimenting with alternative closures to cork for some time. While perhaps not particularly romantic, the various available technologies have genuine advantages, not the least of which, is that they solve the frustrating problem of cork taint, an inherent problem with the treatment and manufacture of cork. Screwcap capsules and Nomacorc® are just two examples of the various closures available.

Bottles in acceptable condition receive a special clinic back label certifying the soundness of the wine.

Penfolds is increasingly using these inert, taint-free closures. Newer vintages of Eden Valley Reserve Riesling, Bottle Aged Reserve Bin Riesling and Reserve Bin A Chardonnay have been bottled under screwcap. It is possible other Penfolds wines will be released with alternative closures. In the meantime, cork producers are working at ways of improving the production and quality of corks. Consumer acceptance is the key to this trend. Regardless, Penfolds Red Wine Re-corking Clinics will remain a feature of Penfolds customer service for many years to come. It is still early days and Penfolds has no plans to stop using traditional cork closures altogether.

Although at first unpredicted, the Red Wine Re-corking Clinics have had a major impact on the secondary wine market. Penfolds' reputation for wine quality and aging potential make it a cornerstone of Australian wine collecting. The overall auction market has embraced the clinics – firstly by offering no obvious difference in market value between bottles in original condition and certified bottles, secondly by discounting older bottles of Penfolds which are 'not in mint condition' and lastly, by rejecting uncertified bottles. The result is that few bottles of poorly cellared wine ever reach the consumer through the secondary market, further enhancing the collector's wine experience and the reputation of Penfolds.

For enquiries regarding Penfolds Red Wine Re-corking Clinics, contact:

PENFOLDS CONSUMER RELATIONS
Tel: 1300 651 650   Australia
     0800 651 650   New Zealand
     020 8917 4687 United Kingdom
     800 255 9966   United States
or visit **www.penfolds.com** to email an enquiry.

Please refer to Cellaring and Service on the Penfolds website for further information on wine valuations, sourcing rare wines and specialist stockists.

The fine wine experience can be enhanced by following a few simple measures. This section highlights the most important aspects of cellaring and serving Penfolds wines.

DOUBLE-DECANTING

There are two reasons to decant a wine: one is to separate the clear wine from the natural sediment that may have formed in the bottle as the wine has aged; the other is to stimulate or enliven the wine by exposing it to the air.

Penfolds encourages the use of decanters for all its red wines, and even some of its whites. There is nothing like a beautiful antique claret jug or a sleek, modern, crystal decanter to create a sense of occasion when you serve a fine old wine.

It is just as good (better, in terms of wine identification at the table) to decant the wine into any clean receptacle, preferably a glass jug with volume markings on the side, rinse out the bottle with filtered or bottled water, drain, and immediately pour the wine back into its own bottle using a clean funnel.

This is called double-decanting. It gives the wine a double aeration, and you can loosely re-cork the bottle if it will be some time before it is served. You will probably find it best to double-decant away from the dining table in a place where there is plenty of light.

Prior to decanting, leave the bottle upright near where it will be opened for as long as possible, at least a few hours and preferably a day or two, or even longer. This will enable any fine sediment to settle.

Take care to minimise movement of the bottle as you open it. In a single movement, pour the wine carefully but steadily at an even rate into your jug in a single movement with as little glugging as possible. The idea is to minimise the likelihood of the sediment being stirred back into the wine.

You can pour over a candle or a small torch so you can stop pouring when you see the sediment enter the shoulder of the bottle, or you can follow Max Schubert's example. Beforehand, simply mark your jug at the 720ml point and stop pouring when the liquid reaches that level. Don't waste the last 25-30ml, with the sediment in it, add it to your gravy – or should we say, jus!

> The fine wine experience can be enhanced by following a few simple measures.

The only exception is with very old bottles, which, if possible, should be decanted immediately before they are served. The ethereal bouquet of a fine old wine near the end of its life may initially seem strong, but it can fade quickly once in contact with air.

CORKS AND CORKSCREWS

Being a product of nature, corks vary. Some seem dense and hard, others relatively soft and spongy. Corks also respond individually to the effects of time and cellaring conditions.

Some of the problems experienced when removing corks – especially from old bottles – can be avoided with the use of a good corkscrew.

> Anyone wishing to cellar Penfolds reds for any length of time will seriously prejudice their quality and condition if storage conditions are poor.

The best types enable you to pull the cork straight up, without dragging it sideways. Also, look for a strong, wire screw that spirals fairly tightly and has a diameter sufficient to gain good purchase on the cork. Avoid any corkscrew whose business end is a pointed rod with a thread cut into it.

Another type of extractor that can be useful has two thin, flat, flexible arms, one slightly longer than the other. The arms are inserted on either side of the cork, between it and the glass, and the implement rocked back and forth until the cork is fully embraced. The cork can then be removed with a side-to-side, twisting motion.

At its Red Wine Re-corking Clinics Penfolds uses the widely available, standard table model Screwpull corkscrew. This has a teflon-coated wire screw and a separate, rigid frame which guides the screw into the centre of the cork and pulls it out automatically; you simply keep turning until the cork separates from the bottle.

CELLARING

The number one cellaring myth in Australia, and perhaps elsewhere, is that bottles should be turned every so often. It is quite possible to guess how this myth may have gained currency, but all that needs to be said is that it is completely wrong.

What is certain is that anyone wishing to cellar Penfolds reds for any length of time will seriously prejudice their quality and condition if storage conditions are poor. Heat is the enemy.

Beware of wide, repeated, day-to-night variations in summer. Slow, gradual temperature change over the seasons is not so bad, but it's still not ideal.

The ideal cellar temperature is a constant 14°C to 16°C, with a relative humidity of 70-75%. The space should be dry, well ventilated and free of odour and vibration. If the wine in your cellar is a significant investment, it is worth using a thermometer to monitor summer temperatures, which should remain below 18°C.

A simple wooden or metal racking system will keep wines well ventilated and provide easy, single-bottle access. Bottles should be stored on their sides, ideally with the neck sloping slightly upwards so that the cork remains wet, the headspace 'bubble' is in the shoulder, and any sediment collects towards the base of the bottle.

If the right conditions don't occur naturally at your place, air-conditioning or temperature controlled wine storage cabinets are high cost options. Alternatively, keep only your drinking wine at home and rent appropriate space for the rest of your cellar, or borrow cellar space from a trusted friend.

Wide temperature variations mean, at best, that your wine will develop more quickly than it would otherwise. At worst, it means ruination. Anyone cellaring fine wine in a warm or hot climate would be foolish not to take the heat factor into account.

> The European idea of serving red wine at room temperature works well in cooler climates. But in Australia or California it could mean serving Shiraz or Cabernet at over 30°C in summer.

SERVING TEMPERATURE

The European idea of serving red wine at room temperature works well in cooler climates. But in Australia or California it could mean serving Shiraz or Cabernet at over 30°C in summer. This is too warm and can ruin the experience of drinking a fine red wine.

The bottle should be cool to the touch, but not cold; a 'cellar temperature' of, say, 15°C is ideal. Do not be concerned if this means cooling red wine in the refrigerator for 30 minutes to an hour.

Temperatures for serving whites are not so critical, but beware of over-chilling, which tends to deaden flavour. It is best to chill white wine as it is needed, either in a refrigerator or in an ice bucket for 20-30 minutes with a mixture of ice and water. Chardonnay, particularly, is often served too cold. The wine's real flavour will begin to emerge only when the chill comes off.

CELLARING AND SERVICE

GLASSWARE

Glassware can make a big difference to the way a wine tastes. Try the same wine out of a tumbler and a fine, thin-walled wine glass. The wine always seems to taste better out of a good glass. Expert opinion is growing that these differences are not merely psychological.

Whilst there are many different glass designs, they tend to be driven by fashion, rather than by the needs of serious wine drinkers. Nevertheless, some companies, notably Riedel in Austria, have developed fine glasses that clearly enhance the fine wine experience.

> Much of what we 'taste' is really what our nose tells us about the wine.

A good, all-purpose wine glass need not be expensive. It should have a total capacity of about 220ml and be slightly tapered or tulip-shaped at the top of the bowl. This helps to concentrate the aroma or bouquet when the wine is swirled around in the glass before nosing. After all, much of what we 'taste' is really what our nose tells us about the wine.

Make sure your glasses are clean, which ideally means washing them separately, rinsing them in hot water and avoiding the use of detergent.

Glasses should be stored upright and aired before use. Do not use glasses straight out of a wooden cupboard or sideboard, or straight from a cardboard box. Sniff a glass straight out of a cupboard or box and you can easily detect the musty or cardboardy smell.

THE PENFOLDS WINEMAKERS

Although Peter Gago frequently notes that the Penfolds winemaking effort is very much team based, with talented staff assisting him to create the wines under Penfolds' masthead, there have been only four Chief Winemakers since 1948: Max Schubert, Don Ditter, John Duval and Peter Gago. All four have contributed to Penfolds' success.

MAX SCHUBERT

Born in 1915, Max Schubert joined Penfolds as a messenger boy in 1931, and became a member of the Magill winemaking team at the age of 21. He was appointed Chief Winemaker in 1948 and, having never formally studied oenology, went on to literally change the course of wine history through his 1951 ground-breaking creation of Grange (then labelled Grange Hermitage). Schubert was honoured many times for his lifetime contribution to the Australian wine industry, receiving Member of the Order of Australia, the Maurice O'Shea Award, South Australian Achiever of the Year, Wine Spectator's Hall of Fame, and Decanter magazine's Man of the Year. He died in March 1994 at the age of 79.

DON DITTER

Donovan John Ditter joined Penfolds in 1942 as a laboratory assistant. Having graduated from Roseworthy Winemaking College, he became a fully fledged winemaker in 1950, in time to witness the return of Max Schubert from Europe and the first production of Grange. He assumed the role of National Production Manager (the equivalent of Chief Winemaker) in 1973 and held that position until his retirement in 1986. With periods spent at Magill, Nuriootpa and the NSW wineries, Ditter's influence over the company's wines was comprehensive. He has enjoyed a long and happy retirement since 1986, living in Sydney, while still making appearances as a wine educator for Penfolds, and sharing his knowledge and enthusiasm for the wines he influenced over the four decades of his tenure with the company.

THE PENFOLDS WINEMAKERS

JOHN DUVAL

John Duval was born in 1950. He joined Penfolds in 1974 and worked with both Ditter and Schubert in the formative years of his career. He took over from Don Ditter as Chief Winemaker in 1986. In 1989, just three years after taking over as Chief Winemaker, Duval was named International Winemaker of the Year at Britain's International Wine and Spirit Competition, as well as twice being named Red Winemaker of the Year at WINE magazine's International Wine Challenge (1991 and 2000).

PETER GAGO

After graduating Dux of his year at South Australia's Roseworthy Winemaking College, he spent four years in sparkling winemaking for the then Penfolds Wine Group. He entered the world of Penfolds red winemaking in late 1993 in time to lead the first 4,000 tonne vintage in the new red wine cellar at the Nuriootpa winery. The following year, his role was expanded. Peter Gago became the Penfolds Red Wine Oenologist, working very closely with John Duval to simultaneously maintain the Penfolds wine style and explore new territories. Appointed Penfolds Chief Winemaker in July 2002, he took over the mantle from his long-time friend and colleague, John Duval. Like Max Schubert, Don Ditter and John Duval before him, Peter, together with his team, continues to challenge winemaking excellence with every vintage.

ANDREW CAILLARD MW

Andrew Caillard MW is a specialist wine auctioneer and widely published wine author. Since 1989 he has been an executive partner of Langton's Wine Auctions and Wine Exchange, Australia's pre-eminent fine wine market place.

Andrew has strong historic links with the Australian wine industry. His great-great grandfather, John Reynell, brought the first grapevines to South Australia. Andrew began his career in wine in Bordeaux, Germany and the United Kingdom. He is a Roseworthy graduate in wine marketing and a Master of Wine. In 1993 he was a recipient of the Madame Bollinger Foundation Medal for Excellence in Wine Tasting.

His work in the secondary wine market is strongly associated with ultra-fine Australian wine and extends well beyond swinging a gavel! As the author of *Langton's Classification of Australian Wine* (now in its third release), *Langton's Australian Wine Investment and Buying Guide* (in its fifth edition) and a substantial body of commentary, articles and market analysis, he has played a key part in underpinning the international emergence of Australian fine wine.

In 2002 Langton's launched its critically-acclaimed interactive wine auction service at www.langtons.com.au, at the same time bringing the wealth of Andrew's Australian wine commentary and analysis to a worldwide audience. The introduction of Langton's Wine Exchange in 2004 has brought a new dimension to the trade in fine Australian wine.

ABOUT THE PHOTOGRAPHER

RICHARD HUMPHRYS

International award winning wine photographer, Richard Humphrys has been working as a commercial photographer in Adelaide, South Australia for over eighteen years. Richard crafts a wide diversity of subject matter into beautiful images to meet the needs of his clients. This fifth edition marks the third *The Rewards of Patience* book in a row for which he has been commissioned to create images.

Richard began his photographic career shooting still life subjects in the studio. For this edition of *The Rewards of Patience* he brings these skills of understanding and controlling light to his vineyard and vintage images. His graphic winemaking and wine tasting photography was taken in an editorial fashion to capture the intimate hands on nature of making fine wine.

Magazines and authors from around the world frequently select images to illustrate their stories from Richard's Stock Library of wine images that can be found on his web site. James Halliday used Richard's grape images exclusively for his recent book *Varietal Wines*. A selection of these meticulously photographed grape studies make up Richard's solo exhibition of limited edition fine art prints which has had several showings around Australia.

www.richardhumphrys.com.au

THIS IS NOT THE END OF THE STORY

You can visit the spiritual home of Penfolds, the elegant Magill Estate Winery, nestled in the Adelaide Hills. The magnificently appointed cellar door offers a myriad of tasting options and provides wonderful insights to the unique personality of this remarkable winery. Not to mention a chance to dine at the award winning Magill Estate Restaurant.

Delve further into Penfolds rich winemaking experience at Penfolds Nuriootpa Winery in the Barossa Valley, where both red and white Penfolds wine legends continue to be created.

Protect your precious Penfolds investment and further your wine cellaring knowledge by attending a Penfolds Red Wine Re-corking Clinic.

Or you can choose to stay in regular contact with Penfolds through their informative newsletter, by registering at www.penfolds.com

And of course, don't forget you can do the simplest and most pleasurable thing of all, just by opening up a bottle of Penfolds and taking that first rewarding sip.

Penfolds Magill Estate Winery and Restaurant
78 Penfold Road, Magill SA 5072
Cellar Door Tel: (+618) 8301 5569
Magill Estate Restaurant Tel: (+618) 8301 5551

Penfolds Nuriootpa Barossa Valley Winery
Tanunda Road, Nuriootpa SA 5355
Tel: (+618) 8568 9408

Penfolds Red Wine Re-corking Clinics
Contact Penfolds Consumer Relations
Tel: Australia   1300 651 650
         New Zealand   0800 651 650
         United States   800 255 9966
         United Kingdom 020 8917 4687

www.penfolds.com